Body, Inc.

Body, Inc.
A Theory of Translation Poetics

Pamela Banting

TURNSTONE PRESS

Turnstone Press
607-100 Arthur Street
Winnipeg, MB
Canada R3B 1H3

Turnstone Press gratefully acknowledges the assistance of
the Canada Council and the Manitoba Arts Council.

This book has been published with the help of a
grant from the Canadian Federation for the Humanities,
using funds provided by the Social Sciences and
Humanities Research Council of Canada.

Cover photograph: Karen Barry

Design: Manuela Dias

This book was printed and bound in Canada by
Friesen Printers for Turnstone Press.

Canadian Cataloguing in Publication Data

Banting, Pamela, 1955–

Body, Inc.

Includes bibliographical references.
ISBN 0-88801-190-3

1. Canadian poetry - 20th century - History
and criticism. 2. Poetics. I. Title

PS8155.B35 1995   C811'.5409   C95-920148-3
PR9190.5.B35 1995

this book is for the boreal forest

from whence it came

For Dot,

who is inscribing the vernacular
"republic" of Wildwood for us,

best wishes,
See you in Calgary,

[signature]

Strawberry Creek Lodge, July '96

What this institution [the university] cannot bear, is for anyone to tamper with [*toucher à;* also "touch," "change," "concern himself with"] language, meaning *both* the *national* language *and,* paradoxically, an ideal of translatability that neutralizes this national language. Nationalism and universalism. What this institution cannot bear is a transformation that leaves intact neither of these two complementary poles.

—Jacques Derrida

Yet I snatch this language that is foreign to me and turn it about in my fashion. . . . I am a foreigner to myself in my own language and I translate myself by quoting all the others.

—Madeleine Gagnon

Christ, these hieroglyphs.

—Charles Olson

Imagine. You can understand seven languages now, even if you can speak only one. You could be a great poet.

—Caprice

A beautiful body begins with a book.
—advertisement for a book on health and fitness

Table of Contents

Foreword

In this book I develop a theory of 'translation poetics,' a poetics radically different from those rooted in mimetic or expressive theories of representation and which from Plato onward have dominated thinking about literary productions. Through readings of some of the long poems and essays of Fred Wah, Robert Kroetsch and Daphne Marlatt, I argue that the postcolonial Canadian long poem is generated *not* primarily through representation but rather through various forms of interlingual, intralingual and intersemiotic[1] translation.

The Preface, "Translation as ' nv s ble tr ck,' " addresses briefly the fields of linguistics, poststructuralism and feminist theory in order to question, first of all, whether and how original writing may be considered translative, secondly, to what extent the relation between speech and writing may legitimately be described as intralingual translation, and, thirdly, why translation poetics is largely ' nv s ble' relative to representationalist poetics. With these questions unfolded, the Preface dilates with speculations about the startling potential we have to translate our very bodies, incorporating them into language and signification, from which they have long been exiled by Western philosophy.

The first part, "The Pictogram as a Medium for Poetry: Fred Wah's Interlingual Translation Poetics," illustrates how Wah's translation of pictographs from the interior of B.C. recapitulates in specifically Canadian and local terms Ernest Fenollosa's and Ezra Pound's prior explorations of the Chinese written character as a medium for poetry. From his *Pictograms from the Interior of B.C.* (1975) to his most recent books, Wah excavates the picto-ideo-phonographic elements of Canadian speech and inscriptions. His translation poetics creates an estranged syntax which graphs his familial, racial and poetic lineages.

The second part, " 'The nightmare and the welcome dream of Babel': Robert Kroetsch's Intralingual Translation Poetics," consists of four chapters. The first chapter examines the relation between speech and writing in prairie poetry generally by interpolating into the arguments of Frank Davey and Dennis Cooley the notion of intralingual translation poetics. The second chapter discusses Kroetsch's "Stone Hammer Poem" as the preface to the translation poetics of his *Completed Field Notes* and analyzes the poetics of *Seed Catalogue* as an answer to his self-imposed question as to how a poet can translate without changing languages. Chapter three deals with the translation of the letters of the alphabet as a generative device in *The Sad Phoenician*. Chapter four focusses on the thematization of infidelity (an unfaithful translation, the translator as traitor, *traduttore-traditore*) as a translation effect in *The Sad Phoenician*.

" 'A new alphabet gasps for air': Daphne Marlatt's Intersemiotic Translation Poetics," deals with Marlatt's feminist translation poetics. The first chapter analyzes ways in which her work has been misread as essentialist and suggests alternatively that she and other experimental feminist writers do *not* write in a specifically feminine mother tongue but rather in an 'interlanguage,' a language which is no one's mother tongue and therefore can only be read in two or more languages at once. Close textual readings of two of Marlatt's long poems, *How Hug a Stone* and *Touch to My Tongue*, illustrate and develop this concept of writing in an interlanguage. The fourth chapter, on her poetic essay "musing with mothertongue," postulates that Marlatt's translation poetics 're-organizes' the body as it has been constructed by phallogocentric discourses.

In the conclusion, "The Promise of Translation," I argue that translation cannot be abstracted, systematized, methodized, or subjected to Cartesian 'universal reason.' It can only take place via the body. In other words, translation can only be performed by a subject who is intimately familiar with the other language, a subject whose body has been initiated into or by a given language. Moreover, that body compounds the difficulties and pleasures of translation, since bodies are sites of differences and resistances. Because translation cannot bypass the materiality of either language or the body, it counters so-called 'universal reason' and method. Translation is therefore a kind of anti-method or, more accurately, a poetics.

Unlike representation, which elides the bodily in favour of maintaining a distance between materiality and its mental reproductions, translation poetics functions only by means of the body's material differences, physical locality and linguistic and other histories. Therefore, long poems composed out of a translation poetics lay claim to an authenticity of languages, experiences and embodied individual and group identities for postcolonial cultures. Paradoxically then, the " nv s ble tr ck" of translation poetics frees Canadians from the colonialist mimicry imposed by representational aesthetics, accommodates and underscores our postcolonial differences, and makes us visible, audible and tangible to ourselves as a people.

I have chosen to focus on selected long poems by Wah, Kroetsch and Marlatt, but readers may be interested to note that translation poetics can also be applied to the long poems of many other poets and the theory of translation poetics further advanced in the application. Furthermore, translation poetics need not be restricted to the long poem or even to poetry; translation poetics is equally applicable to other genres. One could, for instance, analyze the translation poetics of some of the sound and concrete poetry, novels, plays, short stories, experimental prose, fiction-theory, and performances of Douglas Barbour, George Bowering, Di Brandt, Nicole Brossard, Dennis Cooley, Frank Davey, Beth Goobie, Kristjana Gunnars, J.A. Hamilton, Thomson Highway, Thomas King, Ashok Mathur, Steve McCaffery, Roy Miki, bpNichol, Marlene Nourbese-Philip, Stephen Scobie, Andrew Suknaski, Audrey Thomas, Lola Lemire Tostevin, Armin Wiebe, Rudy Wiebe, and several writers who have published with Underwhich Editions. Moreover, because translation poetics functions both as a reading or critical practice and as a 'method' of writerly composition, this book is aimed toward writers, readers, critics, theorists, teachers and professors working in various disciplines. I hope that those with particular interests in Canadian and other postcolonial literatures, translation theory, writing the body, women's writing, feminist and gay and lesbian theory, race, ethnicity, poststructuralism, cultural studies, linguistics, or their own writing will find *Body Inc.* helpful vis-à-vis their projects.

Given the Babelian limitations imposed upon us by different languages, dialects and systems of signs, however, no one person can ever entirely master the field of translation poetics or do adequate justice to all the texts—Canadian and non-Canadian—composed using aspects of translation. To my way of thinking, this necessary community to which translation poetics calls is one of its strengths and beauties as a theory.

I hereby invite others, if they wish, to translate.

Pamela Banting

Notes

1   Intersemiotic translation refers to various forms of translation between different media, between, for example, words and images (paintings, photographs, drawings) or, as I demonstrate in the chapters on Marlatt's work, between words and bodies, text and flesh.

Acknowledgements

I thank Douglas Barbour, Janice Williamson, Jo-Ann Wallace, Claudine Potvin, and Linda Hutcheon for their intriguing, astute, wise and seriously playful commentary and questions about this work at various stages along the way.

Shirley Neuman's personal and intellectual acts of generosity are legendary, and all the legends are true.

Tina Petersen gave me the tremendous gift of her friendship and provided emotional support during the intense period while I was writing this book.

Stephen Scobie and Steven McCaffery contributed both generous commentary and incisive critique of the final draft of the manuscript.

During the revision process, Stan Dragland, Marnie Parsons, Manina Jones, Neal Ferris, Frank Davey, Linda Davey, Aileen Bailey, John Levesque, Dorothy Nielsen, the late Greg Curnoe, and others talked to me about their work and mine. They also shared their gourmet meals, single malt scotch, a day of rollerblading, the Forest City Gallery, and the blue-green sparkle of Lake Huron.

Grace Kehler persuaded me to buy black leather pants at the precise moment when I needed them the most. Charlene Diehl-Jones made my cheeks ache with laughter and my heart swell with love and admiration for her ways. I thank Grace and Charlene for their intellectual, emotional and spiritual vivacity and daring.

At intervals during the time of writing and revision, my beloved friend Christine Wiesenthal and I hiked in the Rocky Mountains and splashed in the Atlantic. We traipsed through Toronto and the Alberta Badlands and drove the windy Cabot Trail. In London, England, we saw the exhibit *Monet in the '90s: The Series Paintings,* which I will never ever forget, and we saw the Rosetta Stone.

I thank Isabel Carrera Suárez of the University of Oviedo, Spain, and Robin Walker for their gracious hospitality and for a series of stimulating conversations about translation poetics, Canadian literature and postcolonialism.

I thank the adventurers who enrolled in my graduate seminar on Translation Poetics in 1993–94. I am indebted to Michael

Bucknor, Margaret Toye, Peter Jaeger, Cathy Grisé, Peter Cumming, Sarah Green, Chantelle MacPhee, Anita Assaly, Sarah King, and Amanda St. Jean for voyaging with me into the hitherto uncharted waters (and occasionally up the creek) of Translation Poetics.

In 1984 and 1987 I studied at the International Summer Institute for Semiotic and Structural Studies (ISISSS) at the University of Toronto, where some of my ideas about translation poetics began to form and be tested in seminars with Jacques Derrida, Linda Hutcheon, Lorraine Weir and Kaja Silverman.

St. John's College at the University of Manitoba is a magical place because of its gifted professors and administrators with heart and vision. In addition to the magic, however, several undergraduate and graduate scholarships from St. John's over the years made it financially possible for me to proceed in my studies. Dennis Cooley and David Arnason spurred me on.

Between 1987 and 1990 I completed the Ph.D. program at the University of Alberta. The Ph.D. was funded entirely by a Social Sciences and Humanities Research Council of Canada Doctoral Fellowship (1987–90) and three successive University of Alberta Graduate Faculty Fellowships, for which I am deeply grateful. A Sarah Nettie Christie Travel Bursary from the English Department at the University of Alberta allowed me to present a chapter of this book at the Bodies: Image, Writing, Technology Conference at the University of California, Irvine, in 1990.

I was fortunate in having Enrique Castro as my Spanish 100 professor in 1987–88. He is a superb teacher, and taking his course and thinking to myself all day long in my beginner's Spanish also impelled this project in translation poetics. Graçias, Enrique.

I am also grateful to SSHRCC for a Postdoctoral Fellowship, during the tenure of which I revised the manuscript and further extended my work on translation poetics, writing the body and postcolonialism. Thanks are due to the Canadian Federation for the Humanities for the publishing subvention which brought the manuscript into print at Turnstone. Thank you to Wayne Tefs for accepting the manuscript with such alacrity and finesse.

Fred Wah, Robert Kroetsch and Daphne Marlatt wrote the many books which made the writing of this one possible, necessary and such a pleasurable task.

I thank Vera Banting for having the wisdom *not* to teach me to read before I started Grade One and for frequently chasing me out of the house and into what some people refer to as "the natural world" or what, in our translation, we call "the bush." I thank Sinclair Banting for working so hard in local politics for fifty years or more to create and sustain a community for all of us to live and grow up in. I thank him also for telling stories.

I thank the conference co-ordinators and editors of the following journals for allowing me to present and publish earlier drafts and excerpts from this work:

" 'A new alphabet/ gasps for air': Translation Theory and the Poetics of Comtemporary Canadian Women's Writing." Presented at the History of the Literature Institution in Canada Conference (HOLIC): Women's Writing and the History of the Literary Institution, University of Alberta, November 9–11, 1989. Published under the title "Body Inc.: Daphne Marlatt's Translation Poetics." *Women's Writing and the Literary Institution/L'écriture au féminin et l'institution littéraire. Towards a History of the Literary Institution in Canada Conference Proceedings (HOLIC)*. Ed. Claudine Potvin and Janice Williamson, in collaboration with S. Totosy de Zepetnek. Edmonton: Research Institute for Comparative Literature, University of Alberta, 1992. 1-19.

"Organ Music: The ReORGANization of the Body in Feminist Experimental Writing." Presented at the Imag(in)ing Women: Representations of Women in Culture Conference, University of Alberta, April 5–7, 1990. Also presented at the Bodies: Image, Writing, Technology Conference. University of California, Irvine, April 26–28, 1990. Published under the title "The Reorganization of the Body: Daphne Marlatt's 'musing with motherongue'." *ReImag(in)ing Women: Representations of Women in Culture*. Ed. Shirley Neuman and Glennis Stephenson. Toronto: University of Toronto Press, 1993. 217-232.

"Fred Wah: The Poet as Theor(h)et(or)ician." *Open Letter: A Canadian Journal of Writing and Theory* 6th ser. 7 (1987): 5–20.

"Fred Wah's Syntax: A Genealogy, A Translation." *Sagetrieb: A Journal Devoted to Poets in the Imagist/Objectivist Tradition*. 7.1 (1988): 99-113.

"The Undersigned: Ethnicity and Signature-Effects in the Poetry of Fred Wah." ACCUTE Conference, Meeting of the Learned Societies, Québec, May 30, 1989. Published in *West Coast Line* 2 (1990): 83-94.

"The (Rosetta) 'Stone Hammer Poem': Robert Kroetsch's Translation Poetics." Canada: A Challenge, Third Annual Conference of the Spanish Association for Canadian Studies, Madrid, Spain, March 8–10,1991. Extended and published under the title "Robert Kroetsch's Translation Poetics: Questions of Composition in the (Rosetta) "Stone Hammer Poem" and *Seed Catalogue*." *West Coast Line* 10 (1993): 92-107.

"The Phantom Limb Syndrome: Writing the Postcolonial Body in Daphne Marlatt's *Touch to My Tongue*. ACCUTE, the Learneds, University of Prince Edward Island, Charlottetown, May 24–27, 1992. Published in *Ariel: A Review of International English Literature* 24.3 (1993): 7-30.

nv s ble
tr ck

Fred Wah
Pictograms from the Interior of B.C.

When I speak of this writing of the other which will be more beautiful, I clearly understand translation as involving the same risk and chance as the poem. How to translate "poem"? a "poem"? . . .

Jacques Derrida
"Letter to a Japanese Friend"

Preface
Translation as " nv s ble tr ck"

Translation theory has until very recently been staged almost exclusively in individual translators' prefaces. Often a practical account of the translator's difficulties and the provisional solutions adopted to overcome or circumvent them, the translator's preface is also the locus of his or her theories about language, the relations between or among different languages, and the relations between source and target texts, author and translator. Flora Ross Amos, whose book *Early Theories of Translation* surveys the field of interlingual translation theory from the medieval period to Alexander Pope, states that "Generally speaking, it has been the prefaces to translations that have yielded material" of a theoretical nature (Amos 1920, x). Despite its tricky and partially invisible title, the preface you are presently reading is intended to reveal the poetry, poetics and translation theories which have drawn me to analyze and to posit a 'translation poetics.' It is itself a kind of translator's preface insofar as it theorizes translation.

Fred Wah's *Pictograms from the Interior of B.C.*, from which the title of my preface borrows, has become something of a tutor text to my critical practice. The visual charms of the transcribed pictographs and their relation to Wah's own verbal 'transcreations' entice me to write myself further into their environs. Their allure does not persuade me to translate the " nv s ble/ tr ck" they perform in terms of meanings transferred between the two systems of pictograph and pictogram. Instead, miming Wah's 'transcreations' between different signifying systems, I wish to read and write a theory of the translative act as a medium for contemporary Canadian poetry.[1]

Both George Bowering and Smaro Kamboureli note and examine the movement in Wah's work between spoken and written models of composition.[2] Bowering, drawing an analogy between Wah's writing and jazz improvisation, comments that "It would be as if speech & writing were to become one." "It is no surprise that when it comes to the composition of poetry, Fred Wah wants to conflate the spoken & the written, out" (Bowering 1980, 16). Bowering insists that Wah's pictograms are " 'transcreations.' That is, they are neither translations nor descriptions. They might resemble Williams' pictures *from* Brueghel" (15). Bowering conceives of speech and writing as radically different and self-contained practices. He writes:

> There is nothing more exterior than writing. The moment it is done it is forever outside. There is also nothing more interior than speech, than the body's saying. It has no meaning save when it accompanies movements inside the mouth & the ear. Speech & writing are therefore eternally separate. Yet the poet survives upon the ambition to entwine them. (Bowering 1980, 12)

Paradoxically, in light of his statement that they are not translations, Bowering's formulation of the difference and nonrelation between the "bodies" of speech and writing and how the poet "survives" on the desire to entwine these two bodies could be recast in terms of translation poetics, as we shall see.

Both Bowering and Kamboureli concur with Wah's statement that his use of language is nonreferential (Nichol 1978, 45). Kamboureli, in her article "Fred Wah: A Poetry of Dialogue," reads "the central aspect of Wah's work [as] the textuality of the world in which human consciousness and the ontology of things are interwoven" (Kamboureli 1984a, 46). She argues that "He is situated on the interface of signifier and signified, relating to objects by contiguity" (47). Locating Wah's position as poet with regard to word and thing as a "dialogue" between reading and writing, Kamboureli concludes:

> Wah's non-referential language, with its implicit resistance to interpretation, prevents him from being a mere beholder of the spectacle of the world. As a reader Wah discovers the narrative inherent in the alphabet of things. As a poet he inscribes himself on the textuality of the world. He is arrested within the dialogue he initiates.
> (Kamboureli 1984a, 59)

Kamboureli constructs a series of parallels between which "dialogue" is enacted: word and thing, signifier and signified, writing and reading. Like Bowering, who sees writing and speech as "eternally separate" but for the poet's attempts to entwine them, Kamboureli imagines the "double discourse" (59) of graph and phoneme displacing the poet bodily from a position of humanist mastery over the objective world and immersing him in "the alphabet of things" (46). Bowering's article hinges on images of the poet engaged in various physical activities—skiing down a mountain, improvising on jazz trumpet, sliding down a scree slope, planting (himself in) a garden, breathing again after suffering the death of his father. Kamboureli's article demonstrates the repositioning of the poet as a subject-in-process in his own language and traces the necessary realignment and reorientation of the poet's body as he "replaces interpretation with perception" (47), "detour[s] from representation" and "shuns mimetic writing and interpretation" (55). In Kamboureli's words,[3] Wah's texts perform a "marriage between the eye and the ear" (49). This marriage supplants the traditional one between hearing and understanding, the ear and cognition (or self-recognition), in poetry which does not challenge representation and mimesis. For Wah, seeing is not the gaze of the humanist ego. Seeing is "the first gesture of the movement toward inscription, the graphic exposure of signs that tells the story of the identity of things and of the poet" (47), such that he is enabled to contextualize himself as an object among other objects.[4] "[T]he eye and the ear work together" at the interface between speech and writing and collaborate with the tongue to give to the audible voice the shape of a letter (49).

Although Kamboureli does not specifically mark her use of the term 'dialogue' or 'dialogic,' its proximity to and interpenetration

with that of 'intertextuality' suggests that it is of Kristevan origin
as well as of more common, general usage. She does attribute her
use of 'intertextuality' (Kamboureli 1984a, 52) to Julia Kristeva's
sense of the term, defined as "the transposition of one or more
systems of signs into another, accompanied by a new articulation
of the enunciative and denotative position" (Kristeva 1980, 15). It
is important to note that both Kristeva's definition of 'intertextuality' and Kamboureli's explication of what she calls "Wah's dialogic
method" (Kamboureli 1984a, 55) are very close to translation.
Intertextuality, dialogism and translation all foreground the writer's
double enunciative position as writer *and* reader. As Kamboureli
notes, "[Wah] starts as a reader soon to become a writer. . . . Wah's
reading becomes a graphic event" (52). The alternation between
what are normally thought of as two distinctly separate subject
positions, writer and reader, allows Kristeva and Kamboureli to
treat composition as process.

Kristeva's use of 'transposition' not only includes the sense of
transformation of language and text but allows her also to theorize
the subject-in-process/on trial [*le sujet en procès*] within signification.
Transformation as 'transposition' affects, and effects, both the text
and the writing subject. The poet is both writer and reader, text and
intertext, textual body and embodied text. As Kristeva explains, her
term 'transposition,' or 'intertextuality,' supplements Freud's terms
'displacement' and 'condensation' (the two fundamental processes
in the work of the unconscious), which entered the field of linguistics through the concepts of metaphor and metonymy:

> To these we must add a third "process"—the *passage*
> *from one sign system to another.* To be sure, this process
> comes about through a combination of displacement and
> condensation, but this does not account for its total op-
> eration. It also involves an altering of the thetic *position*—
> the destruction of the old position and the formation of a
> new one. The new signifying system may be produced
> with the same signifying material; in language, for exam-
> ple, the passage may be made from narrative to text. Or it
> may be borrowed from different signifying materials: the
> transposition from a carnival scene to the written text, for
> instance. In this connection we examined the formation of
> a specific signifying system—the novel—as the result of a

redistribution of several different sign systems: carnival, courtly poetry, scholastic discourse. The term *inter-textuality* denotes this transposition of one (or several) sign system(s) into another; but since this term has often been understood in the banal sense of "study of sources," we prefer the term *transposition* because it specifies that the passage from one signifying system to another demands a new articulation of the thetic—of enunciative and deno-tative positionality. (Kristeva 1984, 59-60)

Kristeva prefers the term 'transposition' over 'intertexuality' or 'translation' because of her investment in exploring 'positionality' as the realm of propositions and judgment. She also exploits the term as a means of distinguishing this process from 'representability.' 'Representability' she defines as the specific articulation of the semiotic and the symbolic for a given sign system. Transposition, on the other hand, implies "the abandonment of a former sign system, the passage to a second via an instinctual intermediary common to the two systems, and the articulation of the new system with its new representability" (60). As a neologism, 'transposition' is perhaps less susceptible than the more common term of 'transla-tion' to generalized and metaphorical usage and to slippage into metaphysical or transcendental presuppositions. It is also at present more flexible: 'transposition' names a translative process that moves not only between, but within, languages and texts and between different realms of signification, such as carnival, only beginning to be conceived as textual.[5]

My own preference for the term 'translation' derives from several impulses. My first impulse is to open that still fairly tradi-tional term to the effects of transposition and thereby to expand its range. Second, I wish to acknowledge and explore the terminology chosen by the authors under study, namely, Wah's adoption and modification of the term 'transcreation' and Robert Kroetsch's and Daphne Marlatt's essays on the relationship of translation to poetic composition. My third reason for selecting 'translation' over, for example, 'transposition' is a reflection of my focus on the process of composition. When a poet sits down in front of a blank piece of paper or a computer screen, she does not sit down to transposition the subject *per se*. Often, however, she does begin to translate.

Fourth, I wish to preserve the link with the history of translation theory and with current developments in that field.

Following Wah's own insistence that the poems are not translations but transcreations, Bowering and Kamboureli eschew translation as a model for his poetic composition. However, in theorizing the relations between reading and writing, and speech and writing, they are in fact discussing what I call 'translation poetics.' In this sense Wah's pictogram " nv s ble/ tr ck" is more than the magic "that is performed when i is removed, or when the eyes are covered" (Bowering 1980, 19). The " nv s ble/ tr ck" is an instance of intralingual and intersemiotic translation. In Wah's interpretation, what the pictograph shows (see the first epigraph to the present chapter) is the appearance and disappearance of a human figure. When the 'i's are removed, Wah says, "the letters, the phonology, breaks up nearly in the same way the pictograph itself breaks up which was very satisfying imagewise" (Nichol 1978, 37). If we read this particular pair of pictograph and pictogram emblematically, we can intimate that in its compositional effects translation is like a palimpsest, or a magic slate in which the marks etched into the wax surface of the underlayer remain when the mark on the plastic film disappears. Translation performs an " nv s ble tr ck."

Because of its relative invisibility and because of the predominance of representational thinking, there has been very little research into translation between speech and writing. J.C. Catford, in his book *A Linguistic Theory of Translation,* insists that between speech and writing there can be no translation. In the first place, he notes that there is no systematic theory of what he refers to as "graphic substance." He finds two instances only of graphological translation: an approximation to graphological translation is practised by typographers who wish to give an 'exotic' flavour to written texts; and persons writing in a foreign language may sometimes produce graphological translations. He emphasizes repeatedly that although in translation there is the substitution of grammar and lexis, and phonic and graphic "substances" (his word) as well, nevertheless the target language (TL) graphological form is by no means a translation equivalent of the source language (SL) graphological form (Catford 1965, 20).[6] Catford excludes the replacement of SL phonology and graphology by TL phonology and graphology from 'total translation' by stating that these replacements do not form equivalents and by arguing that in the absence of equivalence translation does not take place. These replacements are merely consequential upon the replacements of grammar and lexis (22).

Secondly, he refers to the process of switching between the spoken and the written media of language as "transcoding" and emphasizes that transcoding is not translation (42). For any particular language, there is an arbitrary relationship between phonological and graphological units. Conversion from spoken to written medium, or vice versa, is a universal practice among literates, he says, but it is not translation because it is not replacement by items which are equivalent due to their relationship to the same substance.

All of Catford's categories are subject to his a priori linguistic dictum that language is form, not substance. His linguistic theory of translation is formalist: he deliberately sets aside the materiality of the sign. What he isolates and names as 'phonic substance,' 'graphic substance' and even 'situation substance' are excluded from his formalist theory which aims to preserve grammar and lexis, that is, meaning, from contamination by the various substances he precipitates out as extralinguistic. Moreover, his theory of translation is thoroughly imbued with the metaphysics of presence, which prizes the auto-affective elements of the speech act. Although relations between languages can generally be regarded as at least bidirectional (though not always symmetrical), translation for Catford is always only unidirectional—from source text to target text. However, it is precisely this bidirectionality and these banned phonic, graphic and situation 'substances' which I wish to incorporate into my theorization of translation.

Several more recent works of translation theory, by both linguists and those who are not primarily linguists, challenge work such as Catford's. W. Haas, like Catford a British linguist, writing in 1970, just five years after the publication of Catford's textbook, posits a view exactly opposite to Catford's on the nature of the relation between writing and speech. In his book *Phono-Graphic Translation* Haas argues that "The relation itself between writing and speech is different in kind from the reference of either to things outside language" (Haas 1970, 15). Asserting that of course his model of these relations does not work within the traditional view of translation as "the transfer of some neutral extralingual meaning from one linguistic expression to another" (17), he brings the body back into his theory of translation. If such neutral, extralinguistic meaning is what is believed to be transferred between languages and texts during translation, then clearly, he says, it is not possible to call what takes place when meaningless phonemes are matched with meaningless graphemes 'translation.' He criticizes this conception of meaning as "something independent of any language whatever. But since we have never met meanings outside language, we could not say what it might be like to transfer them, a host of migrant souls, from one linguistic embodiment to another" (18). Noting a difference, then, between referentiality and phono-graphic correspondence (both writing and speech refer to 'things') Haas posits the relation between writing and speech as translation. He writes:

> . . . the operation which we perform upon the correspondence between writing and speech is *translation*—proceeding in one direction when we write down what is spoken, and in the other when we read aloud what is written. . . . As we can understand what is said in one language without translating it into another, so we understand what is spoken without writing it down, and also what is written without reading it aloud. (Haas 1970, 16)

While theories such as Catford's aim to preserve referentiality and meaning at the expense of the materiality of language and its "situation substance," Haas's theory is premised upon the lived situations in which the body reads, speaks and writes. While he concedes that there are many differences between phono-graphic translation and interlingual translation, still he does not see these differences as sufficient reason for ruling that translation does not take place between speech and writing (Haas 1970, 18-19). Some of the confusion surrounding the relation between speech and writing, he suggests, stems from the fact that we often mistake the names of letters for nouns. Letters are physical objects, which themselves have no meaning. The same is true of the names of phonemes. Furthermore, he says, we tend to use the same inventory of names for both phonemes and graphemes (23-24), thus habitually blurring the two different media together into one. However, the relation between speech and writing is translative also in the sense that information given in either system is not always translatable into the other (84).[7]

Roman Jakobson's distinctions among three types of translation are useful in clarifying Haas's sense of translation between different media and also in locating the limits of translation theories which privilege interlingual translation as translation "proper." In his essay "On Linguistic Aspects of Translation" Jakobson first points out that "the meaning of any linguistic sign is its translation into some further, alternative sign." Language is metonymic in its associations. Meaning as such is only another name for the deferral of one sign from another. He then sets out his three kinds of translation as follows:

> 1) Intralingual translation or *rewording* is an interpretation of verbal signs by means of other signs of the same language.
> 2) Interlingual translation or *translation proper* is an interpretation of verbal signs by means of some other language.
> 3) Intersemiotic translation or *transmutation* is an interpretation of verbal signs by means of signs of nonverbal sign systems. (Jakobson 1971, 261)

Jakobson's examples of intersemiotic translation include the transmutation from verbal art into music, dance, cinema, or painting, but he does not elaborate upon intersemiotic translation. If, as Haas reminds us, letters are physical objects as well as linguistic signs, then the relation between letters as physical objects and letters as signs might be categorized as intersemiotic translation. The same might be said of the physical sounds of phonemes. However, translation between speech and writing can take place intralingually, interlingually and—if intersemiotic translation were considered more loosely as the interpretation of one set of signs by a different (though not necessarily nonverbal) set of signs—intersemiotically as well.[8]

In a move parallel to Catford's marking off of what he calls the situation substance, Walter J. Ong in his work on the historical transition from orality to literacy almost entirely brackets the body. While Ong traces a process of radical change in the history of consciousness, he steadfastly maintains a speech-based, Cartesian, dualist model of the subject. Thus, in failing to address the body in

11

terms other than the Cartesian split between mind and body, Ong is able to describe the "psychodynamics of orality," for instance, but he is unable to account for the relation between speech and writing. Moreover, his model is a 'progressive' (though nostalgic) one: for him, the order of human history is such that orality precedes literacy, which precedes secondary orality.[9] In the interests of making these various historical stages clear and distinct, Ong does not dwell on the relations between oral signifying systems and written ones. By arguing for the historicity of these stages, he implies that the human individual possesses the power of conscious choice as to the fate of "the original spoken word" (Ong 1982, 81) and its manuscript, print and electronic disseminations. Despite his excoriations of critics whom he insists upon labelling "textualists" (A.J. Greimas, Tzvetan Todorov, Roland Barthes, Philippe Sollers, Jacques Derrida, Michel Foucault, Jacques Lacan) (165) for failing to take into consideration "primary orality," Ong himself fails to explore the operations of speech and writing within the human subject. Such an exploration would deconstruct that subject, with the corollary result that it would emerge as a subject of signs and signification and not a Cartesian, humanist self.[10]

Jacques Derrida, whose work does deconstruct the Cartesian subject, has written copiously on speech and writing and on translation. His work is extraordinarily complex, and any short synopsis of its role in my theorizing of the relation between speech and writing as translation will be reductive. Nevertheless, some general remarks on the importance of translation in his work are in order.

In his "Letter to a Japanese Friend" on the translation of his term 'deconstruction' into the Japanese language, Derrida notes: ". . . (and the question of deconstruction is also through and through *the* question of translation, and of the language of concepts, of the conceptual corpus of so-called 'western' metaphysics) . . ." (Derrida 1988, 1). Derrida's working through of *différance,* the trace structure, the supplement, the *pharmakon,* and other philosophical semes focuses on the structure of signification in alphabetic writing from within mainly the French, German and English languages. In a note appended to a reprint of this letter Derrida quotes from a French dictionary of 1873 in which, along with the mechanical, the grammatical or linguistic senses of the word 'deconstruction' are collected. It is worth quoting this passage in full:

> " 'Grammar: displacement that words are made to undergo when a written sentence is composed in a foreign language, by violating, it is true, the syntax of that language, but also by drawing close to the syntax of the maternal language, in order better to grasp the sense that the words present in the sentence.' This term exactly designates what the majority of grammarians improperly call "Construction"; for in any author, all the sentences are *constructed* according to the genius of his national language; what does a foreigner do who tries to comprehend, to translate this author? He *deconstructs* the sentences, disassembles their words, according to the genius of the foreign language; or if one wants to avoid all confusion in terms, there is *Deconstruction* with respect to the language of the translated author, and *Construction* with respect to the language of the translator. . ." (quoted in Leavey 1990, 193)

This denotation of 'deconstruction' conforms precisely to the linguistic deformation contemporary translation theorists call an 'interlanguage.' The term 'interlanguage,' coined by Larry Selinker in 1972 and further developed by Gideon Toury, refers to the linguistic interference from the mother tongue (SL) during a second-language learner's attempted production of the target language (TL). An interlanguage "enjoys an intermediate status between SL and TL" (Toury 1980, 71). Deconstruction, then, is the construction of an interlanguage—either or both between languages and texts and within a single language and text.[11]

To deconstruct is, in part, to translate. As Barbara Johnson points out, "For Derrida's work, in fact, has always already been (about) translation. His first book was a translation of Husserl's 'Origin of Geometry.' Derrida's theory and practice of *écriture*, indeed, occupy the very point at which philosophy and translation meet" (Johnson 1985, 144). As the English language translator of Derrida's *Dissemination,* Johnson has first-hand knowledge of the difficulty which Derrida's own texts foreground, namely, as Johnson says, "the more a text is worked through by the problem of translation, the more untranslatable it becomes" (146). In the following passage she sums up how this problematic of translation manifests itself in Derrida's texts:

> Derrida's entire philosophic enterprise, indeed, can be seen as an analysis of the translation process at work in every text. In studying the *différance* of signification, Derrida follows the misfires, losses, and infelicities that prevent any given language from being *one*. Language, in fact, can only exist in the space of its own foreignness to itself. . . . Not only, however, is this self-différance the *object* of Derrida's attention: it is an integral part of the functioning of his own écriture. The challenges to translation presented by Derrida's writing have continually multiplied over the years. From the early, well-bred neologisms to a syntax that increasingly frustrates the desire for unified meaning, Derrida has even, in *Living On*—first published in English—gone so far as to write *to* the translator *about* the difficulties he is in the act of creating for him, thus figuratively sticking out his tongue—his mother tongue—at the borderline between the translated text and the original. (Johnson 1985, 146-47)

Language works by deferral and *différance*. The trace structure dictates that any given language functions only through *différance* from itself. Meaning is not irremediably glued to signifiers but only emerges in the interstices between different signifiers. What we call thought takes place between the mark and its erasure: " nv s ble/ tr ck". Thus any text is always already an impossible translation that renders translation impossible (Johnson 1985, 146). In the name of establishing itself as the transparent expression of thought, Western philosophy has repressed translation and the foreignness of language to itself. Derrida attributes the difficulty of translation with regard to philosophy as situated "less in the passage from one language to another, from one philosophical language to another, than already, as we shall see, in the tradition between Greek and Greek; a violent difficulty in the transference of a nonphilosopheme into a philosopheme. With this problem of translation we will thus be dealing with nothing less than the problem of the very passage into philosophy" (Derrida 1981a, 72).

It must be mentioned, however, that in his earlier book *Of Grammatology* Derrida uses the words 'translator' and 'translation' in a metaphorical rather than literal sense, if such a distinction can be made. Speaking about the logocentric view of language and its confinement of writing to a secondary and instrumental function, he argues that logocentrism views writing as merely the "translator of a full speech that was fully *present* (present to itself, to its signified, to the other, the very condition of the theme of presence in general), technics in the service of language, *spokesman,* interpreter of an originary speech itself shielded from interpretation" (Derrida 1976, 8).[12] In a subsequent passage dealing with the Aristotelian perspective on signification, Derrida uses 'translation' as a synonym for the apparently natural signification which obtains in Aristotle between the voice and the mind, mental experiences and things, in order himself to distinguish between such apparent resemblances and the unnatural or conventional symbolization between voice and writing (11).

In light of his later articles and discussions devoted to the problematizing of translation, Derrida's use of the words 'translator' and 'translation' in these earlier contexts functions less to question the nature of the relation between speech and writing than to question the supposed natural resemblances among mind, speech and writing and the kind of translation sponsored by this order of things. The traditional support of translation theory has been the Aristotelian notion that although people use different writing systems and spoken languages nonetheless mental experiences are universal and therefore susceptible to translation. In using the words 'translator' and 'translation' to describe the logocentric view of the relation between writing and speech Derrida does not forfeit these words to the episteme he is deconstructing. For one thing, deconstruction neither prohibits nor licenses such forfeiture. Moreover, when, as in the passage quoted above, Derrida portrays the logocentric perspective on writing using the words 'translator,' 'spokesman' and 'interpreter' (in its double meaning of hermeneutic specialist and translator) he therby personifies, mimes and parodies logocentrism's view of 'being' as presence. In metaphorizing writing as a translator, spokesman and interpreter of speech, he illustrates how the logocentric version of 'translation' contains within it its own deconstruction.

Even as we note the striking similarities between deconstruction and translation then, we must also take under advisement

Derrida's caution to his Japanese friend that "All sentences of the type 'deconstruction is X' or 'deconstruction is not X' a priori miss the point, which is to say that they are at least false. As you know, one of the principal things at stake in what is called in my texts 'deconstruction' is precisely the delimiting of ontology and above all of the third person present indicative: S *is* P" (Derrida 1988, 4). He delimits the possibility for the word 'deconstruction' to be translated within a single language (French, English, or Japanese) into any other word. However, even as he proscribes a statement such as mine that "to deconstruct is, in part, to translate," he alludes, in a letter about translation, to the intralingual translation of the copula verb.[13] My purpose in pointing to the similarities between translation and deconstruction is not to reduce either term to the other but simply to alert the reader to the fact that in places where one is staged the other may also be operant. Translation has deconstructive potential, as translators' prefaces have always lamented.

Furthermore, although he deconstructs binary models of the subject, it has been argued that Derrida's deconstruction of the Cartesian subject has been "generalized to cover all subjects, even those who were never included in that core group of Subjects" (Kintz 1973, 115-16). Therefore Derrida's deconstruction, "a deconstruction of male, white, bourgeois subjectivity, the 'I' generalized to the universality of the 'we,' with the concomitant extension of the applicability of deconstruction to all, indifferently, undifferentiatedly" (116), because it fails to factor in the effects of gender differentiation, which is " 'translated by and translates a difference in the relation to power, language, and meaning' " [sic] (Kristeva, quoted by Kintz 1973, 132), cannot be relied upon entirely for an account of how the act of translation between writing and speech reorganizes the Cartesian subject and its body. My adoption of the word 'translation' and my coinage of the term 'translation poetics' is neither logocentric nor always strictly or solely Derridean.

An additional site at which to theorize the relation between orality and textuality is experimental feminist writing. The experimental writing practices of *écriture féminine* (in France and Québec) and writing the (m)other tongue (in the United States and Canada) are not occupied, as many critics have clamoured, with writing down an exclusively 'feminine' language dredged up from either an originally feminine psyche or a raised feminist consciousness, or from lost and found matriarchal texts and mythologies. Rather they are engaged in the inscription of an 'interlanguage.' As Jane Gallop suggests, the (m)other tongue is a composite that is no one's mother tongue and can only be comprehended in two languages at once (Gallop 1987, 328). Such experimental, feminist writing practices can be described as deconstructive, translative acts excavating and exploring the pictogrammic, ideogrammic and phonogrammic elements of language and incorporating the body's resources of gesture, performance and hysterical practice as well. Instead of rendering the body subservient to the demands of phonogrammic writing, the translation in such writing reverses the logocentric hierarchy of speech over writing whereby speech is viewed as the translation into language of being, writing as the translation of speech, and the body as the imaginary hollow in which these translations of the symbolic take place. Such writing attempts to inscribe the alterity of the scene of reading and writing into our construction of the body. The body becomes a kind of pictogram.

Much feminist criticism has analyzed how women writers incorporate certain body metaphors—the cycle of menstruation, rhythms of desire, the birth process—into the structure of their texts. However, if we conceive neither the female body nor the text as the source, cause or original of the other, then what transpires in this exchange between anatomy and text? To hypothesize the body as pictogram is not to perform a recursive double return—to a 'primitive' form of writing and to the mute flesh. It is not to substitute the body as sensuous original (pictogram) for the body as phonic original (phonogram). The body as pictogram, as the syntax of the phrase suggests, is a metaphor. The body as pictogram is not the body "proper." It cannot be appropriated by 'being' nor by an imaginary interior volume erected by the metaphysics and mathematics of the phoneme properly recorded.

The task is to try to think of the body not as represented, not as "the very expression, moment by moment, of an inward spirit, or a person belonging to himself" (Lingis 1983, 25), but as its own signifier, as a pictogram. "[T]he verbalization, the becoming-conscious, is not the operation that makes the forces that have been marked into signs; the inscribed flesh has been significant long before the voice" (39). Or, as Daphne Marlatt says, the tongue is "the major organ which touches all the different parts of the mouth to make the different sounds—tongue as speech organ. Also, the tongue is a major organ in making love between women [and others]. It's an erotic organ [intertwining] eroticism and speech—lovemaking as a form of organ speech, and poetry as a form of verbal speech" (Williamson 1985, 28). The body can be theorized not as a sum of its internal organs and other visceral parts but as a series of contiguous libidinal surfaces. The body does not pre-exist or subsist outside of either alphabetic writing or the voice but rather is perpetually translating, distributing inscriptions, sounds, vocalizations, touches, tremors, excitations, flows, emissions, pressures, pulses, weights, liquids, thoughts, surges, contractions, pangs, glances, ripples, movements, gestures. . . .

The body is a mobile and lifesize pictogram.

nv s ble tr ck.

Translating is another way of deconstructing the binary between inner and outer. If neither body nor text is construed as the original of the other, then multiple translations—intersemiotic, intralingual and interlingual—can take place between them. In this context, to translate, and to theorize translation, is not always only to write or to speak. To translate can be either to luxuriate in the pleasures of the signifier or to tremble at its terrible powers. As anyone who has ever studied a second language or made strange in a foreign country knows, translation also composes the body. Learning a new language you are compelled to curl your tongue, roll your 'r's, pull down deeper into previously hidden recesses of the throat, thrust your lower jaw forward, experience your lips, click your tongue, activate your shoulders, eyebrows, hands, even implicate your hips. In its play with different languages, with signifier and signified, and with writing and speech even within a single language, translation transforms signs into bodysculpting tools.

Notes

1   Wah borrows the term 'transcreation' from Samuel Taylor Coleridge. See the epigraph to *Pictograms from the Interior of B.C.* and also bpNichol's "Transcreation: A Conversation with Fred Wah."

2   Steve McCaffery's review, "Antiphonies," was the first important reading of Wah's *Pictograms from the Interior of B.C.*, a reading which, along with bpNichol's and McCaffery's major interviews with Wah, conditions the thinking of both Bowering and Kamboureli. McCaffery has subsequently revised and expanded this review and published it as an essay in his book *North of Intention*.

3   She in turn is echoing those of Bowering, specifically the passage from his article which I have quoted in block form above.

4   Kamboureli, analyzing what a 'trans' process means for Wah, explicates the title poem of Wah's book *Among,* in which the poet professes to "tree" himself. Here is how she sees Wah positioning himself in relation to language and things:

> "Treeing" oneself is neither a magical metamorphosis nor an escape up a tree. Wah has not insinuated himself into a paradox, a relationship that does violence to the structure of the sign "tree." "Making inner" does not erase the difference between the tree and Wah. He is not assuming the *physis* of the tree. The transference of the signifier becomes possible partly through Wah's involvement in a process of defamiliarization (*ostranenie*) . . and partly through his partaking in the structuring of nature, the textuality of the world. Wah, by consciously denouncing the being-outside-of-things, contextualizes himself in nature, gaining thus an unmediated understanding of the signification of "tree." "He is situated on the interface of signifier and signified, relating to objects by contiguity." (Wah 1972a, 46-47)

5   Kristeva's use of 'transposition' may also have to do with the translation of the German *Übersetzung.* As Derrida remarks (in English translation), "We would be overlooking the rapport between *Setzen* (the posing of the position, of *thesis* and *nomos*) and *Übersetzung* (trans- and superposing, sur-passing and over-exposing, passing beyond position). We would hardly be translating *Übersetzen* by translating if we translated it to translate" (Derrida 1989, xxiii).

In addition, as Kristeva states, her use of 'position' is Husserlian. See her explication of positionality in *Revolution in Poetic Language*, p. 43.

6   Current translation theory avoids the terms 'original' and 'translation' by using the designations source language and target language (SL and TL) and source text and target text (ST and TT).

7   Haas also states at one point during his argument for phono-graphic translation that "Modern verse is very largely 'bilingual' " (Haas 1970, 87). 'Bilingual,' that is, in terms of the two 'media' of speech and writing.

8   It is worth noting that in his article "Toward the Understanding of Translation in Psychoanalysis" Patrick Mahony describes the interaction of hysteric and linguistic practice as "intersemiotic symptomatology" (Mahoney 1987, 469), thus setting a precedent for retaining Jakobson's term 'intersemiotic' but broadening its interpretation. Mahony states in his introductory paragraph that "Jakobson's attempt at all-embracing categories does not take into account Freud's enormous contribution to the critique of translation" (461). He goes on to substantiate his contention that "Freud's contribution is especially outstanding with respect to Jakobson's third category of intermedium or intersemiotic translation" (467-68).

9   In his book *Orality and Literacy* Ong describes the stage of secondary orality, to which we have acceded with the integration into our daily lives of the telephone, radio and television, as bearing "striking resemblances to [primary orality] in its participatory mystique, its fostering of a communal sense, its concentration on the present moment, and even its use of formulas. But it is essentially a more deliberate and self-conscious orality, based permanently on the use of writing and print, which are essential for the manufacture and operation of the equipment and for its use as well" (Ong 1982, 136). In this book at least, Ong does not consider the computer in terms of secondary orality. His concern is to preserve what he calls "the original spoken word" (81), and so he reads chirographic, print and electronic transformations all as ways of technologizing that original spoken word.

See pp. 135-38 of *Orality and Literacy* for elaboration on secondary orality. See also Dennis Cooley's essays "Placing the Vernacular: The Eye and the Ear in Saskatchewan Poetry" and "The Vernacular Muse in Prairie Poetry." Cooley relies in significant measure upon Ong's distinction between orality and literacy in these two essays. I discuss Cooley's binary mapping of the models of speech and writing onto contemporary Canadian poetry in the chapter "The Vernacular Republic: The Politics of the Mother Tongue in Some Recent Prairie Poetics."

10   In one of her articles on the position of 'woman' in Derrida's vocabulary, Gayatri Chakravorty Spivak suggests that "In the light of Derrida's work, and of Derridian criticism, it is not difficult to understand that traditional phallocentric discourse is marked by, even as it is produced, 'the name of man' " (Spivak 1984, 26).

Spivak connects Derrida's critique of propriation through the disclosure of "the fractured alterity of the scene of reading and writing" (29) with his articulation of a certain "(non)name of woman" (26). Thus Ong's resistance to grammatology and to the work of those others, along with Derrida, whom he regards as "textualists" can be seen as a resistance, in the name of the Father and of 'man,' to the scene of reading and writing. Moreover, as Spivak notes, both the resistance to Derrida's work and its eager reception by prominent adherents have been marked by the failure to take up his renaming the operation of philosophy with the 'name' of woman (35).

11   Speaking in an interview about his career as a philosopher Derrida remarks that he feels as if he has been involved in a twenty-year detour in order to get back to something that literature accommodates more easily than philosophy, a kind of writing that one cannot appropriate, that somehow marks you without belonging to you and that appears only to others, never to you. He says:

> It's fatal to dream of inventing a language or a song which would be yours—not the attributes of an "ego," but rather, the accentuated flourish, that is, the musical flourish of your own most unreadable history. I'm not speaking about a *style,* but of an intersection of singularities, of manners of living, voices, writing, of what you carry with you, what you can never leave behind. What I write resembles, by my account, a dotted outline of a book to be written, in what I call—at least for me—the *"old new language,"* the most archaic and the newest, unheard of, and thereby at present unreadable. (Wood and Bernasconi 1988, 71)

12   This is Ong's position exactly. Ong posits writing as it occurs in both manuscript and print culture as a technique or a technologization of the otherwise unmediated presence of the word.

13   It is worth noting that Ernest Fenollosa also had reservations about the copula verb in the English language. For him the reliance upon the copula "is an ultimate weakness of language. It has come from generalising all intransitive words into one" (Fenollosa 1936, 15). See especially pp. 15 and 26 in *The Chinese Written Character as a Medium for Poetry.*

THE PICTOGRAM AS A
MEDIUM FOR POETRY:
FRED WAH'S INTERLINGUAL
TRANSLATION POETICS

Chinese poetry . . . speaks at once with the vividness of painting, and with the mobility of sounds. It is, in some sense, more objective than either, more dramatic. In reading Chinese we do not seem to be juggling mental counters, but to be watching *things* work out their own fate.

Ernest Fenollosa
The Chinese Written Character as a Medium for Poetry

We have lived long in a generalizing time, at least since 450 B.C. And it has had its effects on the best of men, on the best of things. Logos, or discourse, for example, has, in that time, so worked its abstractions into our concept and use of language that language's other function, speech, seems so in need of restoration that several of us got back to hieroglyphs or to ideograms to right the balance.

Charles Olson
"Human Universe"

The Poet as Theor(h)et(or)ician:
Pictograms from the Interior of B.C.

As the single-word titles of his first five books suggest—

> *Lardeau,*
> *Mountain,*
> *Tree,*
> *Among*
> and *Earth—*

Fred Wah names, but he does not attempt to describe the world in language. In his introduction to Wah's *Selected Poems* George Bowering remarks that a glance at some of Wah's book titles reminds the reader that "here is a poet who responds to the particulars of his ground with an eye to the singularity of each, without any semiological distancing that would be signalled by a 'definite' article" (Bowering 1980, 10-11). Or, as Smaro Kamboureli observes, "Nature predominates in all of [these titles] not as a setting awaiting description but as the natural surrounding in which Wah's presence is embedded in the presence of things" (Kamboureli 1984a, 46).

In these first five books, Wah explored the potential of a reoralized speech model to break through the shielded boundaries of the humanist or logocentric self. The logocentric subject maintains a steadfast belief in his or her own unified, irreducible self-presence as it is manifested in speech. This priorizing of the voice represents, in Frank Lentricchia's words, the triumph of "the ideality of meaning" over "the fallen corporeality" of writing. The metaphysics of presence protects the ideality of meaning by "inventing a residence for ideality—the interior of a consciousness shielded from all exterior contamination" (Lentricchia 1980, 177). The materiality of writing is derogated as the mere transcription of the spoken word. Wah attempted in his early books to penetrate and thereby 'contaminate' this isolate self with phenomena from outside it. Moreover, in his early poetry Wah posited an alternate version of self. Instead of consciousness as the foundation of the self, he proposed the proprioceptive[1] body as the basis upon which to imagine or theorize an alternative self. His poetry flooded and overflowed the strict logocentric division between interior and exterior (and its correlated divisions between subject and object, self and the world) with body in-formation and geo-logical and geo-graphical processes. He merged together on the page the movements of tissues, the snap of synapses and other liminal intelligences which function largely without the mediation of consciousness, and signs and signals from the surrounding geograph. The logic and graph of the 'geo' co-exists in his early work with the logic and recording (note-taking) of the speaking subject.

With the publication of *Pictograms from the Interior of B.C.,* the word 'interior' becomes for Wah a reference not to a psychic or even human 'interior' but rather to a geographical region. He shifts somewhat from dismantling the interior of the logocentric self to exploring both speech and writing insofar as they construct his senses of place and of self. The sense of place, the interior of B.C., is no longer just the poet's home ground and the subject of his spoken address, as it was in the previous books. Now geography is also the site of writing. Locality *is* the scene of writing. Or, as Wah says simply, "Home is where the story is" (Wah 1977, 111). In his poetry, Wah acts as a medium for the intermingling of the materiality of language and the things of the world. Rather than transcribe the world in language, his particular poetic project is to re-embed discourse in the world of things and events. As he has commented, "The language seems very much at home. I don't need a referential language going on" (Nichol 1978, 45). Freed of some of the constraints of referentiality, Wah opens the space of his work to the materiality of language and things.

With *Pictograms from the Interior of B.C.* Wah initiates "a perceptual descent into the graph" (McCaffery 1976, 92), both pictograph and geograph. No doubt part of the seductive appeal of the pictographs[2] for Wah, as for his reader, relates to their perceptual connection with the objects they depict. Unlike alphabetic systems, pictography is a writing system which is not arbitrarily linked through sound with the world but bears instead a direct perceptual relation to things and events.[3] Pictographic characters exist as floating signifiers independent of any specific system of phonetic reproduction. Thus they have the potential to be, in a limited sense, translinguistic. Moreover, the actual presence of the pictographs in his own home territory would have been attractive for a poet so powerfully drawn to inscribing the local.

Wah's account of the genesis of the long poem that is *Pictograms* bears this out. In conversation with bpNichol, he describes how he had decided to write a long poem by translating some Interior Salish texts but found that such texts did not exist. In the meantime he had been looking at John Corner's book, *Pictographs (Indian Rock Paintings) in the Interior of British Columbia,* and, he remarks, "there was this lovely sense of a very clear graphic, graphicness, going on" (Nichol 1978, 35). He began to understand that "this is what I have to work with" (36) so decided to translate the pictographs instead. But this objective, he claims, was thwarted by the lack of any existing substantial code.

Further analyzing the stimulus of Corner's book, Wah had then realized that in his accompanying poems he was responding not to rock paintings per se but to Corner's book of drawings from rock paintings. He was not responding to or writing about objects. Rather text called out to text:

Hey! It Looks like
you got a couple ways in there
and a face, me
no face.
Show me how you do it
and I'll come too.
(*Pictograms,* 7)

Wah's tendency to think in images, the act of looking, was the generative impulse behind *Pictograms*. His image-response doubles Corner's image-response, which in turn doubles the responses of the natives who "themselves disavowed any knowledge or information other than the fact they said they were here when they got here, which couldn't be true. I mean the paintings would not have lasted that long" (Nichol 1978, 37). Just as the origin of the pictographs is concealed and thereby erased, so too the origin (and originality) of Wah's pictograms is doubled and thereby deferred.

Wah repeatedly disavows his source texts and adopts the term 'transcreation' rather than 'translation' to name his compositional process. In the interview with Nichol—the full title of which is "Transcreation: A Conversation with Fred Wah: T.R.G. Report One: Translation (Part 3)"—Wah uses the term 'translation' in its most ordinary sense of interlingual translation in order to distinguish by contrast the process he prefers to call 'transcreation.' The poems in *Pictograms,* he says, range from literal translations to very loose and tangential connections between the pictograph and the corresponding poem. Many of them deliberately improvise upon and deviate from the pictographs with no intention whatsoever of fidelity to the original. He emphasizes that he is not translating the original rock paintings anyway; he's working from Corner's book of drawings of the paintings. His book is a poetic transcreation of Corner's book.

Wah's transcreational poetics privileges looking over translation. In his first books, he attempted to notate the event of his perceiving of primary objects and occurrences. In *Pictograms* he moves to a different locus of activity. In this book he notates the event of his response to a notation. One set of signs attracts another set of signs, and the poet situates himself so as to record and co-sign the crosscurrents of this attraction. Wah says that "language, no matter how you're using it, in all of its aspects, carries with it all of itself. And though we may be aware of any one point, in this case of paying attention to the minimal reference or paying attention to the production, to actually producing something ourselves, that everything else is going on at the same time" (Wah 1978, 58). His notational response to a notation remains grounded primarily at the level of the signifier rather than the signified. As he says:

Glyphs become very interesting to me. . . . And of course I'm very very curious about the ideogram and pictograph and I don't know enough about them. I want to know more about them. OK, so it's *looking,* and the transcreation I think, for me, has been looking and then language and then the formation of language but always after looking at these things. (Nichol 1978, 49)

One of the pictograms is especially mimetic of this visualizing process. Wah remarks about its notation that "the letters, the phonology, breaks up nearly in the same way the pictograph itself breaks up which was very satisfying imagewise" (Nichol 1978, 37).

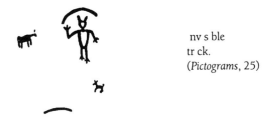

nv s ble
tr ck.
(*Pictograms,* 25)

Paradoxically, the pictogram which most clearly looks like its corresponding (perhaps more accurately, co-responding) pictograph does so when the 'i's/eyes are removed. In this example, Wah's transcreation from pictograph to phonograph undoes the mechanisms of phonology. That is, the resulting poem cannot be spoken. Like a pictograph, it can only be read visually. It is a phono-*graph* or, to use Wah's term, a picto-*gram.* The transcreation of pictograph into pictogram causes pictographic elements of the source language to appear within the phonological target language. In turn, the pictogrammic poem lends a new narrative and a new coding to the pictograph on the facing page: the activity in the drawing becomes a drama of appearance and disappearance. Now you see it; now you don't. Wah's transcreation transforms both source and target texts, source and target writing systems.

In a discussion with Steve McCaffery about the politics of the referent, conducted shortly after the publication of *Pictograms,* Wah repeatedly insists that language for him is primarily a visual experience. He says: "I think in pictures, in images and, though language doesn't elude me in its non-imagic possibilities, basically that's what's happening for me" (Wah 1978, 61). Later in the same discussion he modifies his statement somewhat: "I guess I'm talking about image as not only concrete things you see outside yourself and outside of language but as the idea carried in language. . . . one of my immediate reactions to any kind of language is the 'ideo', 'video', seeing" (62). Pictographs, we recall, do not notate speech sounds; they record observable objects and occurrences. As this emphasis on looking makes clear, even his own written responses to objects, words and texts, though coded in phonetic language, are primarily visual.

Wah's insistence upon the act of looking, then, is frequent, complex and even at times seemingly contradictory. Contradictory, that is, until we recall that 'to look at' is the etymological root of the word 'theory.' *The American Heritage Dictionary of the English Language* traces 'theory' as deriving from the Late Latin *theoria,* from Greek, contemplation, theory, from *theoros,* spectator, from *theastai,* to observe, from *thea,* a viewing. The English word 'theater' also derives from the same root. In "Theoria," the second chapter of his *Applied Grammatology,* Gregory L. Ulmer quotes Martin Heidegger on the meaning of the word 'theory.' Ulmer writes:

> [Heidegger] explains that "theory" stems from the Greek *Theorein,* which grew out of the coalescing of *thea* and *horao.* "*Thea* (cf. Theatre) is the outward look, the aspect, in which something shows itself. Plato names this aspect in which what presences shows what it is, *eidos.* To have seen this aspect, *eidenai,* is to know." And the second root, *horao,* means "to look at something attentively, to look it over, to view it closely." When translated into Latin and German, *theoria* became *contemplatio,* which emphasizes, besides passivity, the sense of "to partition something off into a separate sector and enclose it therein . . ." (Ulmer 1985, 32)

Walter J. Ong is convinced that, by Plato's time, chirographic consciousness, consciousness informed by the technology of writing, had so established itself in the ancient world that Plato was able to conceive of ideas, the look of things, as the " 'really real.' " According to Ong:

> Spoken words are events, engaged in time and indeed in
> the present. Plato's ideas were the polar opposite: not
> events at all, but motionless "objective" existence, imper-
> sonal, and out of time. Forming the ultimate base of all
> knowledge, they implied that intellectual knowledge was
> like sight. . . . Basically, the Greek word *idea* means the
> look of a thing. It comes from the same root as the Latin
> *video* (I see), which yields the English "vision" and its
> cognates. The ideas were thus in a covert sense like
> abstract pictures . . . (Ong 1967, 34-35)

In this context, Wah's work can be seen as a continuation of Charles
Olson's project to find a way of writing which does not continue to
"partition reality at any point, in any way" (Olson 1973, 164). Wah
takes to heart Olson's warning that "[Plato's] world of Ideas, of forms
as extricable from content, is as much and as dangerous an issue as
are logic and classification, and they need to be seen as such if we
are to get on to some alternative to the whole Greek system" (163).
Wah keeps his eyes open to both phenomena and ideas, restoring
them once again to a common and more equal footing.

At this point we can review Wah's characteristic image-response, his response to John Corner's transcribed pictographs and
the meaning of the word 'transcreation.' Ong's statement that Plato's
ideas are "in a covert sense like abstract pictures" recalls Wah's
statements about his immediate reaction to any kind of language
being to form a picture or image in his mind. The effect of Wah's
work then is to add, through a kind of veiled catachresis, to the
meaning of the word 'theory,' which has become generally reduced
in our time to signify the process of abstract reasoning alone,
divorced from seeing or looking. In his first several books, he
concentrated on the acts of seeing and speaking. In *Pictograms* he
turns his gaze to writing. The *gram* is both the materiality of
language and the locus at which theorizing becomes increasingly
possible. In *Pictograms* he is theorizing that there are other kinds of
thought or theory besides those which we commonly acknowledge
as such, namely, logic, rationality, classification, systematization,
hierarchy:

31

The feathers of my mind increase
as I reach for the choices
chance for what else
other than what I knew (know)
another talks to me (I think)
something (things) to see.
(*Pictograms*, 6)

Although Wah claims that no translations of the pictographs could be found (Nichol 1978, 36) so that he was compelled to perform what he calls transcreations instead of translations, this is not entirely true. John Corner's book does include the anthropologist James Teit's dictionary of fifty-two pictographs along with some twenty additional entries appended by Corner himself (Kamboureli 1984a, 52). This is not to suggest that Wah is ingenuous in his claim, but rather that perhaps a certain willful 'blindness' comes into play as a mark of Wah's resistance to translation. The first clue we have of Wah's refusal to translate is the emphasis he places on the fact that he is responding to Corner's *drawings* of the pictographs, not to rock paintings themselves. He declines to read through Corner's *drawings* to the signifieds of the paintings just as he refuses to see the presence of a code that would allow traditional interlingual translation to take place. Moreover, of course, those elements of a text which are not reducible to meaning—namely those partaking of the materiality of the signifier—are those which often are lost in translation.

He also emphasizes that in the process of composition he would select from the panels only certain figures: he did not try to create a narrative that would encompass all the elements of the pictograph. He says that as soon as he had selected out of a panel a few particular figures he would "then get away from that as fast as I could because when I stop to think about it something else is going to happen and I want to stop at that point, i.e. this isn't a meditative process, or a contemplative one, it's very much a time thing" (Nichol 1978, 36-37). Wah does not allow time for passive contemplation or the partitioning and categorizing of perception. He does not allow his thinking, his 'theory,' to spatialize itself. He insists on remaining within the temporal. He sees himself during poetic composition as a medium for a 'trans' process that comes over (to) him (38). He is, in short, a translator.

This 'trans' process includes looking and language, and also narrative. Wah's own personal story enters into the transcreation. For example, his father emerges in the following pictogram:

Northeast
(from family, a few friends)
I turned
since I had accompanied my father
that far
what was in the world around here
became larger
some part of it
then all of it. (*Pictograms*, 17)

And in the next pictogram Wah's trumpet playing in a jazz band known as the Kampus Kings comes in:

How does the jazz go?
Autumn moon a bit drunk
in the tree-tops with Wind
(north) & Pacific cloud banks
about 1959 not quite
jamming it but from here
to the coast one big
triple high C and wetter
than a duck's ass just
a sliver of a harvest moon.
(*Pictograms*, 15)

Although narrative is important to him, he is nevertheless wary of it at the same time. In an interview in *Writing* magazine he says: "I find that I'm not comfortable moving too far into [narrative line]. I'm more attracted to the poem as an activity that informs me about what's going on in language, in my life, in my perceptions. As a poet one way to get into narrative without going into a prose fiction is through the long poem" (Baxter 1984, 45). For him narrative is not the recuperation of a lost past. Rather it is what is *presently* going on "in language, in my life, in my perceptions." When the word 'I' is used in a pictogram, it refers to a figure in the pictograph but "it's also, the figure becomes me," Wah says. "It's a drama" (Nichol 1978, 41).

If narrative is thought of as the dramatic dialogue the poet carries on with himself in the act of writing, then narrative becomes a function of the middle voice. Wah was introduced to the concept of the middle voice in Charles Olson's graduate classes. In "GRAMMAR—a 'book' " Olson wrote that in the middle voice the subject is represented as acting: on himself, for himself or on something belonging to himself (Olson 1974, 29). The middle voice does not occur in English, but it does in Greek. I shall let Smaro Kamboureli describe it: "it is, as its name suggests, neither active nor passive. The action of the verb returns to the grammatical subject that performs the action. That is, the acting subject and the object affected by the action are the same person or the same thing" (Kamboureli 1984a, 58). Because the English language does not have the middle voice, Wah attempts to construct its effects through the manipulation of temporality. He says:

> My sense is . . . that it has to do with tense, it has to do
> with time, middle voice has to do with time. My sense of
> searching for a middle voice has been working between a
> kind of gerundial, participial thing, and a pronoun. Like I
> could say, 'I floating': rather than 'I float' which is too direct.
> A condition . . . 'I floating' . . . if I could state that. I work
> towards that. So I was aware of that [in *Pictograms*] but I
> was aware of that in *Earth.* (Nichol 1978, 48-49)

The use of a kind of synthetic middle voice produces in the pictogrammic poems this double reference of the 'I' as both Wah and a pictographic figure.

In addition to gerunds and participles, Wah relies on subjunctive and imperative constructions, apostrophe, questions, exclamations, lists, and onomatopoeic words to create an impression of the middle voice in English. In the following pictogram, a synthetic middle voice is achieved through recording inner dialogue (action performed for oneself) and through onomatopoeic effects:

> On my way to get a pail of water
> which way
> down by the creek
> down by the dark
> and in the trees the night
> buhdum, buhdum
> bdum bdum bdum. (*Pictograms,* 4)

The time of the poem is the time of its composition. The incident of utterance is the moment of *poiesis*. Event and writing are coincidental.

Even in its personal subjective sense, the pictogrammic I/eye is not a site where Wah as a subject is unquestioningly restored. If, as he says, the eye is that with which one applies "a tactics of syntax to any picture you look at" (Nichol 1978, 49), then similarly the 'I' functions syntactically rather than personally. In the following pictogram, Wah and one of the figures in the panel merge in the instant of the 'I':

> I walked into a battle
> with the forest
> I tried on the buffalo-horn headdress
> things happened to me
> visions and pictures
> two or three signs
>
> I pushed one way
> and I pushed another way
>
> size gave dance to me
> the deer showed me form
>
> the larval, it
> opens up. (*Pictograms*, 23)

Here both addresser and addressee are identical or, in temporal terms, simultaneous. As with the middle voice, the action of the verbs returns to the grammatical subject which performs the action. In this sense, Wah's synthetic middle voice is performative. That is,

35

in the above pictogram the statements accomplish the acts to which they refer. In this performative sense, Wah's identification with figures in the pictographs constitutes a drama.

Roland Barthes contends that the present state of the verb "to write" is exactly middle voice. According to him, in the case of the middle voice, "the subject affects himself in acting; he always remains inside the action, even if an object is involved. The middle voice does not, therefore, exclude transitivity" (Barthes 1970, 142). For the poststructuralist writer, to write "is to effect writing in being affected oneself; it is to leave the writer . . . inside the writing, not as a psychological subject . . . but as the agent of the action" (142). It is in this sense of the middle voice and of writing, then, that Wah's grammatological practice underwrites the dialogical play between pictogram and pictograph, incorporating both the poet and the figure in the pictograph, both the spoken and the written subject(s), both orality and textuality. The double discourse of Wah's grammatology is dramatic and performative, not expressive or demonstrative. Wah's poetic practice moves 'theory' and 'theater' closer again to their common etymological root. In other words, as poet, he neither contemplates things as they are nor expresses truths. He does not maintain a stable position in discourse. He actively looks at things but does not partition reality into separate sectors and then passively contemplate it. He mediates; he does not meditate. His personal self is employed as a vehicle for a knowledge practice; it is not explored for its own sake. Nor are what he calls his image-responses responses to objects and events as much as they are to language itself. He refuses traditional translation as a model of his compositional practice, because it operates primarily at the level of the signified, but he embraces transcreation, which functions at the level of the signifier.[4] For him, narrative is the dialogue of the compositional process itself. Narrative is the story of the story. His approach is theoretical, in the sense established above. He verses himself in the languages of place. He looks at, theorizes, dramatizes, and performs.

WAH CREDITS HIS READING of Ernest Fenollosa for relieving him of the notion that a sentence must be a complete thought (Wah 1985a, 214). In fact, one could read Wah's *Pictograms from the Interior of B.C.* as a response to Fenollosa's influential essay "The Chinese Written Character As a Medium for Poetry," edited and published by Ezra Pound. Just as Fenollosa explores the potential of the Chinese ideogram for estranging and renewing American poetry and poetics, so Wah analyzes the indigenous yet radically 'other' writing system of the pictograph as a medium for poetry.[5]

But while Wah does not reject the sentence as such, he does set aside the concept of the complete thought. For him the creative possibilities lie in the notation of 'inner speech.' The notation of 'inner speech' allows him both to write and to observe the writing process. In a review of *Considering How Exaggerated Music Is,* poems by Leslie Scalapino, a writer whose work he admires, Wah observes:

> She tries to write partly the way someone would talk but also the way someone would think so the writing is like a record of the actual occurrence (and concurrence) of language and thinking where the syntax isn't formal and preset but natural. . . . The syntax moves very quickly so that the sweep of thinking and saying is amazingly particular. She is able to focus on words and thoughts as particles in motion; we don't stop at any point with some glib comprehension but keep adding up, figuring out. (Wah 1983, 9)

Scalapino's work is similar to Wah's but she does not disrupt syntax to anywhere near the extent that he does. Wah praises one sequence in Scalapino's book as "a wonderful illustration of the revolutionary aspect of the larger uses of paradigmatic thought-suffixes; large chunks of mind-rhyme generating further and further prehension" (Wah 1983, 9). Writing partly the way someone would talk but also the way someone would think so the writing is like a record of the actual occurrence and concurrence of language and thinking is precisely the activity which I call Wah's theoretical method.

'Inner speech' is another term for the combined activity that Wah's and Scalapino's double writing or recording is based on. Inner speech, a phenomenon investigated by Russian psychologists and linguists and a concept crucial to discussion of Wah's work, deserves to be treated at some length. One of the best descriptions of inner speech is that provided by A. N. Sokolov in the introduction to his book *Inner Speech and Thought.* He writes:

> In psychology, the term "inner speech" usually signifies soundless, mental speech, arising at the instant we think about something, plan or solve problems in our mind, recall books read or conversations heard, read and write silently. In all such instances, we think and remember with the aid of words which we articulate to ourselves. Inner speech is nothing but speech to oneself, or concealed verbalization, which is instrumental in the logical process-ing of sensory data, in their realization and comprehension within a definite system of concepts and judgments. . . .
>
> . . . however, . . . despite its specificity (soundlessness and fragmentariness), inner speech, far from being an independent entity, is a secondary phenomenon derived from external speech—auditory perception of the speech of other persons and active mastery of all the forms of the spoken and written word. Seen from this viewpoint, inner speech represents a psychological transformation of exter-nal speech, its "internal projection," arising at first as a repetition (echo) of the speech being uttered and heard, but becoming later its increasingly abbreviated reproduc-tion in the form of verbal designs, schemes, and semantic complexes operating not unlike "quanta" of thought. From these psychological descriptions, inner speech emerges as a rather intricate phenomenon, where thought and lan-guage are bound in a single, indissoluble complex acting as the speech mechanism of thinking. (Sokolov 1972, 1)

Inner speech is often invoked in film reception theory to account for the way in which the viewer processes the otherwise separate shots that comprise films. Film theorists suggest that inner speech flows into the hiatus between the individual shots to tell the story of the story. Despite its misleading and very problematic name, at least in English translation, inner speech, as Sokolov points out, incorporates both speech and writing, as well as graphic images: its vocabulary frequently acquires "a very individual, subjective signifi-cance and is complemented by graphic images" (Sokolov 1972, 3).

Furthermore, though silent, inner speech has a somatic, proprioceptive component.

L.S. Vygotsky, whose book *Thought and Language* has been instrumental in the diffusion of the information about inner speech into film reception and critical theory, emphasizes that "inner speech is not the interior aspect of external speech" but is rather a function in itself. According to Vygotsky, "While in external speech thought is embodied in words, in inner speech words die as they bring forth thought" (Vygotsky 1962, 149). "The relation of thought to word is not a thing but a process, a continual movement back and forth from thought to word and from word to thought" (125). He places the syntax of inner speech at the opposite end of the spectrum from that of written speech, with oral speech occupying the middle ground. Each is a separate linguistic function and the grammar of thought differs in each (98-99).

Much of Wah's work consists of the notation of inner speech—examples could be drawn from any of his books—but perhaps one of the clearest examples of the traces of inner speech in *Pictograms from the Interior of B.C.* is the pictogram, quoted earlier, which begins "How does the jazz go?" where, as bpNichol remarks

> with this particular text there's an obvious interpenetration of the two things, . . . it's not a sort of one to one it's actually a flow back and forth between the two [pictograph and pictogram]. It almost goes line for line, almost, not quite, but there's that feeling of going one to the other in the line structure. (Nichol 1978, 39)

In another example, the osprey, which is a "very important personal bird" for Wah (Nichol 1978, 48), comes into the pictogram. Wah comments: "So I don't know if that's [the figure in the pictograph] an Osprey. I'm not saying that the Lilooet Indians knew that that's the Osprey. I don't feel it matters." In an alternating, fluctuating, process and event, inner speech gathers up both Wah's immediate responses to the pictograph and memories from his own personal life story. Rather than categorize and separate the two, the poet allows both into the poem simultaneously, notating their occurrence without editorializing.

One of the most important aspects of inner speech is its inherent dialogism. The units of inner speech combine and permutate like the "alternating lines of a dialogue." They join and alternate "not according to the laws of grammar or logic but according to the laws of evaluative (emotive) correspondence, dialogical deployment, etc., in close dependence on the historical conditions of the social situation and the whole pragmatic run of life" (Vološinov 1973, 38). We have already noted the dialogical play in *Pictograms* between pictograph and pictogram, and between the processes of reading and writing. There are several other dialogues going on within the pictograms themselves, namely, the dialogues inherent in inner speech between thought and language, and between speech and writing, and the proprioceptive dialogue between the body and its experiences. And of course each of these dialogues is in turn carried over into the dialogue between pictogram and pictograph.

It must be emphasized that inner speech is *not* the expression of internal experiences; rather it *is* experience itself. "Experience exists even for the person undergoing it only in the material of signs" (Vološinov 1973, 28). There is no translation from inner to outer; translation takes place only between and among signs. The body produces its own signs in the form of "any organic activity or process: breathing, blood circulation, movements of the body, articulation, inner speech, mimetic motions, reactions to external stimuli . . . and so forth" (28). For Wah, just as experience is its own expression, *noesis* and *poiesis* are simultaneous.

Wah's writing is picto-ideo-phonographic. As the term suggests, picto-ideo-phonographic writing is a double- or triple-valued writing, simultaneously graphic and rhetorical, non-verbal and verbal, which attempts to restore speech to a more balanced relation with such nonphonetic elements as the pictograph and the ideograph. This writing practice mimes the picto-ideo-phonographic inscriptions of non-logocentric cultures in order to subvert the metaphysics of logocentrism.[6] I use the word here to encapsulate Wah's interest not only in the phonetic but also in the tactile, sensual and visual elements of writing. He shares with his teacher, Charles Olson, the belief that the survival, in print, of oral memory devices and rhetorical mnemonic aids "after the oral necessities were ended" (Olson 1980, 155) is a source of decadence in contemporary verse and rejoices that the ear can be freed by script to discover language's other resources. In "Human Universe" Olson notes, paradoxically, that in order to restore these other resources—which he calls "tongue" or "shout"—"several of us got back to hieroglyphs or to ideograms to right the balance" (162). Wah's strategy is to translate pictographs from the interior of B.C.

But Olson's quarrel is not with the act of writing. Nor does he privilege oral composition over writing. The distinction he makes in his essays is between "language as the act of the instant and language as the act of thought about the instant" (Olson 1980, 162). His poetic struggle is against the reductive tendencies of logic, quantification and classification, which are writing effects, as Ong and others have established. What Olson and Wah work toward is a kind of dialogue between speech and writing, which they believe will revivify poetry by opening up new areas of language and consciousness. They push for a grammatological practice that will right the balance between speech and writing and take the reader "to the root of composition itself, where the generalizing intelligence is shunned, altered, or supplanted" (Quasha 1977, 488).

Fred Wah is engaged in a grammatological project to engender a writing practice based not upon expressive or mimetic codes of language but upon the effects of dialogism, polyphony, intertextuality, translation, the slippage of proper names into common nouns, the anti-book book, and a doctrine of signatures. In his poetry he translates intralingually between writing and speech, theory and rhetoric. Fred Wah is the poet as theor(h)et(or)ician.

Notes

1   Proprioception is a concept first introduced to poetics from physiology by poet Charles Olson. In its dictionary definition "proprioception" refers to the stimuli produced and perceived within an organism. Olson imported the idea of proprioception into his poetics of objectism or projective verse. He defined it for poetics as "sensibility within the organism by movement of its own tissues." Although he begins from the physiological notion, he uses the word to displace the humanist " 'subject' and his soul" from its dominion over the rest of nature and to advocate a poetics that will contribute to an ontologic and epistemic shift. Wah did graduate work with Olson in Buffalo in the early 'sixties and has incorporated aspects of Olson's poetics into his own poetry.

2   The terms "pictograph" and "pictogram" are used interchangeably in histories of writing and in the Oxford Concise Dictionary. For purposes of clarity, however, I shall refer to the visual inscriptions, including in *Pictograms from the Interior of B.C.* the reproductions of John Corner's drawings, as "pictographs" and Wah's poetic verbal responses as "pictograms." Within quotations from other sources, the terminology may vary.

3   Most writing system specialists consider pictographs as pre-writing or embryo-writing, not, in other words, as 'true' writing. The definitions of pictography in several books on the history of writing bear traces of the scorn of phonocentrism and ethnocentrism, and the subject is often quickly dispatched. In *The Presence of the Word* Walter J. Ong describes some of the differences, as he sees them, between 'true' writing and pictography. He lumps pictographs in the same category as stone monuments, property marks and totem designs:

> These and similar steps, insofar as they are not merely magical, serve as aide-mémoires. They encode little. The information storage remains almost entirely in the heads of those who use such creations, which are much more triggers than storage devices. . . . True scripts go beyond the earlier aide-mémoire devices. A script is an organized system of writing, not an assortment of more or less isolated signs, and a system which in one way or another undertakes rather to represent concepts themselves directly than merely to picture sensible objects around which concepts may play (35-36).

In a later book, *Orality and Literacy,* he describes how 'true' writing depends upon the establishment of a fixed code, which pictography lacks:

> Pictographic communication such as found among early Native American Indians and many others did not develop into a true script because the code remained too unfixed. Pictographic representations of several objects served as a

kind of allegorical memorandum for parties who were dealing with certain restricted subjects which helped determine in advance how these particular pictures related to each other. But often, even then, the meaning intended did not come entirely clear. (Ong 1982, 86)

David Diringer concedes some additional ground to pictography, namely, that it is not "restricted to the recording of single, disconnected images, but is capable of representing the sequential stages or ideas of a simple narrative." He also mentions that pictograms can be expressed orally in any language without alteration of their content, since the images do not represent any specific sounds (21). It is worth noting that this is also true of Chinese ideograms.

4   Another example of Wah's preference for working with signifiers rather than signifieds can be found in his paralinguistic or homolinguistic translations of Nicole Brossard's work. He writes: "I have found her writing lends itself to [homolinguistic translation] because it is primarily language (and therefore body) oriented. That is, one can feel more literally the actual life in the language without necessarily knowing the full range of reference involved" (Wah 1982b, "Standing and Watching the Writing Writing."). It is of interest to note that in the paragraph immediately preceding this statement Wah draws attention to Brossard's use of the middle voice.

5   In the following two chapters I examine Wah's experimentation with his Chinese name.

6   For amplification about picto-ideo-phonographic writing, see Derrida 1976, *Of Grammatology*, 87-93, and Ulmer 1985, *Applied Grammatology*, 98-100.

. . . Chinese grammar is fluid, not architectural. Whereas in a highly inflected language such as Latin, words are solid bricks with which to build complicated edifices of periods and paragraphs, in Chinese they are chemical elements which form new compounds with great ease. A Chinese word cannot be pinned down to a 'part of speech', 'gender', 'case', etc., but is a mobile unit which acts on, and reacts with, other units in a constant flux.

James J.Y. Liu
The Art of Chinese Poetry

The secret proper name, the absolute idiom, is not necessarily on the order of language in the phonic sense but may be on the order of a gesture, a physical association, a scene of some sort, a taste, a smell.

Jacques Derrida
The Ear of the Other

Wah's Syntax:
A Genealogy, A Translation

Charles Olson's attack on what he called "sprawl" in poetry, namely, the humanist insertion of the ego as barrier between the world and the poem, called for a cutting off of the dead ear of the rhetorical tradition. The poet's job, he insisted, was to pay attention to "the swift currents of the syllable" (Olson 1980, 151), to listen for those properties of language which lately had been overlooked or suppressed in poetry, and not merely to record lips having spoken but rather to listen for the ear of the Other. He urged poets to transgress the boundaries of "inherited line, stanza, over-all form" (148), to travel the periplus of "the workings of his own throat" (158) and to descend into the labyrinth of the ear carried on the bubble of the syllable. For Olson, the rediscovery of the materiality of "that fine creature" the syllable (150), in part through the encounter with alternate systems of notation (Mayan glyphs, Chinese ideograms), challenged the space-time co-ordinates and syntax of traditional verse-making:

> Which brings us up, immediately, bang, against tenses,
> in fact against syntax, in fact against grammar generally,
> that is, as we have inherited it. . . . I would argue that . . .
> the conventions which logic has forced on syntax must be

broken open as quietly as must the too set feet of the old line. But an analysis of how far a new poet can stretch the very conventions on which communication by language rests, is too big for these notes, which are meant, I hope it is obvious, merely to get things started. (Olson 1980, 152-53)

At the time he was composing his literary manifestoes, Olson was aware that any radical challenge to syntax would also constitute a threat to the accepted model of communication and furthermore that it would be impossible to foresee just how far any future poet might be able to push this model. He was also aware that by upsetting the master-slave relationship between logos and syntax he was initiating a long-term poetic project of dynamic and profound potential.

Readers of Fred Wah's work may wonder whether Wah early appointed himself to the task of exploring, through projective verse, these imagined outer limits of communication. Wah's work is, and is generally regarded as, "syntactically daunting" (Ricou 1986, 371). No doubt it is partly due to the difficulty of his syntax that his work has not yet received as much critical attention as it deserves and demands. This is unfortunate because, while the content of Wah's work is intriguing and its 'themes' heartfelt and important, it is his notation which not only makes his work new and exciting but in some respects precedes the development of the content. Long before *Breathin' My Name with a Sigh* and the range of forms the father content generated in that book, *Grasp the Sparrow's Tail* and *Waiting for Saskatchewan,* the figure of Wah's father was very much a textual presence at the level of syntax.

Reviewers from Douglas Barbour to Fraser Sutherland have mentioned or alluded to Wah's syntactical practice. Barbour refers to "a kind of clipped and cryptic musicality" informing the lyrical quality of Wah's poetry, and he suggests that in *Owners Manual* this lyric cry is "subtly subverted toward koan," the word 'koan' exactly capturing both the manifest content of *Owners Manual* as "spiritual guide book" (Barbour 1982, 33) as well as the puzzling and paradoxical nature of its language, which, incidentally, is less pronounced in that book than in some of the others, both earlier and later. Sutherland, reviewing *Waiting for Saskatchewan,* describes Wah as a "resourceful if somewhat inaccessible poet" (Sutherland 1986, C7).

Other reviewers are undecided on the subject of Wah's syntax. N. M. Drutz observes (in an elliptical loop of a sentence) that "Through a loose but not undisciplined syntax, a free association technique of words and images, Wah recreates the cosmos as he sees it, through the medium of memory" but concludes that "the work is marred occasionally by his whimsical syntax," which, together with his images, "are sometimes too enigmatic and private" (Drutz 1981, 176-77). Bruce Serafin is also divided on the subject of Wah's syntax, remarking first that the short section he has quoted from *Breathin' My Name with a Sigh* "contains almost nothing of the vivacity and directness of ordinary speech. It is not talk that it resembles, but rather the excruciatingly fastidious notes of a scientist," producing a cold poetry that makes no attempt to "touch" the reader. However, Serafin notes, "the tiniest shift in syntax registers with the force of a detonation." He concludes that the obscurity of Wah's book is "a necessary obscurity, an obscurity in the service of meaning" (Serafin 1982, L33).

It would be misleading, however, to give the impression that, with notable exceptions, most of the critics have been ambivalent about or confused by the strangeness of Wah's syntax. Especially those who have discussed his work at some length—George Bowering, Smaro Kamboureli, Steve McCaffery, bpNichol—have certainly grasped the significance of his compositional method. Bowering, for example, describes Wah's syntax variously as phenomenological, performative and deconstructive. Kamboureli argues that Wah positions (and problematizes) himself at/as the site of a dialogue between the enounced and the enunciation. Wah's purpose, she says, is to avoid "being a mere beholder of the spectacle of the world" and instead to become "the reader of his own drama" (Kamboureli 1984a, 59). McCaffery places the "grammatical assymetry" of Wah's writing within a project of picto-ideo-phonographic composition. As one in a series of Toronto Research Group (T.R.G.) Reports on translation and compositional processes, Nichol interviews both Wah and his wife, Pauline Butling, on the translative elements of Wah's 'transcreations' in *Pictograms from the Interior of B.C.*

From his first book, *Lardeau,* to his more recent, *Waiting for Saskatchewan* and *Music at the Heart of Thinking,* Wah's writing has not conformed to the rules and conventions of standard English syntax and has followed rather

> . . . a procession forth
> into I like the movement
> in our syntax goes
> something like a river Daphne.
> (*Breathin' My Name with a Sigh*)

His prose poems, for example, exhibit very loose syntactical connections:

> to get it how the river in its mud flows down stream how
> it goes mouth or breath fluid down to the toes outside in
> the wind the dark and stormy brother's sister's blood keep
> coming back into the word alongside itself a bear and a
> bad man/woman family blood keeps it now my daughters
> for the moon and men and their own river a cleft in the
> earth going colour languaging a feeling inside the surface
> feeling out the breadth of my mother/father things I am
> also left over thing put together calendar's event world the
> children's things and wind last night/biography.
> (*Breathin' My Name with a Sigh*)

But in his lined, lyric poems too Wah departs from the syntactical expectations of English. Using a variety of techniques for "making strange the familiar,"[1] he tries to avoid the outworn habits of thought inevitably imposed by the structures of standard English grammar. The beginning of "Mountain" provides a good example of several of these techniques:

> Mountain that has come over me in my youth
>   green grey orange of colored dreams
>   darkest hours of no distance
>   Mountain full of creeks ravines of rock
>   and pasture meadow snow white ridges humps of granite
>   ice springs trails twigs stumps sticks leaves moss
>   shit of bear deer balls rabbit shit
>   shifts and cracks of glaciation mineral
> O Mountain that has hung over me in these years of fiery desire
>   burns on your sides your many crotches rocked

> and treed in silence from the winds
> Mountain many voices nameless curves and pocked in shadows
> not wild but smooth
> your instant flats flat walls of rock
> your troughs of shale and bits
> soft summer glacier snow
> the melting edge of rounded stone
> and cutting of your height the clouds
> a jagged blue
> your nights your nights alone
> your winds your winds your grass . . .
> (*Loki is Buried at Smoky Creek,* 23)

The voice is suspended at the level of the noun subject—naming and renaming, listing, calling, invoking—without verb or predication. As above, both in his prose poems and his lyrics, Wah often omits punctuation, articles and personal pronouns. He breaks lines at points which fracture syntax and seed meaning with ambiguity and lapses. He assembles sheer lists of nouns and repeats words and phrases in almost incantatory fashion. He separates subject and predicate, inverts or undetermines the order of adjective and noun, scatters the poem over the page, and makes abrupt transitions which leave a sentence or a thought uncompleted.

The cumulative effect of these devices is so powerful that even in those poems where the syntax is more or less technically 'correct' one nevertheless has the *illusion* that the poem is asyntactical, or at least more so than it actually is, as in the following extract from "Poem for Turning." Here the extremely short lines and the absence of direct objects or their 'veiling' as verbs fracture the syntactic flow, producing the effect of both real and apparent parataxis:

> in
> heel
> knee
> cut side-hill
> ditch run-off
> move down
> ricochet track
> line shove
> spin out fall
> back fall side
> saw the forest

                    clear the creek rock
                    split the sky
                    open roll dig
                    cover burn
                    fill the fill
                    and cross the bridge
                    turn up
                    turn into turn
                    at it
                    (*Among,* 34)

In this poem of how to move down a mountain, the instructional tone, elicited by the absence of pronouns and by the use of supposedly imperative verbs, is supported by the fast line changes, which force the reader to stay right with the text (as one generally must with instructional manuals) instead of either speeding faster or slowly plodding through it in order to grasp its significance. The fluctuation between the present indicative and the imperative helps to keep the reader situated at the interface between word and world. In this flux the voice fragments among the (absent) first or third person singular or plural (I, s/he, we, or they) of the indicative and an unnamed Other (you) invisibly inscribed by the imperative.

In the previous chapter I suggested that one could describe the drift and fissures of Wah's syntax as a transcription of 'inner speech.' It is sufficient to recall here two aspects of inner speech: first, that, operating as quanta or abbreviated particles of thought, inner speech obeys a paratactical, rather than syntactical, structure. Second, as a function in itself, and not simply the interior projection of external speech, inner speech incorporates somatic and proprioceptive components, speech, writing, and graphic images, without privileging any one mode over another. Inner speech is picto-ideo-phonographic. If it is true, as Mikhail Bakhtin has argued, that a poet's style " 'is engendered from the style of his inner speech, which does not lend itself to control, and his inner speech is itself the product of his entire social life' " (Emerson 1986, quoting Bakhtin, 25), then Wah's style can be seen as a function of his intellectual, social and familial contexts.

Wah credits his reading of Ernest Fenollosa for disburdening him of the grade-school dictum that a sentence must be a complete thought and thus for leading him away from syntactic composition toward a paratactic style (Wah 1985a, 214). Wah finds very limited poetic possibilities in either the sentence as such or in the already completed thought. For him the possibilities lie in a notation that allows him to record the semiotic irruptions and pulsions of the "heartography" within (Wah 1986a,116).

An overview of the general significance of Ernest Fenollosa's and Ezra Pound's collaborative valorization of the Chinese ideogram as a model for composition is supplied by Antony Easthope. He summarizes: "It is not the supposedly iconic feature of Chinese writing that makes it an important model for poetry. Rather it is the way that the writing, in virtue of being ideographic rather than phonetic, foregrounds and insists upon the materiality of the signi-fier" (Easthope 1983, 140). For Pound, he says, the parataxis of Chinese offered an alternative to syntagmatic closure and led him to the image as the furthest alternative to rhetoric, combining the simultaneity of graphic representation with the temporal succession of verbal language (142). Laszlo Géfin concludes his book *Ideogram: History of a Poetic Method* with the observation that although the ideogrammic method has been interpreted by various poets in different "measures"—cumulative and contrastive juxtapositions, fugal, overlapping, collagistic, or elliptical groupings of particulars —poets as diverse as Pound, Olson, William Carlos Williams, Robert Duncan, Robert Creeley, and Gary Snyder, for example, all use these strategies to circumvent the logic and ratiocination of humanistic "positive capability" (Géfin 1982, 137-38).

By now it is a commonplace to note that it is not, strictly speaking, true that, as Fenollosa/Pound wrote, "the Chinese lan-guage naturally knows no grammar" (Fenollosa 1936, 17). Both Fenollosa's and Pound's 'collaborative' and individual analyses of Chinese have been shown to be erroneous in several respects. For instance, although Chinese does not use tenses, declensions and formalized parts of speech, it does of course have recurring patterns, which is after all the broader meaning of the word 'grammar' (Newnham 1971, 99). Despite their misreadings, however, it would be impossible to deny the tremendous influence Fenollosa's and Pound's research had upon their contemporaries and continues to exert over the poetic line (or rhizome) which has grown out of their work. Although a few of Wah's earliest poems could be described as imagistic, *his* encounter with Fenollosa's essay, among other influences, culminated in a different poetic. While the visual (imagistic, pictogrammic and ideogrammic) is undeniably important in Wah's poetry, equally so is his work with parataxis, whereby he emulates in the English language the parataxis of Chinese.[2]

We have already looked at Wah's use of parataxis in "Mountain," a version of which appeared in his first book, *Lardeau*. Another poem from that collection, "Shape-of-a-Bird-with-Stars-in-Its-Eyes," also exhibits some of the "clipped and cryptic musicality" Barbour hears in the later "koan" poems:

> Unnamed glacier
> north
> 25 degrees west
> north
> look north tonight
> at white
> the white hump of ice
> the moon the snow
> bright
> shape-of-a-bird-with-stars-in-its-eyes
> go morning north
> road that way to dawns and breakfasts
> morning grass boots wet
> and some morning don't stop to eat
> with the boots keep walking
> ten miles and find out
> then go into it and into it
> the wet grass morning glacier the
> shape-of-a-bird
> there where I arrive with my wet boots on
> what should I name it. (*Lardeau*)

The language of "Shape-of-a-Bird-with-Stars-in-its-Eyes" is, like the structure of Chinese, paratactical and elliptical. In this poem, as in "Poem for Turning," all the verbs—"look," "go," "stop," "find," "keep walking," "arrive"—except the last one—"should name"—are in the present tense, possibly but not necessarily in the imperative mood. The effect of such indeterminacy of verb is of a recalcitrantly non-conjugating (or perhaps infinitely conjugating) verb. The Chinese verb does not conjugate and has no tenses or moods (Newnham 1971, 84).

Similarly in this poem, naming is endowed with verbal properties; the subject assumes the workload of the predicate. "Motion,"
as Fenollosa observed, "leaks everywhere" (Fenollosa 1936, 11). In
the gradual, line-by-line accumulation of perceptions in lines six
and seven ("at white/ the white hump of ice"), the addition of the
phrase "hump of ice" and the slight variation produced extends the
poem's perceptual process even in the absence, in those two lines,
of a verb. In lines eight and nine ("the moon the snow/ bright"), the
gaze shifts from the sky ("moon") to the earth ("snow") to a purely
visual and somewhat abstracted condition ("bright"). At the word
"bright," the gaze both creates an atmosphere of brightness and
focuses on itself in the act of gazing. As it is doing so, the next line,
appropriately, enacts a naming. And all these shifts and changes and
permutations occur without the use of a verb. The indeterminacy
and the omission of verbs, rather than stilling the poem and freezing
it at the level of nominalization, cause all the other resources of the
poem to spring to action. Even the motion created by the linebreaks
themselves functions in a verbal sense. The named glacier of the
title, unnamed by the first line, is named at mid-point of the poem
only to be unnamed in the last line. In the interstices between
naming and unnaming (which is also a kind of naming) the particulars of the place and the poet's relationship with it are given.

Let us look at one final short poem from early in Wah's poetic
career. The following is a section from Wah's second book, and his
first long poem, *Mountain*:

fucking brown the fall airs
    the end of August rains turn snow
        the dirt is hard around the rocks the leaves are warm
          around those rocks the snow is warm the dirt is
            O so Co-old

The first line is so elliptical it is difficult to know how to read it. Its
semantic content really only emerges (and then only partially) in
the retrospective light of the subsequent four lines of the poem. The
ambiguity of the second line would seem to offer about three slightly
different readings, one focussing on the weather, two on temporality: At the end of August, the rains turn to snowfalls; The end of the
season of August rains shades into the time of snowfalls; It is *now*

the end of August and the rains are turning to snow. In lines three and four, the prepositional phrases "around the rocks" and "around those rocks" float and attach themselves first to the preceding independent clause, then to the one following, eventually setting even the solidly independent clauses into oscillation.

Wah's poems undermine the English language's privileging of the verb and "its power to obliterate all other parts of speech" that, as Fenollosa noted, gives us "the model of terse fine style" (Fenollosa 1936, 29). Alfred Bloom, in *The Linguistic Shaping of Thought: A Study in the Impact of Language on Thinking in China and the West,* describes a fundamental difference between Chinese and English in terms of the approaches of native speakers of each language to theoretical statements and assesses the relative capacities of the two languages for theorization and particularization. It is worth quoting at some length from his experimental results, as they serve to corroborate some of the points in Fenollosa's essay and, more importantly, to clarify certain aspects of Wah's work:

> [By virtue of their structure or syntax] The Chinese sentences . . . call attention to two conditions or two events and then, in addition, stipulate relationships holding between those conditions or events, so that the hearer or reader comes to consider the individual conditions or events on their own terms as well as the intercondition or interevent relationships that link them to one another. By contrast, the entified English sentences convert the subject/predicate descriptions of conditions or events into individual noun phrases and then insert those noun phrases into single subject/predicate frameworks, thereby in effect subordinating the conditions or events to the relationships that link them to one another. The hearer or reader is no longer led to consider the conditions or events on their own terms, but to consider them only as a function of the role they play in the relationships under discussion. The relationships themselves take on a reality of their own, a law-like quality, which derives from the fact that they are understood, not merely as descriptions of observable or imaginable real-world phenomena, but as examples of a different domain of discourse altogether, as theoretical explanatory frameworks designed to provide a clarifying perspective on the world of actual conditions and events

and their interrelationships, while at the same time maintaining a certain cognitive distance from the speaker's or
hearer's baseline model of that world. (Bloom 1981, 46)

Wah's use of the indicative, the imperative and a pseudo-imperative
mood, his omission of pronouns, his elision of standard grammatical particles, and his superadding of the functions of different parts
of speech to a single word or word cluster, like his construction of
a synthetic middle voice, translate not only the Chinese written
character as a medium for poetry but some of the patterns of *spoken*
Chinese as well. That is, Wah does not merely imitate a paradigmatic
model of the Chinese language. He translates a phenomenological,
oral/aural, "lived" Chinese. This translation of Chinese ideogrammic
and speech structures into English deconstructs the meta-discourse
Bloom isolates as attendant upon standard English syntax and
'un-dematerializes' the phonetically-based English word, creating
the conditions necessary for listening, in the same moment, to the
Otherness of both English and Chinese.

Translation has long been a strong interest of Wah's. He has
done a number of homolinguistic translations, from English to
English. In an interview with bpNichol in which they discuss the
writing of *Pictograms from the Interior of B.C.,* Wah says that what he
wanted to do was "to pay attention to all possible aspects of the
'trans' quality, the 'trans' aspect of transcreation, transliteration,
transcription, trans anything" (Nichol 1978, 37-38). In another
interview, Wah talks about "translating" some of Nicole Brossard's
poems into English: "I would sound out the French word and
translate the sound into something that sounds the same in English.
. . . I just got very intrigued by the notion that one could intuit
language by aspects of the language other than meaning" (Goddard
1986, 41). In this same interview Wah is asked to what extent he
feels Chinese. His responses stress the ambivalence of his feelings
of ethnic origin and identity:

> Race is not something you can feel or recognize, and that's
> one of the things I'm investigating in [*Waiting for Saskatch-
> ewan*]. It turns out race is food. I feel Chinese because of
> the food I enjoy, and that's because my father cooked
> Chinese food. But I don't know what it feels like to feel
> Chinese. (Goddard 1986, 41)

Wah is often asked about his ethnicity: he almost always responds not by talking about himself but by telling an abbreviated version of his father's astonishing and poignant story. The following excerpt, from a 1987 interview, is the first published instance I have found in which Wah actually speaks about the influence upon him of the Chinese language:

> My grandparents spoke Swedish, and my father and his parents spoke Chinese. I had to go to Chinese school for a little bit and I think it's made me an awkward speaker. I've always felt awkward about English. I felt that I would never be a good English speaker because my father and my Swedish grandparents felt that. They were always embarrassed about their English and my father was always embarrassed about his English. So I felt embarrassed about mine, too. I thought, "Well, of course, it's because I'm a half-breed." So I've embraced an English which is strange, weird, deconstructed, non-syntactic. I've embraced a more highly personal, jazz-oriented kind of language. (Enright 1987, 36)

Wah's 'Chinese-ing' of English syntax in his poems is a dramatization of genealogy and what he calls 'heartography.' The effect of such 'strange' syntax is as of an imitation of a native Chinese speaker speaking English, perhaps almost an echo of Wah's father's voice. Although the father *content* does not appear until *Breathin' My Name with a Sigh,* Wah's eighth book, at the level of 'Chinesed' syntax the father is present from the very earliest books.

Wah's translation of components of both spoken and written Chinese into his English-language poetry marks him as a one of the inheritors of the Fenollosa/Pound line. Indeed, he allies himself with and is most interested in such language-centered writers as Leslie Scalapino, Fanny Howe, Susan Howe, Lyn Hejinian, Nicole Brossard, and Daphne Marlatt, to name a few (Wah 1986b, 374-79). In *The Dance of the Intellect: Studies in the Poetry of the Pound Tradition,* Marjorie Perloff lists some of the features the language poets have in common, namely, a shared attention to the foregrounding of sound structures, phonemic play, punning, rhythmic recurrence, rhyme and a frequent recourse to prose rather than poetry. An observation from Charles Bernstein's introduction to the *Paris Review* "Language Sampler," quoted by Perloff, is pertinent to Wah's writing:

> . . . there is a claim being made to a syntax . . . of absolute
> attention to the ordering of sound's syllables. . . . Not that this
> is "lyric" poetry, insofar as that term may assume a musical,
> or metric, *accompaniment* to the words: the music rather is
> built into the sequence of the words' tones, totally saturating
> the text's sound. (Perloff 1985, 228; the ellipses are Perloff's)

But if the language poets open their ears to the sound resources of the English language, then Wah's listening is attuned to the music of a triple-valued writing and speech (pictographic, ideographic and phonographic) times two radically different language systems, English and Chinese. In Cantonese, the language his father spoke, the word 'wah' means to say, tell. It can refer to words, language, dialect, and picture. In Mandarin, it means speech (Chao 1947, *Cantonese Primer*, 237). Wah's very own name, then, in both English *and* Chinese, is suggestive of pictographs, ideographs and phonographs. And his syntax is one of the sites where, in a move described by Jacques Derrida as "the patient, crafty, quasi animal or vegetable, untiring, monumental . . . transformation of his proper name, *rebus,* into things, into the name of things" (Derrida 1986, 5), he incorporates his multivalent name into textual tissue.

So while Wah's syntax may seem to the reader to tax the boundaries even of poetic communication, this is, paradoxically, a result of the poet's desire to facilitate communication, with the dead as well as the living. Through the medium of the proper name and the Chinesed syntax in which it encodes itself, Wah translates himself to his father, and his father to himself, and in turn to all readers of his texts. It is our ear, the ear of the Other, our signalling of their difference and even their difficulty, then, that finally 'signs' the Wah text. As Derrida suggests, "The ear of the other says me to me and constitutes the *autos* of my autobiography" (Derrida 1985b, 51). That is, since Wah's writing is translative in nature, it requires a reader's response first to intervene and at some points to divert the oscillation of this doubled translative activity outside its own operation and secondly to ascribe to the work its undecidable 'originality.' That is, someone has to resolve, or at least pose, the following question: if 'Wah' is signed all through these texts at the level of the syntax, then to whom does this signature belong—father? son? or the ghost(s) of (two) language(s)?

Wah's radical syntactic experimentation frees translation itself from its secondary status as mere repetition of the always already written, from the spectacle of 'lip-synching' the original. His work releases the compositional and writerly potential of translation. Translation, for him, is itself writing, not just a transcription of a prior text. Wah's Chinese-ing of English syntax encrypts and disseminates between two languages his name, ethnicity and poetic influences, his genealogy, in short. Derrida conjectures that the desire at work in every proper name can be expressed as a call to "translate me, don't translate me" (Derrida 1985b, 102). Wah's translation poetics simultaneously translates his father's Chinese name and conceals that translation in the now-estranged Otherness of his English mother tongue.

Notes

1   The term is Viktor Shklovsky's. See Wah's interpretation of his own work in his article "Making Strange Poetics."

2   There is a risk in describing the techniques I will be highlighting in Wah's work as a 'Chinese-ing' of English. Parataxis, for example, is not restricted to the Chinese language. However, comparisons between the structures of Chinese and Wah's English syntax can be made.

Everytime I look at my face in a mirror I think of how it keeps on changing its features in English tho English is not my mother tongue. Everytime I've been in an argument I've found the terms of my rationale in English pragmatism. Even my anger, not to mention, my rage, has to all intents and proposes [sic] been shaped by all the gut-level obscenity I picked up away from my mother tongue. And everytime I have tried to express, it must be, affections, it comes out sounding halt. Which thot proposes, that every unspecified emotion I've felt was enfolded in an unspoken Japanese dialect, one which my childhood ears alone, remember. Furthermore, everytime I've broken into my own oftimes unwelcome but salutory silences, I've been left with a tied tongue. All of which tells me that, everytime a word forms on the tip of my tongue, it bears the pulse of an English which is not my mother tongue.

Roy Kiyooka
"We Asian North Americanos: An unhistorical 'take' on growing up yellow in a white world"

The Undersigned:
Ethnicity and Signature-Effects

When Fred Wah's grandfather landed in Canada from China he, like all other Chinese immigrants (with the exception of certain categories of Chinese deemed 'desirable' by the government of Canada—diplomats, tourists, students, and 'men of science'), was subject under the Chinese Immigration Act to a head tax. The head tax was a fee ranging in amount from ten dollars in 1886 to five hundred dollars in 1904 and afterwards, escalating in proportion to racist attitudes and policies on the part of the largely British immigrants previously settled in Canada. Of all the immigrant groups seeking a new life in Canada, only the Chinese had to pay a head tax—a fee for permission to settle here (Chan 1983, 10). Chinese head tax certificates, such as the one which would have been issued to Wah's grandfather, contained the following information: the immigrant's name, age, point and date of departure, point and date of entry into Canada, and, of course, the amount of tax paid. At the bottom right of the document was the signature of the Controller of Chinese Immigration and a photograph of the immigrant. Nowhere on the certificate was there a space for the man's own signature, and his name, which was filled in by an immigration official, was automatically and doubly translated—into the Western phonetic alphabet and into the English language[1].

In my usage here then, the 'undersigned' is the subject whose signature does not appear on the document and whose subjectivity is indicated instead by a photograph, a representation of his physical body. After all, what the Dominion of Canada was interested in was this 'subject's' body and the labour to be extracted from it and converted into capital, not to mention the revenue raised from the head tax itself. The undersigned is the insufficiently signed (paradoxically, in this case, since the ideogrammic characters of Chinese are usually viewed as constituting an excess of signs when compared to the minimalist, phonetic alphabet of the West). He, the undersigned, is the one whose personal and cultural signs are repressed or erased in order that the signs of production (though not reproduction—the Chinese men were not allowed to bring their wives and children to Canada) may circulate rapidly, economically and without interference.

This emblem of the unnaming/renaming staged at the entrance to Canada's geopolitical 'interior' is offered as a device for focussing discussion on the interlingual, intralingual and intersemiotic translations enacted in Wah's writing and as a means of grounding and contextualizing the interplay between ethnicity and signature. In four of his books published after *Pictograms from the Interior of B.C.,* Wah returns to a literal focus on geography, but this geography is the site of absence, the abandoned place of his birth. "Home is where the story is," as he says (Wah 1977, 111), but in *Owners Manual, Breathin' My Name with a Sigh, Grasp the Sparrow's Tail,* and *Waiting for Saskatchewan,* what the story is about begins to incorporate both a local habitation (absent) and a name (under erasure).

In these later texts, especially *Breathin' My Name with a Sigh,* Wah begins to play with his patronymic as a generative device. The sound of his name, Wah, becomes the sound of the breath and the source of a literal in-spiration:

> mmmmmm
> hm
> mmmmmm
> hm
> yuhh   Yeh   Yeh
> thuh moon
> huhh   wu   wu

```
unh    unh    nguh
w_____h
w_____h
```
(*Breathin' My Name with a Sigh*)

Breath is the mediator between outside and inside and, in Wah's case at least, between the world outside, even the air, and identity. The name is both the life, the life breath, and the means by which one can "send signs forward." The name, Wah, is the actual sound of breathing, that divided moment on the lip of speech. As breath, the sign is no more than a sigh. It is the instant *prior* to entering a linguistic system.

But the sigh is also a sign. Or, as Steven Scobie remarks, "the identification of breath and name is the book's starting point, its original si(g)(h)n" (Scobie 1986, 60). The name is a mark. It leaves a trace. The name inscribes itself on the iterable surface of time:

> your name is my name
> our name is bones
> bones alone names
> left-over slowly
> to send signs forward
> found out needed
> knowing names
> parts family imprint
> left shape all over
> us within it
> name signed me name
> as our name
> added-up knowns
> become truths
> said-again things
> left over after
> sedimentary hard
> embedded rock to tell
> (*Breathin' My Name with a Sigh*)

The name is like bones, residue left over after death, the internal made external.[2] Names and bones are traces that can be read. They tell a story in a variety of glyphs and scripts.

Both the front cover of *Breathin' My Name with a Sigh* and the penultimate poem in the book consist simply of a large schwa. The schwa is the linguistic symbol of the upside-down 'e' which represents an indeterminate sound in many unstressed syllables or, in some phonological systems, a phoneme representing the mid-central vowel whether stressed or unstressed. Scobie points out that the word 'schwa' derives from the Hebrew 'schewa,' an indistinct vowel sound that, like all the vowels in the Hebrew language, was not written. "It is not a letter but the absence of a letter" (Scobie 1986, 62). Wah has adopted the schwa, the name of which rhymes with his name, as his sign, or perhaps as a paraph to his signature. When he signs his name and stamps his paraph in red ink beside it, as he has done on the colophon page of my copy of *Grasp the Sparrow's Tail,* the effect is something like that of a Chinese ideograph.

Thus Wah's playing with his patronymic reveals the picto-ideo-phonographic powers hidden in the name. That is, in the first place, the schwa is a pictographic drawing of the dangers encountered in turning the name into a thing. Just as the schwa borders on silence and absence, so the name, the proper noun, threatens to become a common noun: "wa ter/ otter/ [ah[h]]." In a second sense, the Wah/schwa identification suggests that the name verges on becoming an ideogram, perhaps an ideogram for silence. Thirdly, along its phonographic axis, the name gathers to itself the beginnings of all speech, the cry of a baby (wah) and the sound of the breath (wah). Not to mention the wah-wah-wah of a jazz trumpet in whatever key signature you like.[3] In *Breathin' My Name with a Sigh* Wah begins to research his name as a picto-ideo-phonographic reservoir and as a way of exploring the feelings and implications of race and ethnicity.

This picto-ideo-phonographic writing is a grammatological strategy which gravitates toward a kind of writing not predicated on the hierarchization of speech over writing, toward, for example, the writing of China. Unlike the phonetic writing of the West, Chinese ideogrammic writing does not reduce the voice to itself. Ideograms are not simply notations for specific sounds (though some characters do bear phonological instructions): the various Chinese spoken languages use the same ideograms. Picto-ideo-phonographic writing, therefore, is a way of imagining "the organized cohabitation, within the same graphic code, of figurative, symbolic, abstract, and phonetic elements" (Ulmer 1985, 6). It attempts to excise the view of writing as external to speech and speech as external to thought. Wah's story, "within which I carry further into the World through blond and blue-eyed progeny father's fathers clan-name Wah from Canton east across the bridges" (*Breathin'*), is the narrative of the quest for the (name of the) father and for a grammatological practice. For him, the name of the father is also the name of this other writing.

Of course, the actual name of the father, like all proper names, is ultimately untranslatable. A proper name is pure reference, an empty signifier, a signifier which resists translation into any other signifier. Wah's name is doubly untranslatable because his name is or was Chinese: its Chinese characters have been expropriated by the English alphabet in the immigration scene described at the beginning of this chapter. Even Wah himself can only approach his name in the language of its expropriation: "wah water/ wah water."

> when I will be water
> was suh
> in the distance
> ihh-zuh ihh-zuh
> water
> did you hear me wa ter
> wa ter
> otter
> [ah^h]

The ideogrammic name or signature, which had been phoneticized into English, is re-ideogrammatized as it is raised, along with its paraph, the schwa, into the body of the text. Within the text, this oscillation continues as the signature finds breath and is re-phoneticized, re-oralized. In its re-phoneticized form, it becomes contaminated with meaning and therefore translatable as it moves from proper to common noun. Translation acts to cure translation. Translation works to heal the wounds inflicted by that first translation staged at the border between two countries and which is constantly re-staged in the verbal, cultural, historical, geographical, and spiritual elements of the immigrant's life.[4]

Just as the *name* of the father generates the drafts of *Breathin' My Name with a Sigh*, so successive *images* of him generate *Grasp the Sparrow's Tail*. The oscillation within *Breathin' My Name with a Sigh* between ideogram and phonogram repeats itself between these two books. In *Grasp the Sparrow's Tail* too Wah overturns or reverses the rule of phoneticization. He chooses to have this China-Japan diary produced by hand and privately printed in Japan, Japan being both the locale out of which it is written as well as a culture based on the ideogram. Thus it is only appropriate that it is not the phonetic letters of the father's name but rather his image, his *ideo,* which informs the book. The book opens with the dedication "for my Father and his family," followed by a poem about the father in his Diamond Grill restaurant in Canada. "You never did the 'horse' like I do now," the poem begins, announcing a difference between father and son. Son Wah practices tai chi—the "horse" and "grasp the sparrow's tail" are two tai chi forms.[5] The poem is about the son's memories of his father, how he walked and carried himself, and it closes with the recollection "and then you died dancing." These recollected memories of the father are juxtaposed against recurrent "appearances" by Wah's dead father during the son's trip to China and Japan.

Grasp the Sparrow's Tail is modelled on the form of the Japanese poetic diary or *utanikki*. The distinguishing marks of the *utanikki*— its blend of poetry and prose, its concern with time, its rejection of the necessity for entries to be daily, and the artistic reconstitution or fictionalization of fact[6]—are all present in Wah's record of his journey to his ancestral homeland. The pages on the left-hand side are dated, chronological journal entries, printed in italics. The pages on the right, printed in bold face type, are poetic prose 'transcreations' of the journal entries. Here are the first paired entries:

> *July 28*
> *In Vancouver just before trip to China and talk of ways the writing could get done. J's birthday.*

> Her a daughter's birthday think China book out linked to poetry each day something new apparent each word capable of total Chinese character baggage really gain sight of word's imprint to pose itself as action on the world in the context of the journey somewhere get ready for the Canton poem.

Grasp the Sparrow's Tail is a book about imprints and writing: the imprint of father on son, the imprint of language on the world and the world on language, and the effects of the filial inscription, the Canton poem, on the debt to the father for the gift of the name. In this book Wah's double-valued writing, simultaneously ideographic and phonetic, reduces names to initials. His travelling companions are his wife P and daughters J and E. On the left page, he makes a note to himself to *"keep the ears open for possibilities,"* while on the right he reduces the name, the proper noun, past the common noun (which is still within the phonetic economy) to an initial, a written trace, and instructs himself to *picture* "how to staccato Japanese." He plays with English syntax in order to try to think ideogrammically: *"This syntax, have to reverse the English to fit, like"*:

> Tokyo
> windy is
> wind out in the ryokan courtyard
> all night noise in the trees is.

When he walks around the city with his Sony Nude earplugs in "stereo surface to skin technology," he sees pictograms in restaurant windows, *"plastic food in the windows image for each meal."* He watches a painter doing calligraphy. This ideogrammic writing is composed as a hand-eye relation rather than a voice-ear relation.[7] Wah has lost the family information his mother gave him *"so I can't check out actual connections still here in Canton."* In the absence of this information, and due to the radical language barrier, China and Japan are for him, as for Roland Barthes, "empires of signs."

Barthes describes the experience of the Occidental travelling in the Orient as one of being repatriated to language's materiality. Bathing in the plethora of untranslatable signs reactivates the semiotic and libidinal energies of his or her body. Barthes writes:

> The murmuring mass of an unknown language consti-
> tutes a delicious protection, envelops the foreigner . . . in
> an auditory film which halts at his ears all the alienations
> of the mother tongue. . . . The unknown language, of
> which I nonetheless grasp the respiration, the emotive
> aeration, in a word the pure significance, forms around
> me, as I move, a faint vertigo, sweeping me into its artificial
> emptiness, which is consummated only for me: I live in
> the interstice, delivered from any fulfilled meaning. . . .

> Now it happens that in this country (Japan) the empire
> of signifiers is so immense, so in excess of speech, that the
> exchange of signs remains of a fascinating richness, mo-
> bility, and subtlety, despite the opacity of the language,
> sometimes even as a consequence of that opacity. . . . It is
> not the voice . . . which communicates . . . , but the whole
> body . . . which sustains with you a sort of babble that the
> perfect domination of the codes strips of all regressive,
> infantile character. To make a date (by gestures, drawings
> on paper, proper names) may take an hour, but during that
> hour, for a message which would be abolished in an instant
> if it were to be spoken . . , it is the other's body which has
> been known, savoured, received, and which has displayed
> . . . its own narrative, its own text. (Barthes 1982, 9-10)

According to Barthes, the foreigner journeying in an ideogrammic culture experiences an immense surplus of signifiers, which overwhelms his own economy of speech and phoneticization. Enwrapped in the double-valued writing of an "auditory film," he is profoundly aware of sensual intimations, not signified, intellectual meaning. He tunes in to the signifier, the body.

Wah's poetic record of his travels in China and Japan is, if less sexually erotic than Barthes's, strikingly similar in most other respects. For him too, China and Japan are a carnival of scripts, gestures, names, and the body of the Other. It is in these scripts that he "sees" his father. That is, once he is delivered from the referentiality of English, his mother tongue, into the scriptural carnival that is the text of China, Wah encounters his father everywhere. "One morning you were doing tai-chi in a park in Hong Kong." "I saw you riding your bicycle in a large crowd of bicycles moving into town from the outskirts." "I caught a glimpse of you through a window in a roadside eatery gesturing to someone across from you with your chopsticks." The most poignant sighting takes place at the Bhuddist caves near Datong:

> I was about to leave and on a path alongside a wall you
> brushed me. Yes, brushed. I could see it was intentional
> and our eyes met for an instant as you turned and glanced
> over the head of the baby boy you were carrying. Though
> you didn't say anything your face still talked to me. (*Grasp
> the Sparrow's Tail*)

The repetition of the word "brushed" here is critical. In addressing his father Wah has stressed that "what always gives you away is your haircut, your walk, or the flash in your eyes." "It was always your black crew-cut hair which most stood out." "You wore a white sleeveless undershirt and khaki shorts and your brush-cut was shorter than usual, probably because of the extreme heat and humidity." The recognition scene is always precipitated by the father's signature brush-cut. Moreover, as we know, the Chinese calligraphic writing instrument is also a brush. So within the context of the poem, when Wah's father "brushes" him, the stroke is simultaneously a physical caress and an act of writing. The son in the act of writing the Canton poem writes the father, but the father "brushes" the son into the poem as well. The baby boy that the man is carrying could have been, is, Wah himself. Wah's double quest for his father and for a writing practice that will not alienate him from his ethnicity is inscribed by this single deliberate brush. The *name* of the father, and the poet's own signature, in *Breathin' My Name with a Sigh* becomes in *Grasp the Sparrow's Tail* the *image* of the father, which in turn becomes the image of the act of writing itself.

In the same movement, the inscription of Wah's Canton poem becomes "calligraphy." The phonetic English alphabet becomes ideogrammic as it is actually read over the writer's shoulder by Chinese readers:

> As you sit in the warmth of the August morning sun and write this you have attracted a large crowd of Chinese who stop to watch the language flow out onto the paper. You look up at them and ask them in English if they would like to write something on your paper but they simply smile and ignore you. They are interested in the writing and comment to one another and point to the actual incisions you make on the paper, the calligraphy of the foreign letters cutting also into their minds as they recognize something of themselves there. (*Grasp the Sparrow's Tail*)

For the Chinese spectators, the "foreign letters" of the phonetic alphabet would not signify speech but silence, a pure graph. Furthermore, the doubled writing subject of this passage that combines father and son and thereby problematizes the pronoun "you" defeats the logocentrism of phoneticization.

Thus Wah's writing collapses the distinction between form and content. Writing for him has its own exigencies completely independent of the modalities associated with speech:

> ... *I find the writing very relaxing, dialogue set up with mind. Try old-fashioned pen nib and ink supplied in room—stop to go to the inkwell to get more ink with thought of schooldays memory synapse which allows the mind to gather the cloud head of thinking residue and push it out, every strand. The writing during the day has no form or direction except for Father notes. I've been reading Engle's [sic] edition of Mao's poems, good with lots of background notes, so have that floating around as I look, and look. (Grasp the Sparrow's Tail)*

The writing has "no form or direction." The act of writing is not a simple transcription of thought but a "dialogue set up with mind." It is engaged with the material properties of paper and "pen nib and ink." What interests Wah about his own writing act is the same thing that interests him as he watches the Chinese calligrapher at work: "*I like the actualization of the intent which was not an intent but an inclination a 'tropos' which got paid attention to.*" In the book which follows *Grasp the Sparrow's Tail,* this writing without form or direction explodes into several different forms.

In *Waiting for Saskatchewan* the traditional roles of form and content are blurred and even reversed. The father content generates the "threads" or "nodes" that make the book a cohesive structure, while the accumulation of different forms provides the book's actual content. By working to forestall the intrusion of a manipulative narrative line, the diversity of the *utanikki,* the prose poem, and the *haibun* become part of the compositional present that is the poem's content.

By producing this anti-book book Wah has followed through the process he set in motion with *Breathin' My Name with a Sigh* when he transferred his signature from the title page to the inside of the text. The permeable membrane of his proper name, which allows contamination between the inside and the outside of the text, between subject and author, and between content and form, ultimately dismantles the mechanisms of the book as such. For him, in *Breathin'* and his subsequent "signature texts," finding the emotional "relief" of "exotic identity" (Wah 1985b, 62) is also to find a relationship to the geographical relief of home and to the black and white relief of the written surface of the page.

In the context of these processes of contamination and dialogical exchange, however, his name is not neutralized or absorbed. It remains a picto-ideo-phonographic rebus which in disseminating itself throughout the text recuperates some of the losses incurred both in its original translation into English and in the "paraph-raising"[8] operation itself. Derrida describes the net gain possible in this recuperative strategy:

> By disseminating or losing my own name, I make it more and more intrusive; I occupy the whole site, and as a result my name gains more ground. The more I lose, the more I gain by conceiving my proper name as the common noun. . . . The dissemination of a proper name is, in fact, a way of seizing the language, putting it to one's own use, instating its law. (Derrida 1985b, 76-77)

In his texts Fred Wah seizes all three aspects of language—pictographic, ideographic and phonetic—and puts them to use in the name of father, son and grandfather. If language is the element within which one acquires a sense of self and if, through the imposition of another language, this process is blocked such that one can only exist for the Other and not for oneself, then it is through translation that this split self is healed. Or, as Eli Mandel asks in "The Ethnic Voice in Canadian Writing," "Could it be, then, that speaking another's tongue we cannot be ourselves, that the search for the lost self begins when we have been translated into another and will not end until there has been translation, transformation once again?" (Mandel 1978, 276).

It is in the poetry of Fred Wah that the missing signature of Quon Wah is inscribed. The undersigned, then, is also the one who signs *after,* the one who, even before his or her birth, enters into a shadow contract with the ancestors which, at least in some measure, supercedes that other contract entered into in the bad faith of mistranslation. The terms of that shadow contract stipulate that s/he, the undersigned, will translate.

Body Inc.

Notes

1   It should also be remembered that often during immigration procedures the Chinese were forced on the spot to adopt an English name from a list provided by officials. Wah's own grandfather became "James."

I wish to thank Fred Wah and Pauline Butling for sharing with me pertinent details concerning the Wah family's history. For further information about the Chinese head tax see Harry Con et al.. *From China to Canada* and Anthony Chan, *Gold Mountain.*

2   Equally the external made internal. In the case of the translated or mistranslated name, the external sign is repressed, internalized. It becomes concealed somewhere in the cavities of the body.

3   It happens that these phonetic associations are translinguistic.

4   Here I am borrowing Joseph Pivato's list of several forms of translation (Pivato 1987, 63).

5   Fred Wah does "the horse"; he practices tai chi. His grandfather gambled and played the horses, winning enough money to return to China from Canada in 1897, fathering one child and adopting another before coming back to Canada to remain permanently in 1906. His substantial winnings from gambling earned him the (English) nickname "Lucky Jim."

6   See Ann Munton, "The Long Poem as Poetic Diary," especially pp. 97-98.

7   See Chiang Yee, pp. 13-14.

8   I borrow this term from Stephen Scobie.

"THE NIGHTMARE AND THE WELCOME DREAM OF BABEL": ROBERT KROETSCH'S INTRALINGUAL TRANSLATION POETICS

I began with the idea that I could expand our English by investing it with Nordic modes of expression. In the end I felt vaguely ghettoized. Instead of expanding the language I sensed that I had given the cue to have myself confined to an "ethnic" group about which I still know precious little. I believe this is a typical experience.

Because languages came as punishment for wrongdoing, I think the myth of the tower of Babel frightens cultures with a Judeo-Christian orientation into being repelled by multilingualism. Multilingualism seems generally sacrilegious and almost Satanically rebellious. This is something to consider, no less than the myth of Armageddon which seems to be driving the Western world into acquiescence about nuclear war. It was prophesied, so they make it happen. One of our first tasks I believe is to get rid of the myths that bind us and instead allow other languages to flourish, interweave and colour our experience. We will be richer for it and with 3,000 to 4,000 possibilities the mixtures of tone and aesthetic experience are endless.

Kristjana Gunnars
"Words on Multilingualism"

The Vernacular Republic:
The Politics of the Mother Tongue
in Some Recent Prairie Poetics

A phonic diagram of the poetics of Robert Kroetsch's long poems from *The Stone Hammer Poems* and *Seed Catalogue* to *The Sad Phoenician* and beyond might chart his poetic development as a movement from the pub as poem to the poem as hubbub. This transformation from pub to hubbub involves not a progression as such in Kroetsch's work but a move from narrative, tale, anecdote, story, and joke to sound, disruption, textual activity, and perform-ance. It has been suggested, by Robert Lecker among others, that Kroetsch's poetry is structured upon a tension or dialectic between orality and literacy. I shall argue, however, that this explanation is insufficient and that Kroetsch's poetics is based upon intralingual translation, from English to English, using the vernacular and the written as both source and target 'languages.'

Critics Frank Davey and Dennis Cooley have each written at some length about the relationship between speech and writing within the context of prairie poetry and poetics. As a means of clarifying in general terms the poetics and politics at stake in the question of the relation between speech and writing, their work on these issues will be the subject of the present chapter before I proceed in the subsequent four chapters to a consideration of three of Kroetsch's long poems. My purpose in what follows is to show how the terms of their two different arguments approach what I call translation poetics but ultimately veer off into representational poetics instead.

Frank Davey's article "A Young Boy's Eden: Notes on Recent 'Prairie' Poetry," published in his book *Reading Canadian Reading,* questions the politics of prairie poets' use of oral traditions as generative sources for their poetry. Davey draws attention to several problems regarding the appropriation and conversion of the real and/or reconstructed discourse of oral speech communities into literary texts.[1] He argues that a nostalgic desire to "honour" a past vernacular culture can result, paradoxically, in a writer's estrangement from that very culture and even in a colonizing relationship with the subjects of representation: "Literacy offers to represent the interests of orality; the present offers to represent the interests of the past" (Davey 1988, 220). In Davey's view, the prairie poet who does not mark his texts as self-consciously constructed is liable to operate in bad faith: "Here a second generation seeks through writing both to honour a culture it has abandoned and to vicariously enjoy the values of the abandoned culture" (221). From Davey's depiction one forms an image of the reader of such honouring, if less than honourable, prairie poems as comparable to the visitor to a prairie regional museum who tours the displays thanking her lucky stars that, unlike her mother and grandmother, she no longer has to wash clothes with her bare hands on a rough scrub board, with water that has to be hauled and then heated on a woodstove and with suds made from lye. The emotion stirred by such displays, apparently, is not one of political or historical awareness and gratitude or amazement at what one's parents, grandparents and their friends accomplished but one of self-satisfied smugness and gratitude for progress as represented by the names of Viking, Inglis and General Electric.[2]

Perhaps the most important points raised by Davey in terms of the present discussion emerge from his critique of Dennis Cooley's essay, "The Vernacular Muse in Prairie Poetry." Davey argues that Cooley's ideological project fails and that he ends up affirming the binary oppositions he sets out to deconstruct. As Davey suggests, "the oppositions between margin and centre, or orality and print, are less clear-cut than Cooley declares and highly vulnerable to subversion" (Davey 1988, 225). The purpose of Davey's argument is to point to the repressed ideological assumptions underlying much recent prairie poetry, and so he does not substantially develop the notion of the 'opposition' between oral and print cultures, but he does state that "Cooley's emphasis on both 'appropriation' as the way in which an oral discourse can be brought into the written, and on 'use' of 'colonized discourses' as a way of 'speaking from or for minority groups' is, to say the least, problematical" (225). Moreover, Davey isolates what he sees as the two tasks of the type of poet who wishes to conceal his or her own articulation in order to present an unproblematical relationship to the persons or mythologies honoured. The first task is an archaelogical recovery of "what was 'really said' "; the second is translative in nature.

Davey places the word 'translation' in single quotation marks to signal his restricted, unconventional and highly critical use of that term. As distinguished from the archaeological task to recover the "really said," the translational task is to simulate (or dissimulate). He writes:

> Or the task is that of translation—to simulate the 'really said' or 'really thought' in a plausible written text, as [Monty] Reid 'translates' Karst's fragmentary memoirs into coherent monologues, or [Kristjana] Gunnars 'translates' the records of Icelandic 'narratives' by the participants. The resultant texts defer to the illusion of the speaking voice they attempt to produce, and posit a reader who will also wish to produce that voice. (Davey 1988, 227)

According to Davey, the task of the poet who 'translates' from a spoken to a written economy is to inject literariness—the values of coherence, completeness, form, and narrative—into the documentary material and in the process to (re)constitute a written facsimile of the spoken. In these poets' work, he says, translation is a unidirectional practice, working from speech to writing only: "Here writers write 'on behalf' of those who cannot or could not write, or who were on occasion contemptuous of writing skills" (220). The poets pose as faithful translators of their respective ethnic milieux into literate English and literary culture. Davey sees their faithful dissimulation as attempting to represent an unproblematical, because experiental, 'real' which pre-exists the text.

Like Davey, Dennis Tedlock, in an article about anthropologists' translations of native oral compositions into written English verse, also interrogates a politics of translation based on writing down orality:

> What happens, in the passage from the dramatic art of storytelling to the literary art of verse-measuring, is a transformation of the constantly changing sounds and silences of action into regularized typographical patterns that can be comprehended at a single glance by a symmetry-seeking eye. David Antin points to the role of the eye when he questions whether meter plays an important role in the sound of English blank verse, arguing that the printed lines of such verse are best understood not as a "sound structure" but as "a visual framing effect" that "places whatever language is within the frame in a context of 'literature' ". (Tedlock 1983, 61)

The writers whom Davey promotes in his critique are indeed those who 'frame' their texts by foregrounding bi- or multi-directional 'translation' between speech and writing. He offers Robert Kroetsch as an example of a writer who can write about the past by framing his use of vernacular discourse within questioning, self-reflexive structures (Davey 1988, 226, 228). But in valorizing the framing device of self-reflexivity, Davey privileges writing over vernacular speech. The metaphor of the frame—with its territorial, visual, aesthetic, and writerly associations—does not adequately take into account the dynamic *between* speech and writing. Privileging self-reflexivity circumvents the question of the relation between speech and writing. After all, self-reflexivity, or metadiscourse, is present in both spoken *and* written economies. As Paul de Man remarks in the interview appended to the end of his essay on Walter Benjamin's "The Task of the Translator," "If you get popular uses of language, they are highly, infinitely theoretical, they are constantly metalinguistic, they constantly turn back upon language" (de Man 1986, 102).

To a writerly reader like Davey self-consciously "reading Canadian reading," "The project of honouring a particular past, as in Suknaski and Gunnars, is probably more quickly exhausted as a project and a politics than is a project of interrogating (as in

Kroetsch, Arnason and Dyck) how one can write about a past, or (as in Cooley and Sproxton) how particular class interests have entered into the construction of history" (emphasis added; Davey 1988, 228). However, for the reader for whom class, for example, has been a barrier to acquiring a thorough knowledge of and preference for postmodern texts and literary theory, Davey's reading preferences may not be *de rigueur.* Second, it is not insignificant that, in the foregoing quotation, every one of the poets whose work is approved by Davey holds a Ph.D. and is male. Of the two whose work he cites as falsely, inappropriately or naively "honouring a particular past" neither holds a Ph.D. or, at the time he published his article, a full-time, continuing academic appointment. One of them, Kristjana Gunnars (since appointed as professor of creative writing at the University of Alberta), is the only woman in this clutch of poets. Lorna Crozier's work is quoted, but not discussed, in the body of Davey's essay. Moreover, for Davey to choose the phrase 'a young boy's eden' from Patrick Friesen's poem as the title of his article without questioning gender issues along with the politics of style is a serious blind spot, especially when Cooley's essays them-selves, which Davey otherwise so thoroughly and rightly criticizes, are outrageously problematical concerning the issue of gender.

Third, Davey's veiled call for, if not a universal appeal, at least a broader and less regional appeal to "readers in other regions, readers addressed intertextually at moments when the text engages the problematics of writing and historiography" (Davey 1988, 227-28), would seem to militate against his own desire to politicize the textual activities of reading and writing. Surely the local is a valid political constituency. Nowhere does Davey suggest that local ref-erences ought to be edited out of poems, but his call for greater readability based upon framed narratives and self-reflexivity, and for a certain homogenization of poetic discourse, assumes, in the first place, that the proper readers of poetry are the educated who live elsewhere and emphatically not the people about whom or to whom a poet such as Suknaski or Gunnars may be writing. It is dangerous to assume that these two poets, for instance, are not read by the people whose ancestors their poems 'honour' or that they have fewer readers among these communities than among the urban population. Unfortunately, despite his protestations against Cooley's

"rigorous dichotomy between high and low" and despite his contention that Cooley "offers little evidence that the 'high' exists in
Western Canada as a large and valorized body of writing" (222),
Davey's argument in favour of 'framed' texts reminds us of the kind
of culture which prefers its art framed and designated as such. He
himself exports the very kind of high culture which he implies does
not exist in Western Canada as a significant force.

Moreover, Davey is mistaken when he writes as if he assumed
that urban prairie culture has completely abandoned (except for
nostalgia and a certain sense of indebtedness) its participation in
the rural and multilinguistic environment of its roots. Certainly all
of the poets Davey discusses in his essay are highly literate, and
some, though not all, and those not all of the time, live in cities. But
there are other poets as well, largely self-styled, who publish poetry
in the small town and rural newspapers of the places where they
live, who self-publish and, not entirely unlike their urban and more
literary counterparts, sell their books to their friends and neigh-
bours. If such writers go unrecognized, is their reputed 'badness' a
result of their attempts to write in their own voices, or is it
attributable rather to their attempts to imitate the 'high' literary art
of an era which has been abandoned and superceded in the more
populated, more educated, faster-moving centres where books are
much more readily available? It is noteworthy too that while the
majority of prairie people now live in cities, they are not all of the
people. Some people still live in the villages and towns of Alberta,
Saskatchewan and Manitoba, and many prairie poets write with a
profound awareness of the present, not just the past, lives of rural
people who may or may not ever have access to their books.[3]

In short, to gesture as if to politicize textual practices and yet
to appeal for less regional, less vernacular, and more writerly
productions is to advocate a poetics and a politics which ignores
the geopolitical conditions of contemporary prairie life. Ironically,
Davey recapitulates the same error he himself sets out to correct in
Reading Canadian Reading when he criticizes those for whom certain
critical theorists such as some of the French and the Americans
become "nationless, even timeless figures, theorists whose concepts
somehow exist independently of space-time order" (Davey 1988, 8).
Davey's ideological critique borrows too uncritically from figures from

elsewhere and applies their principles wholesale to a very different geography and way of life and artistic production.

Can there be no poetics for honouring the ancestors in voices which meet them halfway, as, for instance, in texts such as those in which, to quote Davey, "Gunnars constructs English monologues for apparently unilingually Icelandic-speaking immigrants" (Davey 1988, 215)? Kristjana Gunnars is multilingual and a proficient and prolific translator. Surely we cannot conclude that her own relationship to the English language and her decision to write her long poems about the Manitoba Icelanders in English must be viewed as unproblematical simply because we too speak and write English. If English is our first language, we seem to require frames in order to foreground that language for us. However, when Gunnars writes in English, is she simply representing lives or speech, or is she translating? Are texts which attempt to honour the past by reproducing real or imagined speech in volumes of written poetry and which refer overtly to themselves as poems and books *effacing* their self-conscious construction, as Davey suggests? Texts written in the English language when another language might be more appropriate to the conventions of realism, and texts which deliberately draw attention to their status as poems and books—are these textual marks and emblems not the very framing devices Davey recommends?

Davey's critique is in other respects a telling, complex and provocative one, and it is not my wish to trivialize or deflate its worth or to soliloquize on behalf of the rural prairies. Nor do I have space here to discuss in detail the texts of Kristjana Gunnars. However, the Icelanders about whom Gunnars has written are not "rustic" or "unsophisticated" (Davey 1988, 218). Icelanders have a history of literacy that extends back nine or more centuries. More importantly, Gunnars in her poems is not merely speaking or writing on behalf of the illiterate, the oppressed or the overworked, nor is she simply recording "what was 'really said.' " Her poems are not representations of actual, prior speech events: they are translations—from vestiges of spoken and written language to literature, from the archive to the book, from Icelandic into English, and from the English of the dominant culture to the English of the Icelanders themselves. If Gunnars gives her Icelanders English instead of Icelandic words, then surely the audience that she has in mind is not only that audience which Davey characterizes as believing itself to have "unproblematical historical connections to the persons or mythologies honoured" (226). The reader reading prairie reading must not overlook or cancel the translation poetics of Gunnars and Suknaski by labelling such work the mere transcription of speech or by reducing it to representationalism. If a frame is required, then the frame or screen of translation is as complex and self-referential as any.

If translation practices the difference between signified and signifier (Derrida 1981b, 20), then texts written out of the history and phenomenological, lived reality of a particular community practice the difference not only between signifier and signified but often also the differences between languages and the differences between speech and writing *in two or more languages.* Putting the word 'translation' into single quotation marks as Davey does results first of all in a failed opportunity to account for the relation between speech and writing, second, in a dismissal of the literary productions of certain 'ethnic' writers as being of limited scope and, third, in an elision of translation poetics in general.

> What I think I do know about writers of our own time leads me to believe that we (and I mean men and women) do not have muses. We have psychology and "shrinks," lovers and pets; but we do not have muses. We have drugs and alcohol and money; we have gurus, astral travel, and Carl Sagan. We have Columbus and Challenger. Have or had Marilyn and Bogey, the Dukes of Hazzard and the Dupes of Dallas, but we do not have muses. (Webb 1985, 114)

DENNIS COOLEY KNOWS INTIMATELY, celebrates joyfully and analyzes brilliantly the constantly metalinguistic, disruptive, subversive, infinitely theoretical qualities of vernacular speech. He writes *about* the vernacular, and he speaks and writes in it too. Cooley is bilingual.

Two of the essays in his book *The Vernacular Muse* deal specifically with the relation between orality and literacy in prairie writing.
Though there are several points of agreement between us, Cooley's
project is more or less the opposite of mine. He sets up (or, more
accurately, reinforces) a dualism within the body between the organs
of the ear and the eye. Then he maps the relation between speech
and writing onto this version of the dualist body, dividing poets into
two classes—speech-centred ear poets and textually-oriented eye
poets. Paradoxically, this traditional, phallogocentric organization
of the body is used to argue for the vitality, exuberance, strength,
merit, and innovation of a vernacular poetry. Thus, although
Cooley's organization of the body and writing provides insightful,
provocative, and delicious readings of several cultural, institutional
and literary texts, a project founded upon the phallogocentric body
can only ultimately fail to create either a truly subversive verse
project or a new version of the body or the body politic.

One of the early symptoms of the collapse of Cooley's argument
is hinted at by the title of the shorter of the two essays, "Placing the
Vernacular: The Eye and the Ear in Saskatchewan Poetry." This essay,
because of its brevity relative to "The Vernacular Muse in Prairie
Poetry," takes the delimited territory of the province of Saskatchewan, not the entire prairie region, in order first to 'place' the
vernacular in terms of poetry at large, to provide a kind of spatially-
limited test case, before attempting to theorize 'the vernacular muse'
within but not solely in relation to geographical boundaries, and
moreover to align the vernacular with a particular organ and faculty
of the body. Cooley refers to his mapping of the body of Saskatchewan poetry according to the organs of the eye and the ear as
divvying it up under two "jurisdictions" (1). Thus he installs an
analogy between the political jurisdiction of a prairie province and
the body as subject of juridical power. The order of the two-part
title of his essay indicates two things: first, that the overriding critical
project is to place, valorize and consolidate the use of the vernacular
in poetry and, second, that specific bodily organs are accessory to
this endeavour. In the history of Canadian criticism, geography has
been the more or less single topographical feature ascribed to prairie
art, often correlated with a thematic approach (themes such as
distance, solitude, meteorological and economic hardship, the

isolated and strained human figure or figures, the failed artist, the failed artist's wife, etc.). Cooley wishes to acknowledge the importance of the geographical imperative in prairie poetry but at the same time to find new and vigorous ways of discussing prairie writing in terms of its linguistic, literary historical, generic, semiotic, and many other properties. He wishes to inject some sexual energy into this staid, old-fashioned, colonial and dismissive vision of prairie writing. In order to effect this radical rereading, Cooley selects the aperture of the ear through which, he argues, vigour can flow from the body to the text and vice versa.

Unfortunately, in both essays Cooley seems to have in mind two implicit figures representing these conflicting and contending views of prairie poetry. The colonialist view is represented for him by "a facsimile Englishman and a transplanted Englishwoman" (Cooley 1987, 169), while the indigenous view is incarnated by the type of street-wise, smart-talking young guy who would likely have been told repeatedly by the strait-laced and strict, if vulnerable, schoolteacher to, in Cooley's vocabulary, "smarnen up." The duality inspired by these two figures is at the root of the most problematical aspect of "Placing the Vernacular." First overlooking the facsimile Englishman, perhaps because of his deemed facsimile virility, Cooley then goes on to use the shorter of the two essays to eject all women writers from his theory of the vitality and generative powers of vernacularly-based prairie poetry.[4] Having ejected women's writing from his main consideration—poetry which transcribes the vernacular onto the page—he proceeds in the lengthier essay, "The Vernacular Muse," to further develop his theory and examples.

It is not until three-quarters of the way through "Placing the Vernacular" that Cooley overtly states that his dichotomy between eye and ear poets coincides for him with gender. Prior to this point, identifying and demonstrating various differences between the two kinds of poets, he begins rhetorically to refer to the former using feminine pronouns and the latter using masculine pronouns. He describes the eye poet, for example, in the following way: "Set apart from what she observes, uninvolved in it other than in her capacity as isolated observer and respondent, unengaged in any dialogue, she looks out upon a world, sometimes as it exists in the mind's eye, a realm that is passive and like as not silent" (Cooley 1987, 6).

This deliberately gendered description of the eye poet might have suggested to Cooley something of the gender politics involved in his poetic stance. Conversely, his description of the male, ear poet might have tipped him off to the social inequities implicit in his binary structure. Cooley praises the male, ear poet for his engagement with an implied reader or auditor: "In oral poetry (and we realize that it too, the poetry *itself,* is authored in solitude) the speaker behaves as if he seeks to be heard, as if he has someone beside him as he speaks and to whom he speaks, even as that audience remains in fact absent to the poet and to the reader. The rhetoric in such poems simulates public exchange" (11). But which scene of public exchange is open to women poets? How do we inscribe "the snap of speech in the street" (19) when the streets are only open to us during shopping hours and after-hours only when accompanied by a man? Or when the topic of "the snap of speech in the street" is frequently how we look or walk or what someone would like to do to us had he world enough and time? How do women poets sing the song of the marketplace when women's bodies are still commodities advertised, bought and sold by men to other men? Where is the auditor who will guarantee us an ear for *our* words?

In order to legitimize the equation he is promoting, and to avoid a discussion of gender politics, Cooley turns to Walter J. Ong for the cause of the personal or private 'inwardness' of the eye poet. Cooley coolly informs us that Ong attributes this inwardness to the development of print culture: it is the fault of the typewriter. Ong, however, does not make the same gender distinctions as Cooley. Although Cooley quotes him on the poet of inwardness, whom Cooley identifies as female, the pronoun Ong uses is masculine (Cooley 1987, 12).

Finally, on page fourteen of a nineteen-page article, Cooley states unequivocally that "It seems to me that what I am calling 'eye' poems tend to be written by women, and 'ear' poems to be written by men" (Cooley 1987, 14). However, having come out with it at last, he moves quickly to add two other hasty generalizations[5] rather than examine or offer any additional reasons for this apparent phenomenon. Instead he rushes on to quote for the second time the same passages from Elizabeth Allen's and Gary Hyland's poems[6] as illustrations of his controversial "jurisdictions." Allen's poem "transplant" is about a woman displaced, out of place, transplanted from the "forgotten & imagined" place of her father's land to the present place from which she is writing the poem. As a poem of displacement, it could have been a clue to Cooley that the lack of an audience to address either in the vernacular or in 'high literary' language might have to do with her condition as a woman and an immigrant. Instead he decides that the "hesitancies in the voice, set into the lines," are indebted to "the technology of writing and of print" which makes possible such "nuance" or "delicacy of phrasing." "You don't have to raise your voice in print culture," Cooley observes (16).[7]

What is perhaps even more revealing, however, is Hyland's "Power Steering," which Cooley applauds because, among other features, "the speech is loaded with the speaker's wholehearted commitment . . . to his fantasy and his desire to win somebody over to his enthusiasms . . , and that as a result it foregrounds the second person in contrast to the first person of the other poetry" (Cooley 1987, 18). This addressee, this second person, to whom the poem speaks is another male who at least potentially shares the speaker's enthusiasms. But what about the third person in the poem? Here is "Power Steering":

> Scrawny's got himself this nifty sorta knob dealie
> ya clamp onto one sidea your steerin wheel
> Gotta be onea the greatest gizmos invented
> Imagine ya got your arm around some dame eh
> ya just grabaholda this here doomajig
> spin it around hard, lay it to the boards
> and no trouble at all ya got yourself a doughnut
> and the dame's smeared against ya real romantic like.
> (Cooley 1987, 18)

What about "the dame" in the poem? Or, what about the addressee who is not a male but a female reader, and who, if the poem functions dramatically and phatically, as Cooley says these kinds of poems do (Cooley 1987, 8-9), finds herself, as she reads the poem, in a doughnut, a UE, a tailspin, a power turn, "smeared against" some guy auspiciously named Scrawny and his sorta knob dealie? The unattractive scenario it presents to this female reader, and perhaps to other readers as well, suggests that it may be a less than ideal example upon which to privilege the writing of one gender at the expense of another.

Using his study of Saskatchewan poetry as a basis upon which to describe women as eye poets, in his longer essay Cooley all but completely ignores their work. Having, he thinks, established the superiority of the organ of the ear and having attempted to show that women poets do not write for the ear,[8] Cooley listens to "the vernacular muse" to pen a hymn of critical praise to the poet who writes poems about male bonding through sports activities and about picking up girls in cars. As Frank Davey correctly points out with regard to Cooley's reliance upon various dichotomies, not just this one: "The repressed ideological project is to deconstruct the culture's inherited binary constructions which have forced it into high/low, father/mother, authority/subversion, centre/margin models. But . . . Cooley is drawn . . . here . . . into affirming these dichotomies by asserting the culturally despised alternative against the privileged other" (Davey 1988, 224).

In the name of a poetry with the laudable aim of engendering "the bold somatic weight of words in the mouth, the whole body" (Cooley 1987, 189), the feminine body is elided and smothered, and prairie women's poetry is "smeared." Having bracketed women's poetry out, Cooley can configure male vernacular speech as the muse in the service of men's poetry. In the conclusion to "Placing the Vernacular," at the point where one might expect some qualification or further insight into the dynamics of the relation between eye and ear, for instance, Cooley comments:

> . . . I will only say we can cultivate *both* of them, enjoy each for what it is. I would add that one of the most exciting forms prairie poetry recently has taken, and may continue to take, lies in a combination of these practices within a single text (not *simply* in the existence of them side by side in different writers or texts). Think of Birk Sproxton. (Cooley 1987, 19)

After pointing out all the limitations to eye poetry and aligning it with poetry written primarily by women, Cooley mildly suggests that we can enjoy both eye and ear poetry for what they are. He then states that the most exciting contemporary texts being written on the prairies combine these two practices or faculties, though he does not elaborate on the dynamics of this combination. The immediate example he offers of this emergent innovative style is another male poet.[9]

Probably the most serious fault of Cooley's two essays though, and the root of his exclusion of women poets from his prairie republic, is his claiming and colonizing of the mother tongue as, and only as, the male vernacular. Cooley claims that his ear poetry "would coincide fairly well with Ong's 'secondary orality' " (Cooley 1987, 5). In fact, however, the poetics Cooley is seeking to valorize would be more correctly described as a second wave of primary orality supported and promoted by male bonding activities.[10] When in "The Vernacular Muse" Cooley provides the reader with a summary of the salient features of orally based expression as isolated by Ong, he does not in fact summarize Ong's category of secondary orality at all. Rather he lists the features of primary orality and then conflates vernacular or ear poetry with primary orality, a condition which, according to Ong, has not obtained for centuries.[11] It is erroneous then to conclude as he does that "With no great effort, we can make extensive and compelling connections between the oral culture Ong describes and certain features of contemporary prairie poetry" (196). As Robert Wilson observes with regard to one prairie province, "Perhaps it would be more accurate to think of Alberta as a verbally reticent culture, or even as post-literate, than as an oral one" (Neuman and Wilson 1982, 171).

By reinvoking a lost, preliterate culture as a license to "reopen some space for orality in the face of a print culture which, allowing for Derrida's larger argument, has consolidated itself as *the* measure of literature, and which in its applications on the prairies works in damaging ways" (Cooley 1987, 197), Cooley is eventually led to the following statement: "But by speaking in the mother tongue, those who have been excluded can call into being an other, another world. In their dream of cultural autonomy, the depreciated language they speak enables them to resist the impositions of a father tongue, which is the respected and learned way of writing, duly installed in academies of one kind or another" (204). Reserving the label of 'father tongue' for the canonical literary tradition and the acts of its enforcers, Cooley co-opts the term 'mother tongue' for male poets writing in the vernacular. With neither father nor mother tongue available to them, and because Cooley apparently cannot or will not 'hear' women's vernacular speech, it is not surprising that women poets are astonishingly absent from his critical purview.

Like Davey who, in "A Young Boy's Eden," dismisses translation as a poetic in the name of a poststructuralist self-reflexivity, Cooley too, anxious to up the ante on prairie poetry by placing it within a postmodern aesthetics,[12] relies too heavily on a plethora of postmodern terms and techniques and fails to consider the crucial question of the relationship between speech and writing in terms of the composition of the text. Like Davey, Cooley also mentions but then overlooks the possibilities of translation as a model for this relation. Commenting on Robert Kroetsch's *Seed Catalogue* he observes: "We're looking here at something close to a documentary muse. The sections taken over (translated) from seed catalogues, where they were offered as commercial come-ons, become in this new configuration wonderfully sensuous, downright sensual" (Cooley 1987, 201). One can hardly fault Cooley for being distracted by the lushly sensual properties of the language of *Seed Catalogue* and thereby overlooking the translation poetics of that book. Indeed Cooley's engagement with the text that he calls "a love song to plants" (202) is a model of critical writing.[13] However, in keeping with his own outlaw stance, Cooley casts the poet as "some kind of literary Robin Hood" (200) and largely misses the poet as translator. Cooley's critical mythology casts Kroetsch as a literary and/but lusty Robin Hood with an agricultural bent, who "gourds up his loins" and sings "his masturbatory song" but laments that "he has no one to receive his seeds / words, to carry them away pregnant with thought." "Orgasmic in his utterance," his is the "spermatic" word (202-203).

Wait a minute. How do we account for this sudden absence of the ear of the other in Cooley's scenario? The vernacular poet, who is, Cooley has informed us, assured of his auditor, appears to be in serious danger of losing touch with him or her. Certainly the desired female auditor is out of earshot. That is, if the vernacular song is "communally based" (Cooley 1987, 196), as Cooley insists, then surely some heterosexual female ear and by extension womb ought to be seduced by its rhythms and rhymes, if not by its persuasive rhetoric or reason. The disappearance in Cooley's theory not of the poet's ear but of the *auditor's* ear collapses his theory in its own terms. The stakes for the male ear poet apparently go beyond the lack of reception and dissemination of his words.

In remarking its absence, Cooley is not necessarily lamenting the lack of successful fertilization. His vernacular muse, as we have seen, seems to promote "male bonding" more than any other kind of union. Despite his exuberance on behalf of playful, polymorphous postmodern representation, Cooley's position remains male, heterosexual and phallogocentric. Di Brandt points to a few of the problems with Cooley's uncritical acceptance of what he takes to be neutral terms in a postmodern program for poetry. In a short essay called "Questions I Asked Dennis Cooley about The Vernacular Muse," Brandt addresses him directly, personally and in a vernacular tone of voice:

> So "plagiarism," you say, didn't begin until after the Renaissance. Cooley, before that people got burned at the stake for stealing words or misusing them. (They still do some places. It's a hell of a copyright.) It's not like words "were openly available in a kind of verbal communism," at least not to be played with the way you want to do, to change the rules. Hell no. And it's not like they're there, even now, "freely," for the taking. . . .
>
> Isn't there a very crucial difference, Cooley, between "finding," "taking," "stealing," "appropriating," and "being given," "offered," "bestowed"? (Remember when women used to have to explain the difference between rape and mutual sex?) "Expropriation" is surely another form of silencing, if you think about it from the point of view of the expropriated. "Speaking from or for" amounts to very different processes if you're talking about language. Doesn't it? You gotta be careful when you're playing around with orality, since it so often, as you say, "belongs" to the already disenfranchised, marginalized people. (Brandt 1988, 95)[14]

It would seem then that Cooley's exile of female poets from his vernacular republic culminates in a number of undesirable outcomes. The relation between speech and writing in poetic composition remains misread, distorted and untheorized. The ear poet finds himself outside the hearing (and the insemination) of a female interlocutor. The exclusive reservation of the vernacular for men bars women poets from the mother tongue and fails even to listen for the vernaculars of women.[15] The consolidation of a binary relation between just two organs of the body, with one, the ear, standing in from time to time for the phallus, reauthorizes traditional binary sexuality and at most only revives men's and women's phallogocentric bodies.

Body Inc.

Notes

1   It is important to remember that for some poets and some communities these manoeuvres of appropriation and conversion, if that is indeed what they are, sometimes also cross language boundaries in the transition between oral and written economies.

2   There are a multiplicity of possible responses to the past available to a second generation. In the first place, one has to remember that the past is never completely abandoned at the birth of the second generation. For instance, one local prairie woman, Shirley Neuman, tells me that even she has washed clothes on scrub boards and heated water and heavy irons on wood stoves.

Too, my remarks in this paragraph are no doubt coloured by my experience of visiting the Swan River and District Museum with my parents, Vera and Sinclair Banting. While touring the museum displays, I was astonished because my parents recognized and had known many of the people represented in the old photographs and documents. Even I, thirty-seven years younger than my father, had known a few of them. The three of us spent the afternoon talking, telling stories, laughing and taking turns informally posing for photographs behind the bodies of mannequins dressed in clothes from the turn of the century. My dad even posed behind a woman's costume, blending gender along with past and present. Mom and I posed together in a double desk as if we had been schoolgirls together.

It may be that, to a degree, prairie history (or rural history) undoes the traditional ideas of history and museum. Our parodic afternoon spent in the museum did not engulf us in waves of nostalgia, naivete or prairie romance. Nor is parody incompatible with a respect for the past.

3   In my own hometown, where my parents still live, private satellite dishes carrying American television programs preceded by several years access for all to a town water system. A small library was installed there within the past year. If I were to write a poem about the day, just over a year ago, my mother first washed a load of clothes without rust in the water and with sufficient water pressure to bring the water quickly into the machine, would I be regarded as nostalgically recalling a bygone era? Would this poem be less respectable than a poem I might write about some urban experience which took place also about a year ago? Would it matter whether I wrote this poem before or after completing my Ph.D.? What if I framed the poem with some self-conscious device that hindered my parents from reading it or made them wonder why I was present in the narrative when I was not there at the time the tap was turned on?

4   Cooley's quarrel with Saskatchewan poet Anne Szumigalski informs his biased use of personal pronouns in this essay. This is confirmed on page 14 of his article, the very point at which he finally says boldly that "eye" poems tend to be written by women and "ear" poems by men. Three

sentences following this remark, Szumigalski's name appears. However, to take Szumigalski on in this veiled way, if that is what he is doing, nonetheless excludes, falsely categorizes and diminishes the work of many other women poets for the sake of a tart response to one woman poet. Moreover, women are largely absent from "The Vernacular Muse," as the article's title suggests.

5   He writes: "I would hazard two other generalizations: for obvious enough reasons vernacular writing often comes from younger writers and native-born writers, iconic work from older writers and immigrant writers." He then cites two examples which, he argues, fit his generalizations, followed by Pat Lane, a male poet whose work would contradict Cooley's scheme, and a female poet, Lorna Crozier, "who hang[s] around both yards" (Cooley 1987, 14).

6   Gary Hyland's poem, "Power Steering," is quoted in full, while only an excerpt from Elizabeth Allen's "transplant" is reproduced. Both poem and excerpt are quoted twice within the article.

7   In "The Vernacular Muse" Cooley, through Ong, acknowledges a difference in the volume and volubility of men's and women's voices. In his footnote number 25, Cooley writes: "The world of high orality, as Ong reminds us, traditionally (but not now, not in an age of electronic amplification that shines into our homes intimate with tête-à-têtes) falls to male dominance for a number of reasons, one of them simple and physiological—the greater volume of sound males normally can muster in public assembly" (216).

8   At least they do not write in the male vernacular, nor do they always write for the male ear.

9   It should be noted that Dennis Cooley's own practice and the editorial decisions of Turnstone Press, of which he is a founding board member, are far more fair and enlightened toward women's poetry than either of Cooley's essays might lead one to think. Books by Kristjana Gunnars, Audrey Poetker, Di Brandt, Jan Horner, Lorna Crozier, Daphne Marlatt, Meíra Cook and Janice Williamson, to name just a few, have been published by Turnstone.

In a strange way Cooley gestures toward both aligning his project with feminism and, as already discussed, setting aside women's poetry. In "The Vernacular Muse," talking about various marginalized discourses, he says "I am here arguing for the third position—that of redoing the discourse—as are numerous feminists" (Cooley 1987, 184). Cooley quotes Josephine Donovan on women and the novel in order to acknowledge that, historically, women as cultural outsiders were in a "good position" to write novels in the vernacular without fear of critical censure. Unfortunately, he does not question why women could write novels in vernacular but not poetry—then or now. Intentional or not, this is another way in which

Cooley exiles women not only from vernacular poetry but from poetry in general.

10   In his two essays Cooley makes use of Antony Easthope's excellent book *Poetry as Discourse* (1983) to lend support to his arguments. In 1986 Easthope published another book, *What a Man's Gotta Do: The Masculine Myth in Popular Culture,* in which he reads various "texts" of popular culture as portraying relationships between men as homosocial. In light of Cooley's assignations of the organs of the eye and the ear, it is interesting to compare Easthope's remark that the masculine body is to be observed and approved by the eye of the father and *not* by the eye of desire. The masculine body shuns the look of desire. Writing about a photograph of male sprinters just exiting their starting blocks, Easthope observes:

> The hardness and tension of the body strives to present it as wholly masculine, to exclude all curves and hollows and be only straight lines and flat planes. It would really like to be a cubist painting. Or whatever. But above all not desirable to other men because it is so definitely not soft and feminine; hairy if need be, but not smooth; bone and muscle, not flesh and blood. The masculine body seeks to be Rambo, not Rimbaud.
>
> . . . Defying gravity in the high jump or the pole vault, puffing itself up like a bullfrog in the weightlifting, the masculine body can impersonate the phallus (Easthope 1986, 54).

It would appear that, on the contrary, Cooley's male poet, or his alter-ego (perhaps I should simply say his 'buddy') personified as the power-turning but physically deficient 'Scrawny' who does not defy but utilizes the forces of gravity to connect physically with a woman, desires to be both Rambo and Rimbaud. The prostheses of the car and the sorta knob dealie on the steering wheel permit even the poet to get the girl.

Cooley is careful to stipulate that female "eye" poets gaze with the look of authority normally associated with the Law of the Father and not with the eye of female desire.

11   See pp. 195-96 of "The Vernacular Muse" for Cooley's summary. See chapter 3, "Some Psychodynamics of Orality," of Ong's *Orality and Literacy* for a discussion of primary orality and chapter 5, "Print, Space and Closure," especially pp. 135-38, where he briefly describes secondary orality.

12   "Such writing is postmodern," Cooley concludes (Cooley 1987, 213).

13   It is to Cooley's credit that in his critical excursion into the language of Seed Catalogue he avoids configuring the sensual richness of fruits and vegetables, and language, in terms of a single gender, at least up to the point where, replying to the real or imaginary woman who would censor such vegetable love he retorts "He speaks of country matters, madam" (Cooley 1987, 202).

14   Kathie Kolybaba, reviewing Cooley's long poem, *Bloody Jack,* also addresses him personally and takes him to task for what she calls a "violent" version of postmodern writing which leaves no room for women readers. She contends that "there's no room for women here, or for the reader: we can be pussies or ladies in bed . . ." (Kolybaba 1985, 43). In an interview with Daniel Lenoski, Cooley confesses to being "bewildered" and "astonished" by this comment in her review (Lenoski 1986, 170-71).

15   See Cooley's "demurral" on pp. 76-77 of his article on "Recursions Excursions and Incursions: Daphne Marlatt Wrestles with the Angel Language" in *Line* 13. This single paragraph interrupts his discussion of Marlatt's work in order to argue that "It doesn't do simply to designate one kind of writing—abstract, discursive, logical, grammatical . . . as a 'male' enterprise. It may not be altogether satisfactory to decide too quickly that certain kinds of writing are exclusively 'female' either." This might seem like a qualification, if not a retraction, of his earlier dichotomy between male ear and female eye poets. However, in the next sentence following he attributes the gender mapping of poetic styles to feminism and specifically to Marlatt's own texts. Here again he is concerned to protect male postmodern poets: "It's hard to think, say, of male postmodern poets, to name only one group, themselves criticized by linguistic standard bearers, as either enforcers or beneficiaries of this 'male' discourse." He then laments feminists' lack of precision in setting up such gender oppositions in terms of writing style (Cooley 1989, 76).

Historically, both Canadians and Americans have experienced the task of commencing a new literature in a mandarin language.

Robert Kroetsch
The Lovely Treachery of Words

Questions of Composition in the (Rosetta) "Stone Hammer Poem" and *Seed Catalogue*

Robert Kroetsch first introduced to the theory and criticism of the contemporary Canadian long poem the metaphor of the postmodern Canadian poet as archaeologist. In his essay "For Play and Entrance: The Contemporary Canadian Long Poem," Kroetsch describes Margaret Atwood's *The Journals of Susanna Moodie* and Michael Ondaatje's *The Collected Works of Billy the Kid* as poems in which "archaeology supplants history; an archaeology that challenges the authenticity of history by saying there can be no joined story, only abrupt guesswork, juxtaposition, flashes of insight" (Kroetsch 1989b, 119). Daphne Marlatt's *Steveston,* Fred Wah's *Pictograms from the Interior of B.C.* and Eli Mandel's *Out of Place* also come immediately to mind. In a parenthetical moment in the same essay Kroetsch reflects on his own long poem: "My own continuing poem is called, somewhat to my dismay, *Field Notes.* Perhaps [Charles] Olson's field is there somewhere, but more specifically I think of the field notes kept by the archaeologist, by the finding man, the finding man who is essentially lost. I can only guess the other; there might, that is, be a hidden text" (129).[1]

However, as I shall argue, the poet as archaeologist is not only a discoverer and hermeneutic interpreter of the past but equally an interpreter in that word's other sense of 'one who translates orally from one language into another.' In his essay "Unhiding the Hidden," Kroetsch meditates on Heidegger's statement about the rootlessness of Western European thought as an effect of the Roman appropriation of Greek words without a corresponding, equally authentic experience of what they say, without, in other words, adequate translation. Kroetsch muses on the parallel between this proto-rootlessness of the English language as it has descended from the Greeks and Romans, and the linguistic dilemma faced by the postcolonial Canadian writer:

> The Canadian writer's particular predicament is that he [or she] works with a language, within a literature, that appears to be authentically his own, and not a borrowing. But just as there was in the Latin word a concealed Greek experience, so there is in the Canadian word a concealed other experience, sometimes British, sometimes American. . . . The process of rooting that borrowed word, that totally exact homonym, in authentic experience, is then, must be, a radical one. (Kroetsch 1989b, 58-59)

Borrowing a Heideggerian phrase, Kroetsch refers to the general program of work in which he and many other Canadian writers are engaged as 'unhiding the hidden.'

'Unhiding the hidden,' then, is for Kroetsch not only a process of archaeological discovery of the past. The poetics of 'unhiding the hidden' involves both archaeology and translation:

> Yes, it is as if we spend our lives finding clues, fragments, shards, leading or misleading details, chipped tablets written over in a forgotten language. Perhaps they are a counting of cattle, a measuring out of grain. Perhaps they are a praising of gods, a naming of the dead. We can't know. (Kroetsch 1989b, 129)

There might be a hidden text, but, to Kroetsch's dismay and delight, it is impossible to translate it. Nevertheless, impossible or not, we *must* translate. The 'radical' process whereby the poet as archaeologist 'roots' the borrowed word in Canada is translation. Like Fred Wah, Kroetsch is monolingual and cannot adequately translate interlingually. However, by translating *intralingually* between speech and writing, he attempts to root the colonial English word in postcolonial Canadian soil and in Canadian tongues.

"STONE HAMMER POEM" can be read as a kind of 'translator's preface' to Kroetsch's long poems collected together in one volume in 1989 under the title *Completed Field Notes*. That is, "Stone Hammer Poem" postulates the translation project which Kroetsch dares himself to prove (or, to use an agricultural metaphor, to prove up) throughout the several individual long poems which comprise *Completed Field Notes*. In this prefatory short long poem, the poet assumes the role of archaeologist-translator, trying to recover the lost connections, to read "the traces, trying to leap the gaps (signifier to signified), trying to un-name the silence back to name" (Kroetsch 1989b, 122-23).[2] In "Stone Hammer Poem" Kroetsch transforms the stone hammer into a Rosetta stone, a stone, that is, with the power to decipher and unlock the disparate pasts of several different peoples—natives, German immigrant farmers and their Canadian progeny.

However, Kroetsch recapitulates the gesture of the translators of the Rosetta stone with a distinctly postcolonial difference. Rather than locate the proper names that will decode the stone's text and in turn other writing systems as well, as with the Egyptian Rosetta stone,[3] Kroetsch continually calls into question the various aspects of 'the proper' associated with the stone as an object in the world, namely, 1) the stone's physical properties, 2) its aspect as owned property, and 3) questions of propriety or its proper location and use. At the same time, he also repeatedly *un-names* the name 'stone hammer.'

The moment it presents itself to the poet as a text to be deciphered and read, the physical properties of the stone hammer become uncertain. Kroetsch writes:

> This stone
> become a hammer
> of stone, this maul

> is the colour
> of bone (no,
> bone is the colour
> of this stone maul).
> (*Completed Field Notes*, 1)

The demonstrative and unequivocal "this stone" undergoes a process of transmutation (or poetic manufacture) in the second line to become a hammer. It changes state from stone to hammer and then, by the third line, to a hammer of stone. Subsequently it becomes a maul and a stone hammer. In addition to these name changes, the stone's colour[4] and other material properties are defined through negation, comparison and reversal of comparison, using the copula verb as a fulcrum around which transformations take place. Kroetsch employs a repertoire of statement, qualification, renaming, comparison, reversal, association by means of internal rhyme, parentheses, and line breaks in order to 'undetermine' the nature of an object as apparently solid and unambiguous as a stone hammer.

Such cautiousness, concern for accuracy, and modification of original impressions mark the practice of the archaeologist recording field notes. But as the repertoire of techniques just mentioned testifies, Kroetsch compiles *his* field notes through a combination of inscription and erasure. In George Bowering's words, "Kroetsch is always erasing, I said. That is how he gets things done. . . . When he erases he doesnt replace, I said. You can see the old words. It's called a palimpsest by an archaeologist" (Bowering 1985, 131). Not only does Kroetsch as archaeologist-poet find a palimpsest at his dig site. His very methods of excavating that site create a palimpsest. In terms of Kroetsch's work, a palimpsest is more than a doubly or multiply inscribed *text*. A palimpsest can be located in other kinds of objects as well, even objects of utility. Moreover, a palimpsest can also be deliberately created as such. In the process of the poet's excavation of it, for example, the stone hammer becomes a palimpsest. But, importantly, it does not become an inscribed text at the expense of losing its physical objecthood, its stoneyness. The stone hammer becomes a palimpsest not through the poet's decipherment of its meaning but, paradoxically, through his recorded hesitations or outright refusal to read it as a text.

As owned property, another element of 'the proper,' the stone goes through many hands. "This paperweight on my desk" was "found in a wheatfield/lost." It

> fell from the travois or
> a boy playing   lost it in
> the prairie wool or
> a squaw   left it in
> the brain of a buffalo or . . .
> (*Completed Field Notes*, 2)

At each juncture of lost and found, both its name and 'proper' function alter. It becomes each of stone hammer and stone maul all over again. It also becomes a pemmican maul and a paperweight. Of course, ultimately, as the title signals, the stone hammer also becomes a poem. As Bowering writes, "By erasing one gets back to the nothing of beginning, but not really, because the erasure is something, a history of the poem's making" (Bowering 1985, 132).[5] This history of the poem's making, this erasure, becomes, paradoxically, the poem. Just as the stone hammer becomes a palimpsest through the poet's written reluctance to decode it, so the poem becomes a palimpsest, and a poem, through his erasure of written words.

Furthermore, every change in ownership of the stone hammer parallels a change in ownership of the site at which it was found:

> Now the field is
> mine because
> I gave it
> (for a price)
>
> to a young man
> (with a growing son)
> who did not
>
> notice that the land
> did not belong
>
> to the Indian who
> gave it to the Queen
> (for a price) who
> gave it to the CPR
> (for a price) which . . .
> (*Completed Field Notes*, 5)

Object, location of the object and the poem all take on aspects of a palimpsest. Neither the stone nor the land are extra-textual. Nor is the poem extraneous to the world of objects. The stone has been shaped and imprinted by many forces: forces of geology and erosion which have shaped the hammer to its present contours and, along with chance, partly determined its functions, time, blood stains, rawhide loops, and now also the forces of grammar, scientific and archaeological methods, ordinary perceptual modalities, habit, curses, and poetry. The land—marked by the retreating ice of the Ice Age, the hooves and bodies of the buffalo, travois lines, the plow, spilled blood, barbed-wire fences, the growing of domestic crops and wild bushes and trees such as saskatoon, chokecherry and cranberry, and the paperwork of numerous land transactions—is similarly textual. The palimpsest, then, encompasses the very lived world of which the stone hammer, a plot of Alberta land and the poet himself are a part. In other words, the largely oral world of the natives and the settlers on the prairies is always already textual. It is not a matter of somehow capturing those previous oral worlds on paper, of representing orality in written form. As "Stone Hammer Poem" reveals, translation between and within languages is already implicated in these oral cultures. Accompanying the passing of the stone hammer from user to user is an exchange of languages. The stone is transferred between, respectively, Blackfoot and/or Cree and German, German and English, and, through intralingual translation within the single language of English, back and forth between orality and writing.

The beauty of "Stone Hammer Poem," however, is that each of the stone hammer, the site at which it is found, and the poem itself retains its physical or material properties and does not become merely absorbed or subsumed by writing and representation. Questions of propriety or 'proper' location or function are raised with regard to the stone at each point of exchange and again at the very point at which its physical utility is apparently suspended:

> He kept it (the
> stone maul) on the railing
> of the back porch in
> a raspberry basket.

> I keep it
> on my desk
> (the stone.
> (*Completed Field Notes,* 6-7)

By continually raising these questions of propriety, property and physical properties, Kroetsch works to guarantee the stone's ston-eyness and prevents it from becoming mere symbol.[6]

If (as he suggests in his author's note on the back cover of the first edition of *The Sad Phoenician*) the ancient Phoenicians moved writing off the sacred wall down to the secular and commercial wharf, then it can be said that Kroetsch builds on the Phoenicians' desacrilizing gesture by refusing to allow us simply to read *through* the (Rosetta) stone hammer to a transcendent text beyond. "Stone Hammer Poem" instructs us, duplicitously, both 'translate' and 'do not translate.' Kroetsch's circumlocutory contra-diction insists that even as we decode the poem, the historical and pre-historical past, and the prairie as the home place we must also continue to read the stoneyness of the stone, the fragment as fragment. It is not that we as readers or as postcolonials have yet to discover the cartouche that will translate the fragments from nonsense into sense. The stone hammer both is and is not a Rosetta stone. As we have seen, it is an implement for the decipherment and translation of ancient and contemporary 'texts.' But unlike the Egyptian Rosetta stone, it is not an official decree passed by a council of priests. Instead, it is a tool for survival—a technology for bringing down a buffalo or an enemy, a pemmican maul for preparing food for winter survival, and an occasional paperweight and translation device on the poet's desk.

As the prologue to his continuing poem *Completed Field Notes,*[7] "Stone Hammer Poem" prefaces and implicates the archaeological investigations of Kroetsch's 'field notes' with the necessity to trans-late and the impossibility of doing so. The temptation to read through the discovered fragments to a signified meaning and simul-taneously to allow these same fragments to retain their nature as fragments, chipped tablets, stone hammers, or stones informs many of the individual long poems which comprise Kroetsch's continuing poem in its entirety. Jacques Derrida's words on the relation between translation and continuance are relevant in this context:

> A text lives only if it lives *on* [*sur-vit*], and it lives *on* only
> if it is *at once* translatable *and* untranslatable . . . . Totally
> translatable, it disappears as a text, as writing, as a body
> of language [*langue*]. Totally untranslatable, even within
> what is believed to be one language, it dies immediately.
> Thus triumphant translation is neither the life nor the
> death of the text, only or already its living *on,* its life after
> life, its life after death. (Derrida 1979, 102-103)

The poet's placement of the stone hammer on his desk, thus removing it sufficiently from its nearly forgotten location in the raspberry basket on the back porch,[8] renders it untranslatable and therefore a text again. Of course, since one of the root meanings of the word 'translation' is 'to carry across, transfer,' this act of re-placement as a literal 'carrying across' from one people to another, from the native to the European, from the nomad to the farmer, and from the farmer to the poet is a 'translation' in itself.[9]

The stone hammer, then, makes intralingual translation between the vernacular and literary language possible. As such, it makes translation "within what is believed to be one language" possible. In setting up the conditions under which translation can take place, the stone hammer functions as a kind of postcolonial Canadian Rosetta stone. The short long poem that is "Stone Hammer Poem" is the poet-as-translator's preface to the comprehensive translation project of *Completed Field Notes.*

IN *SEED CATALOGUE* KROETSCH continues his search for answers to the questions he formulates for himself in "Stone Hammer Poem." In an essay first published under the title "The Continuing Poem"[10] he writes: "Homer's *The Odyssey,* forever being translated into new versions of the poem. How to do that without changing languages" (Kroetsch 1989b, 8).[11] That is, because translation has played an important role in the history of the long poem, the monolingual poet who succumbs to the epic impulse faces a major impediment. How can a monolingual poet translate? How does a poet with only one language compose a long poem?

At no one point has Kroetsch ever discussed his work directly and at length in terms of translation. However, at sundry points in the conversations recorded in *Labyrinths of Voice* he touches on his attraction toward translations. Asked by Shirley Neuman "If the Tower of Babel is very attractive to you, as a positive rather than as a negative mytheme, how do you feel about being monolingual?" (Neuman and Wilson 1982, 119), Kroetsch replies:

> I feel almost crippled. It is sobering to consider how many of the important critical insights have come from people who have more than one language. Steiner is an example —a native speaker of three languages. Multilingual critics have a sense of the conceptual multiplicities behind language. One nice thing that has happened to English is its own unravelling. I'm sure India is going to have a new version of English that will almost have to be translated.

Pursuing this line of discussion, Neuman asks about the role of writing in codifying language. Here is Kroetsch's response:

> Writing codifies but even so there is a breakdown coming. You can pick up two novels written in English right now and sense the enormous differences in their respective uses of English. Of course, I think that speech overrides much of that process of codification even today. That is why an oral tradition is so important. (Neuman and Wilson 1982, 119)

In his answers to Neuman's questions, Kroetsch makes a number of important linkages. He connects translation with critical and theoretical insights about language, with the decomposition of a specific language, and, most crucially for our present purposes, with the relationship between speech and writing. In other places in *Labyrinths of Voice* he allies translation both with the writer's 'misreading' of language—making strange the familiar, ordinary language—and the reader's exploration of the text (Neuman and Wilson 1982, 151). For him, the dream of Babel is juxtaposed with an illusion of freedom associated with "falling out of cosmologies" and "becoming a fragment again" (25). He enthusiastically embraces Neuman's offer of translation as a "trope" for his concept of influence, because, he says, translation contains both metonymy and difference, adding that translation "is metonymy because it's another naming. We can give twenty names and only hope that the nameless thing has been recognized by that" (18). The myth of the Tower of

Babel intrigues him, he admits, more and more: "I now think that it was a great thing, one of the greatest things that has happened to mankind. From the Tower of Babel all of a sudden, we gain all the languages we have" (116).

Without abandoning the oral tradition, the vernacular or the vulgar tongue for high art, but without forsaking high art either, how, Kroetsch asks in the different versions of the refrain to *Seed Catalogue,* do you grow a poet, a lover, a garden, a poem? The answer he invents for himself in "Stone Hammer Poem" and explores further in *Seed Catalogue* is to translate between the spoken and the written registers of a single language, between the oral storytelling of the prairie pub and the hubbub of language made possible by permanent marks incised on a page. A few sentences following his statement about the problem of translating without changing languages, Kroetsch comments both on the general predicament of the Canadian poet and on his own desire in composing *Seed Catalogue.* He writes:

> The seed catalogue is a shared book in our society. We have few literary texts approaching that condition. I wanted to write a poetic equivalent to the 'speech' of a seed catalogue. The way we read the page and hear its implications. Spring. The plowing, the digging, of the garden. The mapping of the blank, cool earth. The exact placing of the explosive seed. (Kroetsch 1989b, 8)

To "write" a "poetic equivalent" to the " 'speech' " of a seed catalogue is, as we shall see, to translate that text without changing languages. It is to translate from writing to speech and from speech to writing.

A palimpsest of a genuine McKenzie's Seeds catalogue is visible at the surface of the page of the first edition of Kroetsch's *Seed Catalogue.*[12] The poem is printed in green ink on Byronic Blue Brocade paper. Just below the surface of the poem, screened in light brown, are text and images reproduced from two catalogues released in 1916 and 1922 by McKenzie's Seeds of Brandon, Manitoba. The images, naturally, are of vegetables, flowers, fruit, grains, grasses, and gardening implements. The light brown text and images exist just at the threshold of legibility, and the reader has to strain a little to decipher them. The sprightly green words of the poem, on the contrary, printed on the right-hand page only, ripple over the surface like new grass or a crop of fall rye.

Surprisingly, Kroetsch relates the compositional method that produced *Seed Catalogue* not to gardening, as might have been expected, but to archaeology. He writes:

> For me, one of those [archaeological] deposits turned out to be an old seed catalogue. I found a 1917 catalogue in the Glenbow archives in 1975. I translated that seed catalogue into a poem called 'Seed Catalogue.' The archaeological discovery, if I might call it that, brought together for me the oral tradition and the dream of origins. (Kroetsch 1989b, 7)

Kroetsch sifts the site of origins, and what he discovers is not a buried city or a lost temple. No dinosaur bones, broken bits of pottery, or even a stone hammer this time. His archaeological method in this instance takes him instead to roots. Actual roots. Roots and vegetables. McKenzie's Pedigreed Early Snowcap Cauliflower, McKenzie's Improved Golden Wax Bean, Hubbard Squash. Flowers too: Spencer Sweet Pea, Imperialis Morning Glory. That is, Kroetsch translates the word 'roots' literally, rather than figuratively, and this translation, to the letter, leads him to the written words of the found text, the seed catalogue, out of which he then translates the poem. Without changing languages.

In translating the written document, Kroetsch rediscovers various spoken forms of the language. That is, the effect of this translation from archival document to long poem is to make us *hear* the written document. Here, for example, is the entry on the Copenhagen Market Cabbage, which opens *Seed Catalogue:* "This *new introduction, strictly speaking,* is in every respect a *thoroughbred, a cabbage* of *highest pedigree,* and is *creating considerable flurry* among *professional gardeners* all *over the world*" (Kroetsch 1977, 32). The emphasis produced by highlighting certain words deemed particularly resonant by the authors of the horticultural catalogue creates a heightened effect. The sales pitch of this passage appeals to 'quality,' emphasizing words pertinent to social class, breeding, professionalism, and internationalism. The contrast between this high-flown, authoritative, British-sounding voice and, a few lines later, the quiet, teasing and intimate speech of a mother to her son ("My mother said: / Did you wash your ears? / You could grow cabbages / in those ears") allows each discourse, both on the subject of cabbages, to read and discover the other. In the month of January, when the seed catalogue arrives in the mail, the promises of spring and new growth (or, as Kroetsch insists, an end to winter) seem hyperbolic. These promises are juxtaposed against the equally hyperbolic promises of cabbages growing in a child's ears. By translating from the archive to the long poem, Kroetsch both oralizes the written document, making us hear the archive once again, and textualizes, and thereby makes strange and 'legitimizes,' informal oral utterance. The co-existence of the two discourses in the text 'unhides' the allusive, poetic elements of each. In addition, translation of the archival seed catalogue into its "poetic equivalent" gives us back the shared text.[13]

By translating between and thereby layering speech and writing over one another, Kroetsch creates a palimpsest in *Seed Catalogue* just as he does in "Stone Hammer Poem." For him, the palimpsest or "text beneath the text" is at the very 'root' of Canadian writing:

> Terry [Heath] insisting we have no tradition and must write out of that. My asserting against his statement a belief in the text beneath the text, an everlasting grope into the shape of that darkness. As with rural people, the complexities and patterns beneath the formulaic speech. Almost the opposite of urban, where the surface is sometimes more complicated than what lies beneath it. But the text beneath the text, as in *Gone Indian,* is at the root of our Canadian writing. The ur-novel that no ONE will ever write. (Kroetsch 1980, 53)

Translating intralingually, within a single language, between speech and writing, obviously Kroetsch does not translate for simple, referential meaning. Rather, he translates in order to preserve the differential characteristics of both speech and writing. As he says in an interview, "I think that when we record speech we have somehow to keep a great deal of that speech present. . . . the page must offer a sense of speechness" (Kamboureli 1984b, 48). Both interlingual and intralingual translation create loss and excess at the borders between texts and between languages (interlingual), and between speech and writing (intralingual). By translating, even between speech and writing, Kroetsch situates his reader at the sites of loss and excess which are produced in every act of translation, sites at which the materiality of the signifier can be rediscovered. By translating intralingually, Kroetsch provides the reader with "a sense of speechness." In his article "The *Délire* of Translation," Keith Cohen investigates the nature and extent of the translator's bondage to the source (or tutor) text and suggests that the excesses and insufficiencies encountered in the process of translation engender a kind of writerly delirium. As Cohen argues:

> In wriggling out of the denotative straitjacket, the transla-
> tor discovers the inherent semantic vacillation of the text,
> the instability many readers may gloss over, the *déborde-*
> *ment,* the superabundance of the original.
>
> It is as though each phrase were an edge, a border
> erroneously delimiting a single denotation. The translator
> must go over this edge (hence *débordement*), unleash in the
> translation this signifying overflow.
>
> In this way the initial constraint is turned into its
> opposite. The illusory bondage by the tutor text yields a
> liberating excess as soon as the unitary is conceived of as
> multiple. And it is the consequential need to remold this
> excess into a new signifying system that provides the *délire*
> (undoing an initial reading through writing) of translation.
> (Cohen 1977, 86)

It is in this way that Kroetsch's intralingual translation poetics works to un-decode the formulaic elements of both speech and writing. Kroetsch constructs a palimpsest of speech and writing in order to "[wriggle] out of the denotative straitjacket" and instead allow the material properties of language to unhide themselves to our ears, eyes, hands, and tongues.

Finally, Kroetsch's translation poetics shows us how, like him, to write right in the book. Kroetsch himself does not write out of a desire merely to interpret or revise the contents of the sacred or culturally and historically hegemonic Book. As we have seen, he understands that developing a thriving postcolonial literature is not at all a matter of establishing a small Canadian niche under the umbrella of the powerful colonial traditions represented by Britain and America. Rather Kroetsch writes right in the literal book (the seed catalogue, the ledger or, in *The Sad Phoenician,* the alphabet book). As Cohen says, translation unleashes the desire to undo an initial reading through writing, to transgress the borders of the book, to appropriate or parody its contents, to go over the edges. He defines translation as follows:

> Translation might be tentatively defined as that process by which the reading of the tutor text is made to give rise immediately to the writing of a new text—a text that does not (as the conventional notion of translation has it) transcribe the original but displaces it, uses it as a conveniently closed foundation and point of departure. In other words, a reading that supplies a writing, or a writing that supplants the reading. (Cohen 1977, 85)

The desire to translate, the desire for other languages, even the desire for other languages within, as Derrida says, "what is believed to be one language," is the desire to figure one's way out into the physical, material world—into the garden, the marketplace, the pattern and tumble of a lover's bed. In other words, the desire for other languages is the desire to exceed the limits of one's own language. As we shall see, Kroetsch's intralingual translation poetics temporarily relieves reader and writer alike of the tyranny of the phonetically based English language. In so doing, he makes it possible for those of us who are, like him, essentially monolingual to transform our bodies back into the flesh which is elided by phoneticism. We can become a fragment again or perhaps a kind of pictogrammic character, digging, plowing, mapping, trading, and loving (in) the world.

Moreover, it is often forgotten that other languages are not just additional or alternate systems of signifiers and signifieds. Even more importantly, other languages are the languages of others. Confronting the materiality of the signifier, therefore, initiates a point of possible conjunction with others. It marks a place where love and friendship can take place, and where community and art can begin.

In "Beyond Nationalism: A Prologue" Kroetsch ventures to characterize the whole enterprise of Canadian writing as a middle-ground perilously situated between the inherited systems of source text and source language and a dispersed target text which can only ever remain fragmentary:

> Canadian writing takes place between the vastness of (closed) cosmologies and the fragments found in the (open) field of the archaeological site. It is a literature of dangerous middles. It is a literature that, compulsively seeking its own story . . . comes compulsively to a genealogy that refuses origin, to a genealogy that speaks instead, and anxiously, and with a generous reticence, the nightmare and the welcome dream of Babel. (Kroetsch 1989b, 71)

What takes place in this post-Babelian middleground, native territory, farmer's field, archaeological site, garden, bush, or at the poet's desk is a poetics of translation. The moment of the discovery of the Americas continues, in Canada, in the burdensome debt and the seductive promises of translation.

In composing "Stone Hammer Poem" and *Seed Catalogue,* Kroetsch theorizes a postcolonial writing practice based not on representation but rather on translation. "How do you grow a poet?" is his refrain. The parallel between the physical work involved in plotting, digging, sifting, stringing, and seeding a garden in spring and conducting an archaeological dig is plain. But given our preconceived notions about writing as representation, the parallel between archaeology and translation is not at first as readily apparent.

But when you come from a distant place, a bookless oral world, as many of us still do,[14] and when later you enter a world full of books, you do not simply transcribe your oral world onto paper, as mimetic or expressive theories of representation suggest. Conversely, when you leave a world full of books and emigrate to another country, you cannot immediately resort to mimetic or expressive representation either. In both cases, you know you must first learn the new tongue. First things first. And you realize that you *must* translate—between languages and/or between the world of orality and that of written words.

Notes

1   For further discussion of the archaeological impulse in contemporary Canadian writing, see the conversations with Robert Kroetsch in Neuman and Wilson's *Labyrinths of Voice.*

2   This is Kroetsch's description of Fred Wah's undertaking in *Pictograms from the Interior of B.C.,* but I shall argue that it can be applied to the compositional process of "Stone Hammer Poem" as well.

3   The translation of the Egyptian Rosetta stone provided the key to the decipherment of Egyptian hieroglyphics.

4   As George Bowering notes, "So far he has told us what colour the object is, but he has not mentioned a colour" (Bowering 1985, 132). See Bowering's word-by-word analysis, almost a translation itself, of "Stone Hammer Poem." See also Russell Brown's essay "Seeds and Stones" Unhiding in Kroetsch's Poetry," which treats "Stone Hammer Poem" at some length.

5   Bowering says that the first section of "Stone Hammer Poem" "is a western Canadian reconstruction of Keats's ode on an old urn; an act that Keats's poem suggested someone meditate and perform. We infer a succession all the way form sylvan historian to Prairie archaeologist, a code transmitted from ditty to Dawe" (Bowering 1985, 133). I would reconfigure what Bowering refers to as Kroetsch's reconstruction of the Keats poem as his intralingual translation of it.

6   I am not arguing that the stone hammer is symbolic of the Rosetta stone but rather that within extremely different cultural and historical contexts the functions of the two stones vis-à-vis translation are similar. I would argue that Kroetsch's technique prevents the stone hammer from becoming symbolic of the Rosetta stone.

7   In an interview with Roy Miki, Kroetsch says: "I was tempted at one point to frame the whole poem with Indian material, to open with "Stone Hammer Poem" and to end with those Old Man stories which I—how many are there, I forget. Are there twelve?" (Miki 1989, 124). He confesses that this secret ending failed. This failure of ending and of poem, of course, are part of Kroetsch's aesthetics of failure, the failure in this case of the postmodern poet to write the epic poem and which, paradoxically, generates the contemporary long poem. Ironically, it was in part "Stone Hammer Poem," the prologue, that threw out the count in terms of epic numbers. Miki suggests that after *The Ledger* and *Seed Catalogue* Kroetsch might have ended his long poem. Kroetsch replies: "No, I think I pretty quickly recognized that I couldn't stop then—given my epic impulse I had to go for 12 at least. I've gone past 12, so now I'm hoping that at 24 I can quit, and that my continuing poem is going to cease at section 24. But there's a prologue that is, or is not, counted into the counting. So then you start to play that little trick on yourself" (126).

8   Bowering describes the raspberry basket as "a little museum" (Bowering 1985, 143).

9   Perhaps an additional meaning of the word 'translation,' namely, 'carried into heaven without death,' was invoked when the stone hammer first stopped the plow in the field, inspiring the exclamation "*Gott im Himmel.*" It is worth underscoring that the stone hammer is not passed directly from hand to hand but alternately lost and found. In the interval, the need for translation arises.

10   This essay is now included under the title "The Moment of the Discovery of America Continues" in *The Lovely Treachery of Words.*

11   *The Ledger,* which appeared between the publication of "Stone Hammer Poem" and *Seed Catalogue,* is also translative. I focus here on *Seed Catalogue,* however, because it has had a more significant impact upon contemporary Canadian poetry and because the translation poetics of *The Ledger* became more evident in light of *Seed Catalogue* than in isolation.

12   The first edition of *Seed Catalogue* was designed by Eva Fritsch.

13   Kristjana Gunnars astutely connects roots, rootedness and hearing in Kroetsch's poetry when, in conversation with him, she observes: "Even when your mother says you've gotta wash your ears because you could grow cabbages there. This has everything to do with what you hear. The plants you have grown in the soil, where you are rooted, and also what you hear: grows in your ear" (Gunnars 1987-88, 61).

14   Kroetsch himself grew up on a farm "way hell and gone out in Alberta" (Kroetsch 1989b, 9).

Thus the Biblical myth is reversed, the confusion of tongues is no longer a punishment, the subject gains access to bliss by the cohabitation of languages *working side by side:* the text of pleasure is a sanctioned Babel.

Roland Barthes
The Pleasure of the Text

I write because I do not want the words I find: by subtraction

Roland Barthes
The Pleasure of the Text

The Archaeology of the Alphabet
in *The Sad Phoenician*

Robert Kroetsch's *The Sad Phoenician* is generated out of two mistakes. One is the lovely mistranslations of Chinese ideograms by Ernest Fenollosa and Ezra Pound in their explorations of the Chinese written character as a medium for American English-language poetry. The second is embedded in Kroetsch's back cover note from *The Sad Phoenician*:

> It was the Phoenicians who moved writing from the temple, down to the wharf. Not, I'll make you a god; rather, I'll make you a deal.
> They wrote down the sound, not the picture. That was the astonishing thing. They wrote down the sound. They freed the reader from the wall.
> Fenollosa and Pound were mistaken when they praised the ideograph and returned us to the arrested image. The Phoenicians—they'd heard that one before. Hey, they said, the ship is leaving. Get that cargo sorted and counted, the destinations marked. They needed an alphabet they could learn fast, write fast, send anywhere.
> The poem as hubbub. Freed from picture, into the pattern and tumble of sound. Poetry as commotion: a condition of civil unrest. Now listen here.
> The poet, not as priest, but as lover.

Kroetsch's statement about Fenollosa's and Pound's mistaken praise of the Chinese character must also be read as a deliberately partial and restrictive mistake or Bloomian 'misprision.' On the one hand, Kroetsch confines the effects of their praise of the ideograph to the Imagist movement initiated and then rapidly abandoned by Pound (though still important for hundreds of poets who are even now writing in the English language). On the other hand, he invokes the translation poetics of both Fenollosa's "The Chinese Written Character as a Medium for Poetry" and Pound's long poem the *Cantos* as generative texts for *The Sad Phoenician.* Kroetsch's cover statement amounts to an apology for the long poem and the translation poetics which generate it.

The Sad Phoenician celebrates the process of translation from its very first page. The stylized letter 'a' which, following the front cover and title pages, announces the text's opening (although one could also genuinely argue that the book begins with its back cover blurb, thus suggesting the possibility of an oriental reading order for the occidental book) constitutes a facsimile of a letter in the Phoenician alphabet:[1]

This lower-case 'a' with part of its bottom portion erased functions as both an instance and an emblem of graphological translation, a form of translation in which a source-language (SL) graphology is replaced by an equivalent target-language (TL) graphology (Catford, 62). But this 'a,' caught in the very process of translation, retains its own visual and linguistic identity and does not *imitate* a letter in the Phoenician alphabet. The clue that imitation is not being practiced here lies in the fact that the Phoenician alphabet did not include vowels: it was actually a twenty-two character syllabary. Thus it is not imitation or representation but translation that is signalled at the beginning of *The Sad Phoenician.*

It is important to stress that writing as representation and writing as translation are different, if related, textual enterprises. Translation is not mimetic, not a metaphor. Paul de Man, in a useful article analyzing (he calls it 'translating') Walter Benjamin's essay "The Task of the Translator," sets up a distinction between the translator and the poet which, while de Man relies on versions of the poet and the translator which have been challenged and surpassed, nevertheless helps to clarify the distinction between translation and representation. De Man writes:

> Of the differences between the situation of the translator and that of the poet, the first that comes to mind is that the poet has some relationship to meaning, to a statement that is not purely within the realm of language. That is the naiveté of the poet, that he has to say something, that he has to convey a meaning which does not necessarily relate to language. The relationship of the translator to the original is the relationship between language and language, wherein the problem of meaning or the desire to say something, the need to make a statement, is entirely absent. Translation is a relation from language to language, not a relation to an extralinguistic meaning that could be copied, paraphrased, or imitated. That is not the case for the poet; poetry is certainly not paraphrase, clarification, or interpretation, a copy in that sense; and that is already the first difference. (De Man 1986, 81-82)

De Man, following Benjamin, suggests that translation resembles philosophy, literary criticism or theory, and history more than it does poetry because like these other derived or secondary processes translation is not mimetic: it does not resemble the original the way, for example, children resemble parents, nor is it an imitation, copy, paraphrase, or metaphor of the original (De Man 1986, 82-83). Philosophy, criticism, theory, history—like translation, all of these disciplines are intralinguistic: "they relate to what in the original belongs to language, and not to meaning as an extralinguistic correlate susceptible of paraphrase and imitation" (84).[2] Or, as de Man succinctly points out in an interview immediately following his article, "you could not possibly get from the translation back to an original" (97). Unlike representation, the faithfulness of translation is not to some bit of meaning, truth or an abstract idea. Rather it is a relation of fidelity between language and language.

In *The Sad Phoenician* Kroetsch plays with and blurs this distinction between the translator and the poet. Instead of practicing the art of mimesis, Kroetsch practices a poetics of translation. Constantly short-circuiting his own desire to say something, to make a complete statement, he falls back relentlessly into sentence fragments, aborted replies and linguistic play, into, in short, the relation between languages. The graphic stylization of the letter 'a' provokes questions of translation. Is the letter in the process of appearing or disappearing? Is the English letter 'a' retracing the path of its historical development by composing itself out of the Phoenician and/or Greek alphabets? Or is it decomposing, eroding, or regressing toward the Phoenician? Are we as readers being alerted to a process of composition as decomposition?[3] Or is the English alphabet being translated into another alphabet or another language which may or may not share the same alphabet?

These mobile, gesturing letters pose still further enigmas. For example, is the written trace composed, or decomposed, by speech? Or by the laugh, the cry, the lie, or the, ha, snort?

> and   even if it's true, that my women all have new lovers,
>   then laugh, go ahead
> but   don't expect me to cry
> and   believe you me, I have a few tricks up my sleeve myself.
> (*The Sad Phoenician,* 9)

Is the letter generally in a state of flux with regard to speech? Does the voice translate the letter in ways we have not previously considered? Will the composing or decomposing letter, moving toward origin or destination, source or target, reach such an end point? What or where is this destination? In its state of graphic composition/decomposition, is the English phonetic character being imbued with pictographic or ideographic residues?

In order to begin to address some of these complex questions, we must look briefly at ways in which translation is imbricated with alphabetic or phonetic writing. Jacques Derrida, reading Rousseau, has this to say about the relationship of alphabetic writing to the voice and to languages:

> The trader invents a system of graphic signs which in its principle is no longer attached to a particular language. This writing may in principle inscribe all languages in general. It gains in universality, it favors trade and makes communication "with other people who [speak] other languages" easier. But it is perfectly enslaved to language

> in general the moment it liberates itself from all particular languages. It is, in its principle, a universal phonetic writing. Its neutral transparence allows each language its proper form and its liberty. Alphabetic writing concerns itself only with pure representers. It is a system of signifiers where the signifieds are signifiers: phonemes. The circulation of signs is infinitely facilitated. Alphabetic writing is the mutest possible, for it does not speak any language immediately. But, alien to the voice, it is more faithful to it and represents it better. (Derrida 1976, 299-300)

Alphabetic or phonetic writing introduces a supplement into the structure of representation. Whereas pictography appears to mime the thing itself or the signified, phonetic writing uses sound analysis to record signifiers that are in a sense nonsignifying. "Letters, which have no meaning by themselves, signify only the elementary phonic signifiers that make sense only when they are put together according to certain rules" (Derrida 1976, 299). Phonetic writing bypasses mimesis and goes directly to a radical translative process whereby letters translate phonemes, and phonemes translate other phonemes. Phonetic writing functions by translating intersemiotically between the audible voice and visible letters.

The stylized white alphabet collected on the front cover and the title page of the first edition of *The Sad Phoenician* looks something like a Semitic alphabet, especially if it is somewhat estranged—when, for example, the book is turned upside down or held up to a mirror. To Smaro Kamboureli the new alphabet looks like "something between the classic Greek alphabet and the Latin alphabet" (Kamboureli 1984b, 49). Through this graphic stylization the reader is reminded that in addition to the interlingual translatability of an alphabet, various alphabets themselves, such as the Phoenician and the Greek, have been acquired and developed by means of translation from other alphabets and systems of notation. Giovanni Garbini describes the development of the first Semitic (or Phoenician) alphabet as a translation from the Egyptian alphabet and provides an illustration of the process:

> The ideal would have been to find as many monoconsonantal Semitic words as the monoconsonantal signs in the Semitic alphabet, but since Semitic has very few monoconsonantal words, the difficulty was avoided by using

only the first consonant of longer words (the acrostic principle). In Egyptian a quadrilateral indicated a house and had the phonetic value *pr;* in Semitic, "house" was *bet,* therefore the quadrilateral sign was adopted to express the corresponding Semitic word, but only in relation to the first consonant, i.e. *b.* Another example: in Egyptian a wavy line represented "water", *nu* and had a phonetic value *n;* in Semitic "water" is *mem (maym);* at this point the wavy line adopts the value *m.* This procedure was applied to all the consonants; as far as possible, Egyptian signs with the new Semitic phonetic value were used and examples were drawn—this is worthy of note—from the whole Egyptian graphic system rather than from the Egyptian "alphabet".

Thus was born the first Semitic alphabet . . . but this Semitic translation of Egyptian signs could only have taken place in a Semitic region dominated by Egyptian culture such as Palestine (Garbini 1988, 89-90).

Similarly the Greeks' appropriation from the Phoenician alphabet of consonantal signs which the Greeks themselves did not use, in order to express Greek vowels (the Phoenician language used vowels but their script did not reflect them), is a species of graphological translation. Even alphabets themselves, then, are created by, and function as technologies for, translation.

The archaeology of the letter 'a' marks Kroetsch's poetics in *The Sad Phoenician* as one of archaeological decipherment or translation. Indeed, Shirley Neuman characterizes the exchange between speech and writing in the book as the barter or trade that eventually leads to archaeology. She writes:

"At sea," the Phoenician is "a trad[er] in language," bartering speech for writing, writing for speech, and scattering the artifacts of that barter around the Mediterranean of the poem, leaving them to be found out of context, fragmented, transformed into other uses, all use lost. The poem becomes, to use a favorite Kroetsch metaphor, an archaeological site of language. The dig turns up allusions, puns, clichés. Puns proliferate, sometimes literary, sometimes colloquial, often morbid, intentionally bad, nearly always based on cliché. (Neuman 1983, 111)

By translating between alphabets and between the economies of speech and writing, Kroetsch is able to translate without changing languages. As in "Stone Hammer Poem" and *Seed Catalogue,* this intralingual, phonographic translation inscribes a palimpsest. In *The Sad Phoenician* the palimpsest is composed of the rubbed out, written over, over-written, disrupted, disintegrated fragments of the oral rhetoric of the poem:

but	I gave her tat for tit
and	that reminds me, I owe myself a letter too, a gentle apology for sins of omission, ha, emission, well, let the chips fall
but	I was only joking when I suggested, we could go down together, hoo
and	a rose by any other name

(*The Sad Phoenician,* 17)

A palimpsest, originally a handwritten manuscript which has been written on, erased and then written over again, is created at the surface of the page in this text not by writing over writing but by rubbing out (figures of) *speech.* The Sad Phoenician, the speaker in and of the poem, prunes popular expressions and cultural clichés ("a rose by any other name"), reverses their ordinary order ("tat for tit"), makes substitutions and emendations ("sins of omission, ha, emission"). The particular letter of the alphabet at which he is currently situated, 'e' in this case, along with the element of sexual play, dictates the emendation of a single letter which changes "omission" to "emission." In the lines above, he puns on at least two meanings of the word "letter" as 1) a written symbol or character representing a speech sound, and 2) a written or printed communication directed to an individual or organization. Both of these meanings are implicit in the phrase "I owe myself a letter too." Settling with himself the debt of a letter, he chooses not the letter 'o' (which perhaps reminds him of scenarios he would sooner forget or repress—scenes of owing, debt, lack, absence, failure) but the letter 'e.' That is, he chooses "sins of emission" over sins of "omission."

A third definition of "letter," namely, the literal meaning of something, is what gets the Sad Phoenician to that word in the first place. That is, he takes his own reversed cliché "tat for tit" literally (moreover, literal and equivalent exchange is what the expression 'tit for tat' in its ordinary form connotes), and this reminds him that he owes himself a letter of apology for what may have been, controversially perhaps, either sexual failure or sexual promiscuity: "sins of omission, ha, emission." If he "gave her tat for tit," and somehow this revenge strategy reminds him that he owes himself a letter too, then it would follow that the "tat" he gave "for tit" must have been a letter or writing of some kind. Bundled together in these few lines, then, are sexual emissions, oral ejaculations, letters, and writing traded for sexual favours ("tat for tit"). Throughout the entire poem, of course, including earlier on the same page where he refers to his own "sterling insights into the pseudonymous works of poor dear Kierkegaard," as well as in the Silent Poet Sequence, yet another definition of "letter" as literary culture or learning, or literature as a discipline or profession, is in play. Moreover, the penis, which often functions in Kroetsch's work as a kind of a letter,[4] is also much in evidence as a privileged signifier throughout the entire long poem. In short, the letter, in several senses of the word, generates the poem.

Letters beget other letters. Kroetsch uses the arbitrary order of the alphabet both to generate and to structure his text. A crucial question which must be asked in this context is, if an alphabet "represents the phonological system at the rate, more or less, of one sign per phoneme" (Barber 1974, 49), then what is the ratio between the single composing/decomposing letter of the alphabet on the left-hand page and the profusion of language on the right-hand page? Clearly the economy of *The Sad Phoenician* is not based on a one-to-one ratio but rather on an economy which alternates between insufficiency and excess. This non-equivalent economy must be taken into account, of course, if one is arguing that a translation is taking place in this text. How are we to explain this blatant violation of translation equivalence between the letter and the spoken word, between the disappearing letter and the volubility of speech?

One way of resolving this problem is to recall that the English alphabet is not English at all but borrowed from Latin (which derived from Phoenician) and shared by many languages. As bpNichol explains in one of his articles on notation, "The 'Pata of Letter Feet, or, The English Written Character as a Medium for Poetry":

> Well really the alphabet is Phoenician eh? And of course the same one is used in French and Spanish and Portuguese and and and. So at a certain point when i bring my poems down to the level of the letter i also begin to move freely between languages, or between certain languages, or at least in a space where the particularity of my language is over-ridden by the particle clarity. . . . It is also true that at this level of things you are very in touch with the essential arbitrariness of signs. (Nichol 1985, 93)

This access, at the level of the letter, to other language systems is boosted in Kroetsch's *The Sad Phoenician* by the graphic estrangement of the English written character to the point where it borders on other writing systems which do not use the same alphabet or even exclusively phonetic characters. Thus, using the phonetic alphabet to generate his text, the poet as "a kind of Phoenician" "trading in language" (Kroetsch 1979, 13) translates, paradoxically, away from phoneticism and toward a mixed script,[5] a picto-ideo-phonographic writing system.

At the same time though, excavating and deciphering puns, homonyms, redundancies, and slippages, he also performs an archaeological cryptanalysis of the English language, specifically western Canadian English. Cryptanalysis is "The study of secret codes and ciphers with the object of decoding or deciphering them" (Barber 1974, 246). However, rather than decoding or deciphering fragments of old texts or archival records into either standard or poetic English, Kroetsch's poetic cryptanalysis works to un-decode or un-decipher (in other words, to encrypt) the formulas of speech and writing.

The source language which he encrypts is the rhetoric of ordinary figures of speech:

> but   frankly
> and   I don't think a little frankness would kill any of us,
>   I had my peek into the abyss, my brush with the
> verities,
>   such as they are, my astounding fall from innocence,
> you
>   better believe it
> but   I'm all right, don't feel you should worry, the
>   responsibility is mine, I can take care of myself

and   the next time you feel like deceiving someone, why not
       try yourself
but   I have my work to sustain me, my poetry, the
satisfaction
       of a job well done . . .
(*The Sad Phoenician,* 11)

Using, in addition to the order of the alphabet, the translation machine of alternating 'ands' and 'buts' throughout the entire poem, Kroetsch juxtaposes cliché after cliché almost without interruption, as in the above quotation. Abyss, brush, better believe it, responsibility, job—all of these words are brought to us by the propulsion of the letter 'b' and the voice whose moralizing, self-pitying, smug, complaining, vengeful rhetoric rants on throughout the poem.

Obviously, translating within a single language, Kroetsch does not translate for referential meaning; he translates in order to preserve the differential features of speech and writing. As he says, "I think that when we record speech we have somehow to keep a great deal of that speech present. I feel that writing on the wall was often a denial of speech, while the page must offer a sense of speechness" (Kamboureli 1984b, 48). Rehearsing a short history of rhetoric in his essay "Figures," Gérard Genette describes a rhetorical figure as "a gap in relation to usage, but a gap that is nevertheless part of usage; that is the paradox of rhetoric" (Genette 1982, 48). For Genette, this gap, this spacing, between the present signifier of the rhetorical figure and the virtual signifier which could have been used in its place (usually thought of as the 'meaning' of the figure) creates the texture of a palimpsest. Rhetorical form, he says, "is a *surface,* delimited by the two lines of the present signifier and the absent signifier" (49). He continues:

> That is why the treatises of rhetoric are collections of examples of figures followed by their translation into literal language: "The author means. . . . The author might have said. . . ." Every figure is translatable, and bears its translation, transparently visible, like a watermark, or a palimpsest, beneath its apparent text. Rhetoric is bound up with this duplicity of language. (Genette 1982, 50; the ellipses are Genette's)

Genette also discusses the politics of the rhetorical figure. Explaining why the distinction between ordinary language and poetic language is an insufficient criterion for defining the figure, he notes that "the vulgar tongue also has its rhetoric, but rhetoric itself defines a *literary usage* which resembles a language *(langue)* rather than speech *(parole)*" (Genette 1982, 50). Conversely,

> Once it has emerged from the vivid speech of personal invention and entered the code of tradition, each figure has as its task merely to intimate in its own particular way the poetic quality of the discourse of which it is part. The "sail" of the classical ship has long since ceased to be the mark of a concrete vision; it has become, like Quevedo's "bloodstained moon" a pure emblem: a standard, above the troop of words and phrases, on which one may read not only "here, a ship," but also "here, poetry." (Genette 1982, 58)

The ultimate aim of rhetoric, according to Genette, is not to concern itself with the originality or novelty of figures, which are qualities of individual speech. "Its ultimate ideal would be to organize literary language as a second language within the first, in which the evidence of signs would assert itself with as much clarity as in the dialectal system of Greek poetry, in which the use of the Dorian mode signified *lyricism* absolutely, that of the Attic mode *drama,* and that of the Ionian-Aeolian mode *epic*" (Genette 1982, 58). Genette concludes his essay by asserting that the rhetoric of modern literature is precisely a rejection of rhetoric: "What can be retained of the old rhetoric is not, therefore, its content, but its example, its form, its paradoxical idea of literature as an order based on the ambiguity of signs, on the tiny, but vertiginous space that opens up between two words having the same meaning, two meanings of the same word: two languages *(langages)* in the same language *(langage)*" (59).[6]

The rhetoric of *The Sad Phoenician* suggests that Kroetsch simultaneously delights in, rejects, and delights in rejecting the rhetoric of common speech. After listing a series of examples of a central figure he calls "the x of x," a catachresis which he catalogues throughout Kroetsch's work, Ed Dyck concludes that "these are all extreme examples of the very figure of figurality in the Western poetic tradition" (Dyck 1987-88, 88). Dyck's point is that subtraction, like its opposite, abundance, is also a kind of style, and therefore a species of rhetoric. Following Genette, if Kroetsch produces a rhetorical anti-rhetoric, he also employs subtracted figures of speech (even as he empties them of their content or meaning) in order to open a space for two languages within the same language. For him, poetic composition is more than the transcription of a spoken or preconceived poem. The long poem is "A method, then, and then, and then, of composition; against the 'and then' of story" (Kroetsch 1989b, 120). That method of composition is translation. In *The Sad Phoenician* the poet is not the "translator, traitor" (Italian *traduttore-traditore*) invoked throughout the entire history of translation theory. He is the poet as translator/ trader.

Notes

1   *The Sad Phoenician* was designed by Glenn Goluska. As with Kroetsch's *Seed Catalogue* and Fred Wah's *Pictograms from the Interior of B.C.,* I do not restrict my reading to the words of the text but include also its design elements. Many long poems foreground both the materiality of language and of the book.

2   See my discussion of Gérard Genette later in this chapter. Genette points out that the relation of signifier to signified in a rhetorical figure is actually the relation of one signifier to another, one of which poses as the signified of the other (Genette 1982, 47).

3   In Gregory L. Ulmer's reading of Derrida, decomposition is defined as deconstruction extended from a mode of criticism to a mode of composition (Ulmer 1985, 59).

4   See one of Kroetsch's poems about lovemaking, "Conservative Streak," where the following lines describe the act of penetration: "(my/ poet's metaphor neatly/ inserted like a weasel's whiskers" (Kroetsch 1977, 43).

5   Mixed scripts contain some combination of phonological signs, ideograms, determinatives (which do not represent anything pronounceable but simply indicate to what semantic category a neighboring word belongs), and pictograms. See Barber, p. 8.

6   Genette's theory that modern literature rejects rhetoric but retains its idea of literature as two languages within a single language compares with W. Haas's comment, quoted in the notes to my Preface, that "Modern verse is very largely 'bilingual' " in terms of speech and writing (Haas 1970, 87).

Translation, Infidelity and the Sadness of the Sad Phoenician

Robert Kroetsch allies the sadness of the Sad Phoenician with the cultural predicament of non-native Canadians in general. Such Canadians, he says, "experience the sadness of arriving late" into the global world, "and with that comes our recurring need to recover a beginning. You see, like the Americans we see ourselves as new people, but we don't believe what we see" (Kamboureli 1984b, 49). We are an invisible people. Disembodied, we are each our own double. Earle Birney first summed up the Canadian dilemma in his subsequently much-quoted line that it is only by our lack of ghosts we Canadians are haunted. However, if Kroetsch is right and we are invisible even to ourselves, then how are we to recognize a ghost in the event one should manifest itself? He sees the task of the Canadian writer as persuading us as readers into an individual belief in and collective vision of ourselves.

We saw in the previous chapter how the letters of the alphabet are translated in *The Sad Phoenician*. Like the alphabetic characters, the 'figures' of the lovers in the poem, both the poet and the women, also undergo translation. In several of Kroetsch's long poems, the performance of rhetoric and the rhetoric of sexual performance double and undo one another. In *The Sad Phoenician* the figure of

129

the poet is that of an unfaithful lover and unfaithful translator who, paradoxically, generates authenticity of feeling and of language.

The Sad Phoenician thematizes infidelity from its very first line. The book opens with a statement of infidelity: "and even if it's true, that my women all have new lovers" (Kroetsch 1979, 9). With only the briefest hesitation, the voice informs us that 'his' women all have new lovers. Whether 'his' women were untrue to him and ran off with other lovers, or whether they simply moved on after his own infidelities, or what indeed has happened, is unclear. However, the fact that he expects responses of laughter and derision to his declaration ("then laugh, go ahead / but don't expect me to cry") underscores an image of the male lover who believes himself simultaneously capable and incapable of controlling his female lovers' sexuality and who thereby invites our scepticism and suspicion. Why should he expect us to laugh at his misfortune, unless perhaps out of a sense of justice attained? His anticipation of our laughter, his determination not to demonstrate the sadness or remorse of the wronged lover, and his description of the women as several and as a generic group under his possession, multiplying their number with the word "all," suggests he may be something of a Don Juan. Or, to put it another way, perhaps closer to the speaker's own perspective: although he may be something of a Don Juan, it is the women who all have new lovers.

In this same opening line, questions of faithfulness are also raised in terms of linguistic fidelity. The first phrase simultaneously announces the truth of the statement which follows, and retracts it: "and even if it's true." Truth in love and truth in language are placed on par with one another from the very first line of the poem. After questioning the truth of his own statement that his women all have new lovers and inviting the laughter of scorn, however, the speaker demands that his words be believed ("believe you me"). What we are to believe, though, is that he has "a few tricks" up his sleeve. He is nothing, he says, if not honest. It is "true" that he'd be off like a shot to see the girl from Swift Current, "but the woman in Montreal is not so evasive, not so given / to outright lies, deceptions." When she receives his letter, he predicts, she will confess her infidelity by admitting that "darling, I was following a fire truck / and quite by accident found the divine, ha, flicker." Like the poet himself, she will, he thinks, readily confess her infidelities. "Virtue will out" (Kroetsch 1979, 13) in the form of truthful statements, if not in emotional and sexual loyalty.

All of these linguistic and sexual fidelities and infidelities—of tongue, letter and body—are staged on the page facing the one on which the letter 'a' is suspended in translation between English and Phoenician, English and English. In *The Sad Phoenician* the question of fidelity—of word and deed, in translation as in love—is radically foregrounded. Drawing an analogy between the crisis of fidelity in marriage and in translation, Barbara Johnson describes how both linguistic and sexual infidelity depend upon a prior promise or contract. She remarks: "For while both translators and spouses were once bound by contracts to love, honor, and obey, and while both inevitably betray, the current questioning of the possibility and desirability of conscious mastery makes that contract seem deluded and exploitative from the start. But what are the alternatives? Is it possible simply to renounce the meaning of promises or the promise of meaning?" (Johnson 1985, 142-43). The Sad Phoenician's duplicitous way with truth and fidelity suggests that, despite their overt content, his rhetorical utterances may be less absorbed by questions of truth or falsity, even in 'his' women or in women in general, than with promises and the act of promising. It is his promises, more so than his confessed sexual behavior, which nominate him as a type of Don Juan. His amorous quest is to explore whether or not it is possible to love without the promise of meaning and the meaning of promises.

In fact the Sad Phoenician is such a Don Juan that he cannot resist attempting to seduce the reader too with his promises. Despite his obfuscations, denials, wisecracks, false humility, sexism, and so on, he is nevertheless intent upon making us believe him. The Sad Phoenician wants to be believed. As if the preceding stanza were something less than frank, the words "but frankly" begin the section of the poem devoted to the letter 'b':

> but   frankly
> and   I don't think a little frankness would kill any of us,
>   I had my peek into the abyss, my brush with the verities
>   such as they are, my astounding fall from innocence, you
>   better believe it.
> (*The Sad Phoenician*, 11)

"Believe you me" has metamorphosed into "you better believe it" and at the end of the same page "you bet you me," a movement from belief to betting but still within the rhetoric of promising. Having just let us know with the words "but frankly" that he has already lied to us or at least misrepresented the truth in stanza 'a,' he promises in stanza 'b' to tell the truth. By implicitly, and only implicitly, confessing a lie, he promises the truth. He tells the truth by confessing a lie. After all, in confessing he is speaking the truth, if not with regard to the original sin at least with regard to the act of lying about it. However, his confession, his overstated frankness, his brush with the verities and peek into the abyss seem just a little too close to his "astounding fall from innocence" to be wholly reliable. His desire to cast his lovers as the deceivers and himself as the deceived though not entirely innocent party (and therefore the one to be believed) and the mixture of promising with cursing ("she'll get her just reward") causes his promises of truth, honesty and trustworthiness to fail. His "peek into the abyss," we suspect, may not amount to much more than a peek into the brush, or the bush, or the a-b-c's.

Though his promises fail utterly, the Sad Phoenician continues to make them. In promising, he seeks the success or felicity he may (or may not) have sought in sexual and emotional relationship. Through rhetorical performance he seeks sexual performance. His discourse is that of seduction. The act of promising, of course, is not only seductive; it is also performative. As Shoshana Felman reminds us, the very acts of promising, swearing, apologizing, and so forth produce their designated events. Therefore, "performative utterances, inasmuch as they produce actions, and constitute operations, cannot be logically true or false, but only successful or unsuccessful, 'felicitous' or 'infelicitous' " (Felman 1983, 16). As Kamboureli correctly notes about the poem, "But [the Sad Phoenician's] love for language overtakes the other aspects of love. I think that the way he talks about his different women is a sort of practice, a praxis almost, the trying out of language, in all its possibilities, rhetorical and others" (Kamboureli 1984b, 50).

Indeed *The Sad Phoenician* is written almost entirely in the performative. Kroetsch uses all five of J.L. Austin's categories of the performative—verdicts, orders, commitments, behaviors, and expositions[1]—in the book. As Felman shows, however, Emile Benveniste, refining and modifying Austin's categories, removes from the category of the performative all clichés, failures, and implicit and pervasive speech acts. " 'Since they have fallen to the rank of simple formulae, they must be brought back to their original sense in order for them to regain their performative function,' " according to Benveniste (quoted in Felman 1983, 21). As I have argued in the previous chapter though, Kroetsch does not simply employ clichés in their exhausted form. He defamiliarizes them through using them in great abundance and juxtaposing them against one another, reversing their traditional order, breaking them off prematurely, punning, interjecting with 'ha,' and so on. Thus he restores them to their performative function. Writing about autobiography in *Field Notes* Shirley Neuman analyzes how Kroetsch's use of clichés paradoxically generates authenticity of language and self. In her detailed analysis of the section "The Silent Poet Eats his Words" she writes:

> The poems recreate the clichés in which *I* gives voice to his loss, his self-pity, his sense of returning lost; doing so, they expose those clichés and allow the poems *as poems* to become original and witty statements of a feeling which is in no way diminished or anaesthetized as it would be if the cliché were allowed to remain simply cliché. They effect that most difficult thing: they distinguish between genuine feeling and its inauthentic expression without denying the feeling. The poet IN the poem experiences death of language and Self, he "eats his own words"; the poet OF the poem triumphs by saying "I" dialectically. He is simultaneously both where he is, the site of the poem, and where he "might have been," the subject of the poem. (Neuman 1983, 114)

Neuman persuades us that "By synchronizing his two voices, his autobiography ceases to be an act of memory and becomes an act of speech, becomes an act of continuing self-enunciation" (Neuman 1983, 115).

What renders the language of *The Sad Phoenician* performative rather than constative is the continuing bi-directional translation between speech and writing. That is, the decomposition of the oral clichés composes the poem. This composition as decomposition can only be accomplished through the technology of writing. The estrangement of the clichés made possible by writing them down and then, for example, erasing parts of them causes their constative, common-sense truth values to be rendered performative instead and thereby diverted away from the criterion of constative truth or falsity to become instead successful or unsuccessful, felicitous or infelicitous. For the Sad Phoenician, as for Don Juan, language is performative not informative.

The Sad Phoenician's rhetorical performance, his trying out of language, is closely tied to his discourse on women. His lament, however, is not the traditional morbid abjection incurred by a lost great love but the mild revenge of the slighted and powerless lover who acknowledges his own part in bringing on his misery and who moreover openly revels in the language of complaint. His rhetorical *tour de force* of clichés, hyperbole, braggadocio, and false humility, on the current of which each of the women he imagines as his enters the poem, undercuts his repeated insistence upon truth, frankness and fidelity. The infelicities of his performance with women are inauspicious with regard to his rhetorical performance. His promises are not very promising.

Just as his fragmented and circumlocutory rhetoric undermines itself, so his catalogue of misfires, losses, and blown encounters testifies to the infelicities of sexual performance. For example, despite his contention with regard to the girl from Swift Current that he had been "the cause of / her sweating, her shortness of breath" (Kroetsch 1979, 9) and that she now "follows large flocks of birds, I hear, calling my / name" (13), still she was the one who scorned his offer "of sex / in a tree house" (9) and "moved in with that photographer from / Saskatoon" (13). All of his women make rather audacious, if somewhat unconventional, claims to the autonomy of their own desires—running after doorknobs, following fires to firemen, refusing to become mere fantasy objects and pursuing their own fantasies instead.

At the letter 'h' ('h' for hero, himself, halo, Who? him, bird in the hand), the Sad Phoenician openly confesses to an inveterate infidelity: "and when the goat wears a halo, then I too shall be / faithful, believe me; a man faithful, a woman satisfied" (Kroetsch 1979, 23). Having begun this stanza with a skepticism (genuine or faked, it is impossible to ascertain) about the ability of a man to satisfy a woman, he concludes it on the same note, with a jab at the notion of the hero (and repeating an earlier pun on 'sea' and 'c') along the way:

> but   there's no satisfying women, so why try; the hero; yes,
>   right, by all means, dead on: a quest for a woman who
>   might be satisfied, the holy grail nothing, poor old
>   Who?him gets it into his brief case, he puts out to sea,
>   so to speak, for himself.

(*The Sad Phoenician*, 23)

"But there's no satisfying women, so why try" is a rhetorical question if ever there was one. In the same way that, by acknowledging his several lovers' new lovers, he evacuates from the poem woman as figure of the beloved, the Sad Phoenician also purges the poem of pretensions to the heroic. Whereas Ezra Pound's *Cantos* translate *The Odyssey* by changing languages, Kroetsch composes *The Sad Phoenician* by translating within a single language. Whereas the *Cantos* open with the line "And then went down to the ship," Kroetsch's long poem begins "and even if it's true, that my women all have new lovers, then laugh, go ahead." In Kroetsch's poem, the hero does not put out to sea to return, eventually and after much diversion, to the faithful Penelope. His hero puts out to sea/c so to speak for himself (if one reads that last line eliding the comma). The Sad Phoenician as poet/lover/translator/trader sets out to sea/c in order to speak (and write) for himself rather than in a borrowed language.[2] In an earlier passage he refers to himself not as a Greek, like Odysseus, but as "a kind of Phoenician, with reference, that is, / to my trading in language, even in, to stretch a point, / ha, my being at sea" (Kroetsch 1979, 13). He names himself as a Phoenician trader, making reference to the invention, translation and dissemination of the alphabet (one of its destinations being, of course, Canada, where the original Roman borrowing of the Greek word into the Latin context is recapitulated). He refuses fidelity to a language which, like the women in the poem, is both his and not his.

However, although he mocks the idea of a woman satisfied, and though his stated mission is to speak for himself, his rhetorical query "so why try" suggests that along with temptations toward the ocean-going, seaworthy heroic he does not renounce this other traditional aspect of the epic quest either. Kamboureli postulates that "After reading the poem many times I decided that it's not about love. It's about sex and about the erotic, and the Sad Phoenician is sad because he doesn't want to, or cannot, love. . . . But his love for language overtakes the other aspects of love" (Kroetsch 1979, 49-50). I have already suggested that the desire of the Sad Phoenician is the desire for an Other and for another language. As Shoshana Felman makes clear, these are the desires of a Don Juan:

> The desire of a Don Juan is thus at once desire for desire and desire for language; a desire that desires *itself* and that desires its own language. Speech is the true realm of eroticism, and not simply a means of access to this realm. To seduce is to produce language that enjoys, language that takes pleasure in having "no more to say." To seduce is thus to prolong, within desiring speech, the pleasure-taking performance of the very production of that speech.
> . . . The question of man's [sic] eroticism is raised, through the Don Juan myth, as the question of the relation of the erotic and the linguistic on the stage of the speaking body . . . (Felman 1983, 28-29)

Even if it is true, that his women all have new lovers, and if there is no satisfying women, so why try, then who, we might ask, is the Sad Phoenician trying to seduce in his poem? If the girl from Swift Current, the woman who follows fires to firemen, she who lives in a submarine, she who runs after doorknobs, etc. are all past history, then to whom is the poem directed? Is the poem the letter the poet threatens periodically to send to his various lovers? If "To seduce is to produce felicitous language" (Felman 1983, 28), then are the women in the poem essential only to generate linguistic felicity, as Kamboureli proposes? Is the paradoxical authenticity of the performative cliché seductive? Is "I love you" (Kroetsch 1979, 35) a cliché too? Are these clichés examples of "language that enjoys, language that takes pleasure in having 'no more to say?' " Can the desire for felicitous language itself write the poem, or is an Other, one woman or several, needed? If so, how many women does it take to write a long poem?

The women, marked in the text according to their curious

desires, are inscribed iconically: the woman who lives in a submarine, the woman who developed a thing for adverbs, etc. The Don Juanian poet may be constructing an alphabet or catalogue composed of women and their erotic enthusiasms. It is worth noting, for instance, that it is at the letter 'w' that the poet recounts an old version of the making of the alphabet. 'W,' of course, also stands for 'woman.' At the letter 'e' he proposes that some woman, probably the woman from Nanaimo, "shall henceforth be referred to / as A; right eh / and henceforth, everlastingly, A she shall be" (Kroetsch 1979, 17). Later he says of her that "X marks the known, the spot where she was / but isn't" (19). The woman from Montreal becomes Ms. R (19). Ms. R becomes Miss Reading (39). The "cheeky ass umbrella" of the woman from Swift Current is the shape of the letter 'm,' at which letter this part of her anatomy is remembered.

The figures of the women in the text, the letters of the alphabet and the rhetorical figures of speech circulate reciprocally as signs in the text. Although they inspire the sadness, gladness and perhaps also the madness of the Sad Phoenician, the women do not represent the figure of the female as the erotic but passive muse. Their own erotic quests and involvements far overshadow his. Kroetsch has used aspects of the traditional dichotomy between male and female in some of his earlier work, but in *The Sad Phoenician* and others of his later texts the figure of the woman as lover is neither the figure of immortal woman as Muse (Twigg 1981, 109) nor as either prop or ruin of representation. By lifting the restrictions on subjectivity the figures of the Others in *The Sad Phoenician* (including the reader) function to open the text to picto-ideo-phonographic inscription.

Now we can begin to understand more fully both why the Sad Phoenician is the Sad Phoenician of Love and why he is sad. The sadness of the Sad Phoenician of Love derives not only from the personal facts that his women all have new lovers and that as a poet he has not attained the recognition he thinks he deserves. His sadness is a poet's sadness. David A. White describes Heidegger's sense of a poet's sadness:

> Renunciation as a word names the domain in which ontological relations occur between poet as speaker and entities as spoken about, ultimately entities tranformed into things through the agency of language. . . .

Renunciation names the domain in which the poet experiences the awesome power of the word. . . . Sadness is similar to renunciation in that its ontological sense involves both the name for a distinctive psychological state and the connection between the name and the word as an indicator of the ontological dimension. Thus, the sadness experienced by the poet is neither mere dejection nor melancholy but is sadness resulting from the realization of the necessity of renunciation. In the first book of *The Prelude*, Wordsworth observes that

> The Poet, gentle creature as he is,
> Hath, like the lover, his unruly times. . . .

For Heidegger, these "unruly times" are not durations of experience which could be avoided or mitigated if only the poet had greater self-control or if the situation were otherwise. They are essential in an ontological sense; that is, they describe the condition through which poetized language is possible as language. The poet is not sad as a prelude to the toil of creating his poem or is not sad in retrospect, gazing abjectly upon its poorness in light of hopes for what it could have been. Sadness is a type of feeling, but feeling must not be reduced to a purely subjective reaction without ontological import simply because of its immediately private nature. (White 1978, 81-82)

The sadness of the Sad Phoenician, then, is not of a purely private nature but points rather to the ontological relation between word and thing, language and subjectivity, and self and Other. Surely the Sad Phoenician's sadness is also a form of gladness. Indeed the abundance of language within the poem is an indication of celebration and joy, despite the rhetoric of complaint, neglect and bravado. Although a poet's sadness derives from the ontological separation between word and thing, nevertheless it is this very separation which makes writing possible. As Kroetsch says, "You write the poem with your life by not creating a safe boundary between poetry and life. It would be nice if there sometimes were a clear boundary, but in fact the two keep spilling back and forth; exchanging. And it's not just from life into art. Art does things to our lives too. You write a poem and then it backfires on you and alters your life" (Gunnars 1987-88, 67). In Kroetsch's aesthetic, the separation between word and thing, like the separation between languages, is a fortunate thing. Recall his statement that Canadian literature "comes compulsively to a genealogy that refuses origin, to a genealogy that speaks instead, and anxiously, and with a generous reticence, the nightmare and the welcome dream of Babel" (Kroetsch 1989b, 71). The poet's sadness at the separation between language and life, and between languages, generates the poem, which in turn alters both life and language.

The problem for Kroetsch as a Canadian writer is to be able to gain access to his own unique senses of identity and place and the connections between them in a language overdetermined by cultural inheritances both his and not his. Hence he is faced with the necessity of locating himself through rhetorical circumlocutions, of deconstructing identity through the performance of gender, of writing the poem only by refusing to authorize it, of composing by decomposition, of translating from English into English. In *Writing and Madness* Felman describes the investments of translation in the lifting of psychic repression and, we might add, a poet's sadness. She writes:

> The very essence of repression is defined by Freud as a "failure of translation," that is, precisely as the barrier which separates us from a foreign language. . . . And while it is, no doubt, impossible—by passing from one language to another—to cancel out the "failure of translation," to suppress or lift the barrier of repression, it must be possible to displace that barrier, to *make it visible* in order to subject it to analysis. . . . "A national, mother-tongue cannot be dreamt: it makes a subject dream in its own dream. *But the dreaming of one language may be the waking of another,* and when it is night in one zone, it may be day in another." If the "failure of translation" between languages is in some sense radically irreducible, what is at stake in the passage from one language to another is less translation in itself than the translation *of oneself*—into the otherness of languages. To speak about madness is to speak about the difference between languages: to import into one language the strangeness of another; to unsettle the decisions language has prescribed to us so that, somewhere between languages, will emerge the freedom to speak. (Felman 1985, 19)

The desiring and desired Others of *The Sad Phoenician* function to translate the poet out of self into the Otherness of languages. Writing as translation deconstructs the notion of identity as the supplement of the self.

The Sad Phoenician, dedicated to Kroetsch's formerly Greek, now Canadian wife, and, indirectly, within the context of his *Completed Field Notes,* to "that reader I call Ishtar, that undiscoverable and discovered reader towards whom one, always, writes" (Kroetsch 1979, 270), is dedicated finally to the Other's words and to the ability of writing to assuage the sadness both of the poet and of a people who, as Canadians, "experience the sadness of arriving late" into the world and do not quite believe what we see (Kamboureli 1984b, 49). "Freed from picture, into the pattern and tumble of sound" (*The Sad Phoenician,* cover note), we are freed not into our own uniquely Canadian use of the English language so much as we are released into the Otherness of languages and of language (rather than silence) itself. Freed, by the infidelities to language made possible by translation, into a belief in our own utterances, the text makes us possible. A national language cannot be dreamt, but it can be, and in fact always is, translated out of another language or languages. Because non-native Canadians experience the sadness of arriving late into the world, even those of us who are not poets become silent poets. But our sadness carries us to the place where language intersects with the things of the world.

The Sad Phoenician is the long poem as love poem.[3] While it is true that the Sad Phoenician's "love for language overtakes the other aspects of love" (Kamboureli , 50), it is not that the poem is "not about love. It's about sex and about the erotic, and the Sad Phoenician is sad because he doesn't want to, or cannot, love" (49). The love for language does not supercede the love for the Other, as we have seen. The sadness of the Sad Phoenician of Love is also a reflection of his desire for the authenticity of experience. His sadness is that of desire for an Other *and* for the Other's language.

The words "I love you" (Kroetsch 1979, 35) are not empty cliché. They are performative in that they enact the real to which they refer. It is impossible to renounce the meaning of promises and the promises of meaning, because the language of promising is not constative but performative. And it is impossible to renounce (what we perceive as) the real. It is possible, though, to say 'I love you' in every conceivable phrase but that one. Every place in the text where a cliché reverses itself, fades or breaks off, there is in that silence, that erasure, that subtraction, a palimpsest which makes visible and invisible at once the words 'I love you.' If, as Barthes claims, "The stereotype is that emplacement of discourse *where the body is missing,* where one is sure the body is not" (Barthes 1977b, 90), then conversely the emptying of the cliché allows the body (of the lover and also of one's self) not to be missed and also to stop missing, which always makes one sad. Kroetsch's emphasis upon the "speechness" of speech stems from his concern that the reader reading, like the writer writing, read/write from an embodied subject position. His project as a poet is through language to make us visible, embodied subjects in the lived world.

Notes

1   (1) Verdicts: speech acts that constitute the exercise of judgment (condemning, acquitting, estimating, evaluating, etc.).

(2) Orders: speech acts that constitute assertions of authority or the exercise of power (commanding, giving an order, naming, advising, pardoning, etc.).

(3) Commitments: speech acts that consist in the assumption of an engagement with respect to a future action (promising, contracting, espousing, enrolling, swearing, betting, etc.).

(4) Behaviors: speech acts linked to a social posture (congratulating, apologizing, greeting, etc.).

(5) Expositions: speech acts that consist in a discursive clarification (affirming, denying, questioning, asking, remarking, etc.).

(Felman 1983, 19)

2   Travelling from sea to 'c,' or sea to sea, may be the archetypal journey for the Sad Phoenician as Canadian poet. Ironically, journeying 'from sea to sea' in Canada means sailing across not oceans but miles and miles of dry land.

See also Kroetsch's poem "Mile Zero" (and the history of its composition) in *The Stone Hammer Poems* and *Advice to My Friends*. It is reprinted in *Completed Field Notes*.

3   The Sad Phoenician is the Sad Phoenician of Love. A section of the poem was initially published with the title "This Is A Love Poem," but Kroetsch says that he felt "there was too much direction given to the reader by that original title" (Kamboureli 1984b, 49).

"A NEW ALPHABET/ GASPS FOR AIR": DAPHNE MARLATT'S INTERSEMIOTIC TRANSLATION POETICS

In the language I speak, the mother tongue resonates, tongue of my mother, less language than music, less syntax than song of words, beautiful *Hochdeutsch,* throaty warmth from the north in the cool speech of the south. Mother German is the body that swims in the current, between my tongue's borders, the maternal loversoul, the wild tongue that gives form to the oldest the youngest of passions, that makes milky night in the French day. Isn't written: traverses me, makes love to me, makes me love, speak, laugh from feeling its air caressing my throat. My German mother in my mouth, in my larynx, rhythms me.

Hélène Cixous
"Coming to Writing" and Other Essays

Unlimited Inc.orporation

Daphne Marlatt's recent texts can be read as translative acts which research and incorporate the pictogrammic, ideogrammic, and phonetic elements of language, as well as the resources of gesture, performance and hysteria. The three phases of the present chapter work to clear ground for such a reading. I begin with a critique of Lola Lemire Tostevin's article "Daphne Marlatt: Writing in the Space that is Her Mother's Face," published in the special Marlatt issue of *Line,* as just one example of how a representationalist reading fails adequately to account for Marlatt's poetics. In the process, I point to ways in which representationalism and essentialism are inextricably entwined. My detailed examination of Tostevin's argument is intended not to pillory it but rather to demonstrate with precision some of the intrinsic limitations of representationalist aesthetics and to propose that translation poetics offers an alternative to these highlighted misprisions. The second phase of the chapter discusses some specific problems and gaps within feminist poststructuralist criticism which may be addressed by translation poetics. I would suggest, for example, that translation poetics offers new ways of analyzing writers' relationships to language, writing and speech, reconfigures the relations between and among different kinds of semiotic practices, and allows us to rethink memory and even the body. Translation poetics overlaps with, differs from and challenges general grammatological and poststructuralist poetics. The chapter concludes by reconfiguring the feminist and poststructuralist aspects of Marlatt's work as part of her translation poetics.

Lola Tostevin criticizes Marlatt for what Tostevin frames as a nostalgic desire for origins. She holds the view that Marlatt's double recourse to the maternal body and to the roots of words is reductive, regressive and essentialist. Her article attempts to draw attention to what she perceives to be the impure elements in Marlatt's writing, namely, an imagined nostalgia for origins as represented by the use of etymologies, traditional symbolism, the maternal body, and utopianism. Unfortunately and ironically, Tostevin, beguiling herself with the etymology of "etymology," ends up misreading, reducing and essentializing Marlatt's work. She writes:

> Wordplay, the etymological breakdown of words, the story of language within language, has allowed many women to establish a newly found intimacy with language. Granting a word an ultimate definition, a final authority in its most ancient meaning, posits an origin, a truth, with which some women have felt comfortable. (Tostevin 1989, 35)

Etymology has allowed "many women"/"some women" such as Marlatt (though not Tostevin herself, the suggestion is, who allies herself with the French poststructuralists) to bed down in a "comfortable" "intimacy" with patriarchal authority and truth. Tostevin's sexual and gender metaphors cross (and double-cross) one another as she proceeds in the next paragraph to question this etymological impulse by framing it as a "search" for the lost or repressed mother and furthermore by describing this search for the maternal as *filiation*:

> This genealogy, the *filiation* of a direct line leading back to a fundamental original signification, parallels the search for the lost mother on which traditional Western philosophy and literature are based and contradicts the open-endedness and new beginnings of *l'écriture féminine* which attempts to displace and exceed authority, truth, and the illusionary essence of origins.

Tostevin employs the French rather than the English form of "filiation" in part to indicate that she is working from within the system of the French poststructuralist critique elaborated by such figures as Jacques Lacan, Jacques Derrida, Jean-Paul Sartre, and Hélène Cixous, for example, all of whom she invokes in her article. She uses the French term to direct the reader to the inference that women writers' search for the absent mother is allied, paradoxically, with the very phallogocentrism which they are trying to evade, a phallogocentrism which is successfully deconstructed by the French critics and, by implication, Tostevin herself in her article.[1]

The bilingual Tostevin positions herself as speaking the "languages" of both the French and the Canadian critical milieux. However, yet another paradox imposes itself on her critical narrative when she finds that the problem with "Marlatt's theory" is that it "differs" from that of Cixous:

> Marlatt's theory differs from Hélène Cixous' theory of *écriture féminine* which also emphasizes textual play and language as presence, but which does not maintain a source, does "not say originary, because obviously there is no origin" [Conley 1984, 130]. If each of Marlatt's books is an additional ring in the progression of a dynamic circular chain that grows and moves from past to present, each book also conveys a nostalgia for a source, an origin. . . . (Tostevin 1989, 35)

The context surrounding the particular phrase quoted from an interview with Cixous by Verena Andermatt Conley has to do with the provisionality of words and terms (libido, economy, masculine and feminine, *écriture féminine*) and with how Cixous can use these various "linguistic instruments" without enclosing herself within their various systems (Conley 1984, 130-31). Therefore it actually runs counter to Tostevin's purpose of pointing out the lapses in Marlatt's work. That is, if French feminist Hélène Cixous can be permitted the use of certain key words without being entrapped in the various systems they carry with them, then surely Canadian feminist Daphne Marlatt may be permitted a similar license. Instead, the impression Tostevin leaves us with is that to differ from Cixous is merely to dream comfortably on the couch of nostalgia rather than that of analysis.

Despite her strenuous critique of Marlatt, throughout her article Tostevin makes a few positive remarks about the aesthetic and feminist merit of Marlatt's work and her generosity toward other writers. Surprisingly, though, she chooses for the most part to borrow her praise from other critics. She quotes Frank Davey's statement from his 1974 book, *From There to Here,* that Marlatt's *Rings* is "a book whose linguistic structure is 'one of the most beautiful in our literature' " (Tostevin 1989, 33). She relies on his words to make the point that " 'The phenomenological method of *Frames* results in some extraordinarily elaborate and detailed evocations of consciousness' " (32). Quoting Laurie Ricou, she writes that "There's little doubt that 'Marlatt is convincing' " (33). She also counts on this male critic to say that *Touch to My Tongue* is " 'the most overtly feminist of Marlatt's books' " (36). She concludes her article with the compliment that, despite the contradictions within her work, Marlatt's "main story has remained that of language, and few people in Canada tell it so well" and with an allusion to "the generous dialogues" Marlatt has had "with so many writers during the last twenty years" (39).

A much more serious problem with her article than the curious secondhand praise, though, is that she makes little attempt to consider the *effects* of Marlatt's feminist aesthetic. The issue for Tostevin seems to be (and the use to which she employs the quotation from Cixous is telling) whether or not the *word* "origin" or any of its synonyms appears in Marlatt's texts or her statements about her poetics. For example, while Tostevin concedes that "Much of Marlatt's use of etymology proliferates meaning" she does not illustrate or analyze this proliferation but moves immediately, without so much as a comma's pause, to complain "but more and more her work relies on originary/original meaning" (Tostevin 1989, 35). She then quotes a passage from Marlatt's poetic essay "musing with mothertongue" dealing with etymology. Here is the quotation as Tostevin reproduces it:

> hidden in the etymology and usage of so much of our vocabulary for verbal communication (contact, sharing) is a link with the body's physicality: matter (the import of what you say) and matter and by extension mother; language and tongue; to utter and outer (give birth again); . . . to relate (a story) and to relate to somebody, related (carried back) with its connection with bearing (a child); intimate and to intimate; vulva and voluble. . . . (Tostevin 1989, 35)

Tostevin elides several of the clauses which deal most specifically with the linkages between language and the body. Her point in citing this quotation seems to be that it includes the word "etymology" and appears to link the tracing of word origins with a parallel regression back toward the figure of the mother. But here is the full paragraph from Marlatt's text:

> hidden in the etymology and usage of so much of our vocabulary for verbal communication (contact, sharing) is a link with the body's physicality: matter (the import of what you say) and matter and by extension mother; language and tongue; to utter and outer (give birth again); *a part of speech and a part of the body; pregnant with meaning; to mouth (speak) and the mouth with which we also eat and make love; sense (meaning) and that with which we sense the world;* to relate (a story) and to relate to somebody, related (carried back) with its connection with bearing (a child); intimate and to intimate; vulva and voluble; *even sentence which comes from a verb meaning to feel.* (Marlatt 1984b, 46; my italics)

What Tostevin removes from the quoted passage are the body parts. With these parts excised, the body is present only in a more abstract sense and the passage then seems to valorize a model of communication constructed upon serendipitous connections between language and the maternal body. However, the passage in full deals not with originary meaning at all but rather with constructed, phenomenological, lived reality, with connections between the materiality of language and the physicality of the body, neither of which—language or body—Marlatt privileges as the origin of the other. Moreover, the linguistic model implicit in the passage is not one of communication but rather of translation, as we shall see.

Although it is indeed the case that, as Tostevin writes, "*Touch to My Tongue* is nevertheless centred in traditional symbols of the feminine, making it difficult to disassociate them from overdetermined associations" (Tostevin 1989, 36), surely it is the task of the critic to make the effort to distinguish Marlatt's use of these symbols from their patriarchal connotations and to discover whether or not they do retain their patriarchal function within the context of the lesbian feminist text. In failing to address these possible differences,

Tostevin contradicts her own concluding remarks that "It would seem more vital than ever that in our newly created spaces we discover not only the multiple differences that exist between men and women, between women and women, but perhaps *more importantly, within each woman*" (39; my italics). Does it follow that if a woman writer employs symbols drawn from patriarchal tradition her use of them will be traditional? Even if her symbolism were in fact conventional, would the text as a whole then necessarily recuperate or reinforce traditional structures and values, assuming that symbols do not perform the entire work of which a text is capable?

Tostevin invests heavily in what she perceives to be the aims of the poststructuralist enterprise. However, other critics working in and with problematical poststructuralist texts have produced complex and satisfying solutions to similar problems, which she might have drawn upon. To select just two, there are the examples of Paul de Man's discussion of Walter Benjamin's use of conventional symbology in his essay "The Task of the Translator" and Réda Bensmaïa's illumination in *The Barthes Effect* of Roland Barthes's use of ancient rhetorical terms, neologisms from Latin and Greek roots, foreign words, and other obscure devices. De Man, dealing with the problem that Benjamin's text "seems to relapse into the tropological errors that it denounces," suggests the following: "Whenever Benjamin uses a trope which seems to convey a picture of total meaning, of complete adequacy between figure and meaning . . . he manipulates the allusive context within his work in such a way that the traditional symbol is displaced in a manner that acts out the discrepancy between symbol and meaning, rather than the acquiescence between both" (De Man 1986, 89). Bensmaïa demonstrates that Barthes uses " 'preciously ambiguous' semes" not to reify old signifieds but rather to float them, to summon other codes:

> But contrary to what would occur for the concepts of a philosophical system, for example, the semes are never taken up in order to define or exhaust them. . . . As the words . . . are selected and scrutinized, the discourse *is produced* as a "translation" of these words in an "other site" and as an unfolding of all their potentialities. (Bensmaïa 1987, 20)

I will return to the issue of discourse produced as a translation in another site later in my discussion of Marlatt's etymological work.

Moreover, Cixous, more than any other of the French feminists, has been charged (wrongly, I think) with the same kind of essentialism and nostalgia for origins that Tostevin is troubled by in Marlatt.[2] Toril Moi, for one, levels the same accusation against Cixous that Tostevin marshals against Marlatt, namely, that her "global appeal to 'woman's powers' glosses over the real differences among women, and thus ironically represses the true heterogeneity of women's powers" (Moi 1985, 125). The strategy of Moi's essay is to compare points of convergence and divergence between Cixous's thinking and that of Derrida. The convergences are duly noted and applauded while the divergences are dutifully described as regressions —moments of biological determinism and essentialism. But what is missing, by her own admission, from Moi's analysis (as from Tostevin's) is the kind of closer investigation of Cixous's work that will, as Moi concludes, "confront its intricate webs of contradiction and conflict, where a deconstructive view of textuality is countered and undermined by an equally passionate presentation of writing as a female essence" (126). It is ironic indeed that both Tostevin and Moi sacrifice plurality in order to plead for *différance*. Tostevin compares Marlatt to Cixous and finds the former lacking. Moi compares Cixous to Derrida and locates "lack" in Cixous. This regression toward the source as represented by either Cixous or Derrida differs not at all from what Tostevin argues is the effect of tracking etymological associations in the dictionary.

This controversy within feminist critique over essentialism and biologism in the work of important women writers indicates a series of untheorized gaps pertaining to the relations between corporeal and linguistic substances. This theoretical hiatus causes us to misread the colloquy between the body (specifically, the body gendered as feminine) and, for example, metaphor and symbolism, between the body and the archive or the dictionary, and between writing and speech in the practices of *écriture féminine* and writing the (m)other tongue.

Much of the feminist criticism published during the past twenty years has examined how women writers incorporate certain female body metaphors, especially maternal metaphors, into the structure of their texts. However, I would suggest that the exchange between the text and the body gendered as female is a form of translation— intersemiotic translation. Roman Jakobson defines intersemiotic translation as an interpretation of verbal signs by means of signs from nonverbal systems (Jakobson 1971, 261). I would add that translation between bodies and texts occurs bidirectionally. That is, not only does the verbal system of the text incorporate the signs of the nonverbal system, the body (menstruation, childbirth, lactation, orgasm, hysteria, etc.), as images or narrative "material." The body, organized (incorporated) by language, but always also retaining its "fleshiness," never wholly absorbed, mastered, expressed, or mimed by language, mothers its own tongue. The body, to borrow Elizabeth Grosz's words, "its epidermic surface, muscular-skeletal frame, liga- ments, joints, blood vessels and internal organs, as *corporeal surfaces* on which engraving, inscription or 'graffiti' are etched," is also the place where inscriptions "coagulate corporeal signifiers into signs" (Grosz 1989). If the body is the locus where desire is inscribed, it also writes, speaks, gestures, signs, sighs, and sings back. The body translates. Hysterical fantasies, for example, can translate them- selves into the motor sphere, there to be staged in pantomime (Mahony 1987, 466). And, as in even the most traditional forms of interlingual translation, this intersemiotic translation alters the "original."[3] The "original" (body or text) cannot be restored as such on the basis of the translation alone. Both the corporeal and the textual imprint, act upon and irrevocably change one another.

These remarks about the body as translator and the connection with the preceding critique of Tostevin's article will become clearer as we proceed for an interval through a double reading of Cixous and Marlatt. Barbara Freeman, in her article "Plus corps donc plus écriture: Hélène Cixous and the Mind-Body Problem," addressing the issue of essentialism in Cixous, analyzes brilliantly Cixous's rhetorical deployment of the body. Freeman convincingly demon- strates that "At the very moment that Cixous's critics accuse her of employing the body in order to ground sexual difference outside of language, they themselves do exactly what they ascribe to her; conceive of the body as if it were 'a universal, biological given,' and thus in 'essentialist terms' " (Freeman 1988, 61). Freeman believes that "Anatomy, the body, can no longer mean what Cixous's critics take it to mean once its priority in relation to the text has been called into question" (66). Cixous's contribution, neither essentialist nor anti-essentialist, is to corporealize the text and metaphorize the body such that neither term can be accorded the original or source (or, I would add, source text) of the other. Body and text are co-constitutive. Freeman interprets Cixous's notion of a feminine "essence" as "non-essentialistic in that, identical to that which destabilizes any notion of essence, it is able to inscribe (or invent) a possible non-essential feminine specificity" (68). Against Domna C. Stanton's argument in "Difference on Trial: A Critique of the Maternal Metaphor in Cixous, Irigaray, and Kristeva," Freeman asserts that there is a difference between metaphor as a collapsing of difference into sameness and metaphorization as a textual strategy:

> What I am calling Cixous's "corporealization of the text" does not assert a *likeness* between two terms, but rather functions so as to locate difference where none had previously been seen to exist. To say, for example, "the mother is also a metaphor" is not to imply a similarity between the maternal body and rhetorical trope, as Stanton would have it, but rather to displace the opposition between body and text and to locate each as already *within* its other or opposite. While metaphor may (or may not) assert similitude, metaphorization as a strategy insinuates difference; for if the "mother" is a "metaphor," so too the "metaphor" must also be a "mother." Here the copula is employed so as to undo, not affirm, copularity, for through the metaphoric process the identity of both terms [is] displaced and undone. (Freeman 1988, 70)

Domna Stanton surveys extensively the work of Cixous, Irigaray and Kristeva, but she fails to analyze the textual strategies of these writers and fails also to re-examine metaphor in the light of the work it can perform within poststructuralist texts. Instead she shops through the works for short guilty phrases and culpable individual terms (" 'the essence of femininity,' " " 'rebeginning,' " " 'the Mother goddess,' " " 'woman-voice,' " etc.). Except for block quotations, she seldom quotes an entire sentence from any of her three subjects; her critique amounts to little more than synonym detection in a large number of texts. When she proposes metonymy as a possible alternative to metaphor, her solution is unconvincing (and conventional, authorized by the masters) because the reader suspects that, following Stanton's own methods, a similarly reductive definition of metonymy could be found and supplemented by a survey of individual words and phrases. Stanton's failure to acknowledge the value of the physical, textual work performed by writing ultimately dismantles her argument. Although she assumes an ostensibly poststructuralist stance, her devaluation of writing and her reliance on the conventional interpretation of metaphor reveals that stance to be no more than a posture exercise. She is working from within a rhetorical, rather than a writerly, landscape of signs.[4]

While Lola Tostevin's endeavour to open up discussion of apparent contradictions within Daphne Marlatt's writing and poetics is, in some respects, useful, her assumption that Marlatt's use of etymologies and of lesbian and maternal bodies is a recourse to "origins" and essentialism is not. Moreover, this assumption leads her to impose upon Marlatt's writing the very expectations and standards that Tostevin herself argues against in advocating the pluralization of differences. Paradoxically, her attempt to purge Marlatt's writing of metaphysics imposes upon it an aesthetics of purity, unity, coherence, clarity, and the logic of non-contradiction. The ending of Marlatt's novel *Ana Historic* will be unsatisfactory to "some readers," Tostevin contends: "Because the formal strategy of the novel so brilliantly subverts cohesion and narrative syntax and is not bound by master plot or one heroic voice—on the contrary, the narrative voice embodies many voices—its climax, both literal and literary, is unexpectedly conventional in its utopian vision" (Tostevin 1989, 38). At this point, near the climax of her own article, Tostevin, who had earlier distanced herself from "many women" and "some women," now inscribes herself under the rubric "some readers." Tostevin formulates herself, in other words, as a textually constructed, though gender neutral, subject. It is of some significance that, after initially subsuming her personal voice to those of other critics such as Davey and Ricou, this climactic revelation of her presence in the text as a non-gendered "reader" coincides with the point at which she argues that sexuality, pleasure, women's imagination, and utopian visions are limited solutions to complex social problems. Ironically, that is, the climax of her argument for the pluralization of differences between and within women coincides with the apparition of a non-gendered subject.

Several additional questions and issues emerge with regard to Tostevin's critique of *Ana Historic*. In the first place, if the formal strategy of *Ana Historic* subverts narrative conventions, then, logically, part of its subversion may well extend to claiming the right to subvert what is conventionally thought to be the subversive by providing an "unexpectedly conventional" climax to an otherwise deconstructed narrative. Secondly, is the climax in fact utopian? More generally, is "a writing of *jouissance* which cultivates, culminates in the pleasure principle and evokes the imaginative power of women writers" utopian (Tostevin 1989, 38)? If so, by whose standards? Is Tostevin's own isolation and privileging of a single narrative climax in *Ana Historic* consistent or inconsistent with her valorization of subversion and the deconstruction of master plots? Is not the expectation and requirement of a single climactic event one of the primary master plots? Although Tostevin states that "When Marlatt writes, 'mouth speaking flesh. she touches it to make it tell her present in this other language so difficult to translate. the difference,' it is evident that she is referring to *the* difference, keeping it within the traditional concept of binary opposition" (38), it is not at all evident that Marlatt is referring to binary opposition rather than to Derridean *différance* and to the act of translation between the body and language.[5]

In short, contrary to Tostevin's argument for a deconstructive writing practice, she herself imposes an aesthetic derived from a rhetorical, logocentric and metaphysical critical tradition. Thus she misrepresents and falsifies the deconstructive project she positions herself to speak for and legislates for the very nostalgia she would excise in Marlatt.[6] Furthermore, she ignores the aesthetic or textual *effects* of Marlatt's writing strategies.[7]

At this point, let me offer some alternative interpretations of Daphne Marlatt's poetics and raise some questions about the interpretation of feminist poetics in general. Her concept of metaphor, for example, is very close to that of Cixous as outlined above. In conversation with George Bowering almost twenty years ago, Marlatt discussed metaphor not as a reduction of two terms to a single one but as multiplicity simply there, to borrow a phrase from *Steveston*. She said:

> Metaphor has to do with the way things both are & are
> not themselves, are other things. The way we usually refer
> to it is: you have a discrete thing over here, you have a
> discrete thing over there, & there's an invisible bridge
> which is the metaphor. I don't understand that. Anything
> can be anything else, depending on one's point of view,
> one's specific vantage point. (Bowering 1979, 43)

American poet Charles Olson—for whom in the summer of 1963 Marlatt wrote a paper on etymology which would turn out to be a lead in to "all the writing I would subsequently do . . . it opened up language for me" (Marlatt, quoted in Wah 1980a, 8-9)—theorizing the poem as an energy transfer rather than the interposition of the individual as ego, criticized various rhetorical devices which force us to "partition reality" and thereby isolate us from what he saw as the active intellectual states, metaphor and performance. Simile, for him, was anathema. In the essay "Human Universe" he wrote: "All that comparison ever does is set up a series of reference points: to compare is to take one thing and try to understand it by marking its similarities to or differences from another thing" (Olson 1973, 164). The trouble with such classification is that it only ever accomplishes a description. Description robs things of their particularity and their "thingness" and robs us too of our experience of them. As a remedy to this kind of verse-making, Olson imported the idea of "proprioception," the sensory reception in our bodies to stimuli arising from within, from physiology into his poetics of projective verse. As Fred Wah says in his introduction to her "selected" volume *Net Work,* Marlatt is one of the most disciplined proponents of proprioceptive writing (Wah 1980a, 15). Her understanding of and usage of metaphor is informed by Olson's body-oriented, proprioceptive poetry and poetics and must therefore be considered in that context.

Secondly, an alternative to conceiving of Marlatt's work with etymology and mythology as essentialist might be to cast it as an inscription of "the proper name effect."[8] In Greek mythology, the nymph Daphne chose to be metamorphosed into a laurel rather than be sexually assaulted by Apollo. If a writer's name were Daphne, it would be almost mandatory for her to explore the complicity of that name both with gender relations and with mediations between women and the natural world, not to mention the name's duplicitous implication with poetry and poetics.

However, any examination of etymology as a sign of the proper name or signature effect would have to confront the extent to which *for the woman writer* the proper name effect is deconstructive and the extent to which it is complicit with patriarchal practices. That is, are the effects of raising the signature into the text the same for writing subjects configured as feminine as for those configured as masculine? Does bleeding the proper noun into the common noun function to disappropriate even as it appropriates, as Derrida suggests? Or, for the woman writer, is this intralingual translation and erosion of her proper name just more of the (logic of the) same? In the following passage, Derrida describes the net gain possible in the recuperation of the proper name:

> By disseminating or losing my own name, I make it more and more intrusive; I occupy the whole site, and as a result my name gains more ground. The more I lose, the more I gain by conceiving my proper name as the common noun. . . . The dissemination of a proper name is, in fact, a way of seizing the language, putting it to one's own use, instating its law. (Derrida 1985b, 76-77)

Does the woman writer raise her signature into the text in order to purchase real estate there, to "occupy the whole site," to gain "more ground," or is she trying to claim additional territory and simultaneously to decolonize territory traditionally designated as female, territory Marlatt, for example, refers to as a "sensorium." As she says:

> For instance, if I talk about our sexuality as a hidden ground, then I have to make a distinction between ground that is laid out, gridded, cleared for use, dry land versus unmapped, uncharted, untamed land that is wet and swampy and usually discarded. So there is a difference within the landscape metaphor. (Williamson 1985, 27)

What degree of "properness" can we assume adheres *for women* to the proper name? For women, property (ground), propriety, naming, and language have always been extremely problematical. To what extent is the strategy of "The more I lose, the more I gain" for women a practice of self-denial and self-abnegation which has proven ineffective in our individual and collective struggles for equality? To what extent might feminist writers' experiments with etymology and mythology represent not a return to origins or an impulse toward a masculinist version of essentialism but perhaps an "improper" version of the proper name effect, one which pays homage not only to the differences among women but to both the differences and the similarities within our collective inheritances at once?

In questioning the degree of applicability of Derridean textual practices to the analysis of women's texts, Linda Kintz's article "In-Different Criticism: the Deconstructive 'Parole'" is helpful. Kintz argues that Derrida's deconstruction is of, by, and for the white male subject, and she charges that Derrida's caution to women not to reproduce the dialectic of sex "anchor[s] his theory to a dialectic that appears to be unsusceptible to transformation" (Kintz 1973, 132). According to Kintz:

> Derrida's brilliant readings have been centred on a Subject who is male, white, European; then that critique of subjectivity has been generalized, like a metaphor that substitutes the genus for the species. The Subject, the general term, covers the more limited one, the male of the dominant class, but it claims universality, a pattern or experience characteristic of all human beings. The deconstruction of the Subject has thus been generalized to cover all subjects, even those who were never included in that core group of Subjects. We have gone from Subject to subject, with no pause for gender differentiation, or for race and class distinctions. (Kintz 1973, 115-16)

Kintz diagnoses Derrida's concern that women speaking like men will perpetuate the dialectic as his failure to "factor in gender or colour as disruptive and inappropriate threats to the specular dialectic" (131). Like Barbara Freeman and Naomi Schor (whom Freeman quotes), who think that "playing off 'essentialism' and 'anti-essentialism' as antagonistic and mutually exclusive may not lead feminist theory in productive directions" (Freeman 1988, 69), Kintz concludes that it is possible and desirable to work on more than one project at a time, even apparently oppositional or contradictory tasks. As Kintz proclaims:

> We must take seriously, even as we work to undermine
> them, the effects of gender differentiation, which is "trans-
> lated by and translates a difference in the relation to power,
> language, and meaning" [*sic*] . . . But what we are begin-
> ning to notice is that there are (at least) two dramas of
> subjectivity, and if we keep at it, if we keep refining our
> terms, we may find a way to talk about activity that is not
> simply an analogy for masculinity. Because we are past the
> time when women need to be shown our absence from
> history and language, we might carry on a project that is
> a dialogue—a continuing dream of utopian indifferentia-
> tion, of "incalculable choreographies," while we also take
> the time to find ways to theorize our activity as culturally
> constructed, gendered subjects, speaking bodies, real fic-
> tions. Such a dialogue may help us theorize what meta-
> physics has always missed: "le moi corporeal." (Kintz
> 1973, 132-33)

My point is that in our critical practice we must continue to search
for ways of talking about feminist writing strategies which do not
simply invoke or reproduce monological models of textual "activity"
the way Stanton reproduces traditional assumptions about the
functions of metaphor and applies them wholesale to Cixous,
Irigaray and Kristeva and the way Tostevin reproduces strictures
about essentialism with regard to Marlatt's work.[10] Gender must not
be elided in or by rhetorical, deconstructive or reader-response
methods of interpretation. As Julia Kristeva notes (in the sentence
misquoted in the passage from Kintz's article above), "Sexual difference—which is at once biological, physiological, and relative to
reproduction—is translated by and translates a difference in the
relationship of subjects to the symbolic contract which *is* the social
contract" (Kristeva 1981, 21). Gender is a function of the translation
between various discourses (power, meaning, sexuality) and the
body; and the gendered body translates in reply. The subject that is
translated textually is also translated sexually. Or, in Grosz's metaphor of inscription and reinscription: "As well as being the site of
knowledge-power, the body is thus also a site of *resistance,* for it
exerts a recalcitrance, and always entails the possibility of a counter-
strategic reinscription, for it is capable of being self-marked, self-
represented in alternative ways." We must not attempt to censor this

translation, this reinscription, this "mouth speaking flesh," simply because we have yet to learn how to decipher its significations and how to respond.

Marlatt's archaeological project is to recover and reappropriate the gendered body from under the weight of the dictionary, that archive which regularizes and legitimizes our use of language. Through her archival, etymological excavations she tries to re-collect and re-member lost body memories. In "musing with mothertongue," she writes: "if we are women poets, writers, speakers, we also take issue with the given, hearing the discrepancy between what our patriarchally-loaded language bears (can bear) of our experience and the difference from it our experience bears out—how it misrepresents, even miscarries, and so leaves unsaid what we actually experience" (Marlatt 1984b, 47). For her, etymology is "almost like a racial memory, verified in the recording of the relationships of words to various civilizations" (Williamson 1985, 27). The memory encoded in etymologies is a function of successive generations' experiences of language, body and world. We are born into language, as language is born in us:

> the beginning: language, a living body we enter at birth, sustains and contains us. it does not stand in place of anything else, it does not replace the bodies around us. placental, our flat land, our sea, it is both place (where we are situated) and body (that contains us), that body of language we speak, our mothertongue. it bears us as we are born in it, into cognition. (Marlatt 1984b, 45)

Unlike official linguistic accounts of language, Marlatt's experience of language tells her that signs are not split into signifier and signified. Our "mothertongue," as she calls language, does not "replace the bodies around us"; it does not substitute words or syntactical units for our experience of others and of the world. Rather, mothertongue/language is part of our continuous relation to our world, at once *both* mind and body, cognition and feeling, self and Other. As she asks:

> where are the poems that celebrate the soft letting-go the flow of menstrual blood is as it leaves her body? how can the standard sentence structure of English with its linear

authority, subject through verb to object, convey the wisdom of endlessly repeating and not exactly repeated cycles her body knows? or the mutuality her body shares embracing other bodies, children, friends, animals, all those she customarily holds and is held by? how can the separate nouns mother and child convey the fusion, bleeding womb-infant mouth, she experiences in those first days of feeding? what syntax can carry the turning herself inside out in love when she is both sucking mouth and hot gush on her lover's tongue? (Marlatt 1984b, 47-48)

She juxtaposes women's physical experiences and body memories against linguistics and against the kind of memory associated with writing as that term has been patriarchally conceived—writing as men's expression of their interaction with the world.

Throughout Marlatt's poetic essay, the body, lingering imprints and residues of embraces, and the presence of the Other (writer, reader, lover) in the text supplement writing understood as tangible, material, black marks on the page representing the rhetorical use of the voice and thereby supplanting the rest of the body and its signifying potential. The tongue, the organ which, as she says, "touches all the different parts of the mouth to make the different sounds," is also a major organ in making love (Williamson 1985, 28). Lovemaking, then, is a form of organ speech just as poetry is a form of verbal speech. Desire is not contained in language, nor is desire expressed through language. According to Marlatt, desire "moves through your body at the same moment as it moves through the language." In the words of phenomenologist Maurice Merleau-Ponty, whose work has also been influential in shaping Marlatt's poetics, "all corporeality is already symbolism" (Merleau-Ponty 1970, 98).

Etymology is for Marlatt a source of delight, inspiration, historical information, memory, and collaboration, as this excerpt from one of her letters to Betsy Warland demonstrates:

anyway i discovered that, as the Weekley Etymological Dictionary notes, "lust" has developed "peculiar" & negative connotations only in English because the Latin in the Bible was early translated into the "lusts of the flesh." in other languages lust has life-affirming senses: Old Norse *losti,* sexual desire; Gothic *lustus,* desire; Latin *lascivus,*

> wanton, playful; Greek *lilaiesthai* (isn't that a lovely
> sound?) to yearn: Sanskrit, *lasati*, he yearns, & *lasati* plays.
> there's a quote from Francis Bacon in the Webster's 3rd
> Internat.: "the increasing lust of the earth or of the planet"
> which is the closest i found to "fertility of the planet." an
> intense longing, a craving, is one of its other senses.
> (Marlatt 1989a, 30)

As Marlatt remarks in conversation with George Bowering about her novel *Ana Historic,* "the trouble with writing fiction is that it replaces memory. You may remember it until you write about it, *and then the writing itself replaces the actual memory"* (Bowering 1989, 96-97; my italics). Her etymological archaeology is *not* a privileging of origins but rather, through the process of writing, a kind of deconstruction of the text, a reconstruction of lost memory tissues and, by extension, a construction of new bodies.

In other words, just as the word "lust" has acquired its present meaning because of a Christian translation and appropriation of the term, writing for Marlatt is part of a translation process which radically alters memories, both forgotten and recalled. In "musing with mothertongue" she describes the woman writer's place as "that double edge where she has always lived, between the already spoken and the unspeakable, sense and non-sense." As she realizes, writing from this double edge, "risking nonsense, chaotic language leafings, unspeakable breaches of usage, intuitive leaps" (Marlatt 1984b, 48), simultaneously releases life in "old roots" and inscribes a new old mother tongue. This translation of the old roots is both possible and necessary because in its common usage even the very word "mother tongue" implies a language which has been alienated, superseded or annulled by another. As Kaja Silverman observes, the term "mother tongue" attributes to women sole knowledge of that language within which lack can be experienced and known (Silverman 1988, 20-21). Theorists of the process of the subject's entry into language routinely posit this entrance into signifying systems as a choice between meaning and life, significance and insignificance. They are more than willing to surrender or abandon the presymbolic or semiotic in the Name of the Father (i.e., the symbolic, the native language). However, for Marlatt, meaning is always already constituted in the sonorous envelope, the eye contact and the gestural hieroglyphs of the "mother tongue." Here the word "tongue" becomes inadequate: this domestic vernacular pervades the whole body and actually blurs the boundaries between two bodies. Furthermore, this bond with the mother and the feminine more generally need not, should not and in fact cannot be irretrievably re- nounced, forfeited or signed away in negotiating the social contract.

Marlatt does not write "in the Space That Is Her Mother's Face" as Tostevin contends. She writes in the spaces between and among languages. Translating from a source language—the mother tongue as native language, the vernacular—which is never entirely pure or unitary, into a target language—often notated as the (m)other tongue—which does not exist as a language separate unto itself either, the feminist writing practices which engage both Cixous and Marlatt, *écriture féminine* and writing the (m)other tongue, involve the exploration of writing as a process of translation into a language which emerges *only* in the act of translation. Such writing inscribes an "interlanguage," a separate, yet intermediate, linguistic system situated between a source language and a target language and which results from a learner's attempted production of the target language (Toury 1980, 71). Patriarchal discourse structures the very ideas of "woman" and "mother." Therefore, as Jane Gallop urges "The question of language must be inserted as the wedge to break the hold of the figure of the mother. *Écriture féminine* must not be arrested by the plenitude of the mother tongue, but must try to be always and also an other tongue." The (m)other tongue is a composite that is no one's mother tongue and can only be comprehended in two languages at once (Gallop 1987, 328-29).

Écriture féminine and writing the (m)other tongue excavate and translate the pictogrammic, ideogrammic and phonetic elements of language and incorporate the body's lesser-analyzed signifying resources of gesture, performance, hysterical practice, and lovemaking. There are more ways of relating to mothers and to bodies than patriarchy has dreamt of. Like poet Di Brandt, we ask questions of our mothers and fathers. Like Brandt and Cixous, we listen in so many languages, hear in other ones. And we translate:

learning to speak *in public* to write love poems for all the
world to read meant betraying once & for all the good
Mennonite daughter i tried so unsuccessfully to become
acknowledging in myself the rebel traitor thief the one who
asked too many questions who argued with the father &
with God who always took things always went too far who
questioned every thing the one who talked too often too
loud the questionable one shouting from rooftops what
should only be thought guiltily in secret squandering
stealing the family words the one out of line recognizing
finding myself in exile where i had always been trying as
always to be true whispering in pain the old words trying
to speak the truth as it was given listening in so many
languages & hearing in this one translating remembering
claiming my past living my inheritance on this black earth
among strangers prodigally making love in a foreign country writing coming home. (Brandt 1987, "Foreword")

Notes

1   The English term "filiation" refers, somewhat vaguely, to "the
condition or fact of being the child of a certain parent." The word's use in
law is more specific. In law, "filiation" is "the assignment of paternity to
someone, as a bastard child." It is perhaps needless to add that the verb
'filiate' derives from a Medieval Latin term meaning "to acknowledge as a
son." It is worth noting too that the third meaning of the word set down in
The American Heritage Dictionary of the English Language, 1971 edition, is
"the act or fact of forming a new branch, as of a society or language group;
expansion or division." The act of forming a new branch of a language group
is precisely what Marlatt is engaged with in her poetry and poetics.

2   As I am attempting to show, Tostevin's charge is more generic than
specific to Marlatt. My article "The Body as Pictogram: Rethinking Hélène
Cixous's *écriture féminine"* analyses Toril Moi's critique of Cixous at some
length.

3   Because I have argued that neither text nor body precedes the other
or functions as the original of the other, I cannot subsequently use the term
"original" without placing it in quotation marks.

4   It is not my wish simply to draw attention to the logical throwbacks
in Tostevin's, Moi's and Stanton's work and to insist in turn, as each of them
does, that these logically inconsistent, impure elements be discarded.
Rather, my point is that if we are in the process of moving between systems,
between modernism and postmodernism, rehetorical and poststructuralist

interpretations, we need to rethink not only such questions as binary oppositions, questions of origin, essentialism, and biological determinism but our aesthetic, rhetorical and critical practices as well. We must not be content simply to spot the synonyms for "origin" or "body." Instead, we must pay increased attention to and revise our thinking about the physics and labour of textual work.

5   For further discussion of the translation poetics of *Ana Historic,* see my article "Translation A to Z: Notes on Daphne Marlattt's *Ana Historic.*" See also Janice Williamson's article "It gives me a great deal of pleasure to say yes: Writing/Reading Lesbian in Daphne Marlatt's *Touch to My Tongue.*"

6   Tostevin's strictures and the demands she attempts to place upon Marlatt's texts are a demand for purity, logical purity in this case. Whenever the cry for purity arises, however, one must ask exactly what it is that, by contrast, is deemed unpure. In the context of Tostevin's argument, the phrase "the Space That Is Her Mother's Face" figures as a synecdoche for the mother's body.

7   Dennis Cooley's article, "Recursions Excursions and Incursions: Daphne Marlatt Wrestles with the Angel Language," in the same issue of *Line* as Tostevin's piece, does perform a close reading of important aspects of Marlatt's use of language. Similarly alert to the apparently contradictory streams in her work, Cooley reconciles the contradiction first by accepting that "[Marlatt] wants to write this way . . . and she chooses to do so for good reasons" and then by considering some of these reasons. For example, he finds that Marlatt's writing "derives from a phenomenological and not particularly from a structuralist or poststructuralist base" (Cooley 1989, 71).

8   For amplification about the proper name effect, see Derrida's *Signéponge/Signsponge* 24-36 and *The Ear of the Other* 50-53, 76-77. See also the "Roundtable on Translation" in the latter volume.

9   See by contrast Tostevin's narrative account in her book *'sophie* of her attempt to speak—literally and in person—to Jacques Derrida about the absence of both woman and women from his theoretical discourse (Tostevin 1988b, 43-48).

His discourse is full of words he cuts off, so to speak, at the root. Yet in etymology it is not the truth or the origin of the word which pleases him but rather the *effect of overdetermination* which it authorizes: the word is seen as a palimpsest: it then seems to me that I have ideas *on the level of language*—which is quite simply: to write (I am speaking here of a praxis, not of a value).

Roland Barthes
Roland Barthes by Roland Barthes

Writing Under Embrasure:
How Hug a Stone

In "Unlimited Inc.orporation" I argued that Daphne Marlatt's etymological work was not a return to the origins of words or to an exclusively female language but rather part of her poetics of translating in the direction of a (m)other tongue. In this and the next two chapters, I will attempt to document this interlanguage in Marlatt's *How Hug a Stone* and *Touch to My Tongue*. Although "musing with mothertongue," the poetic essay appended to the latter volume, is a wholly integral component of that text, its richness dictates that it be treated at considerable length on its own. Accordingly, chapter four, devoted to "musing with mothertongue," culminates my present argument about how Marlatt's feminist translation poetics reorganizes the body.

If William Carlos Williams's long poem *Paterson* is, as he announces in the equation which immediately precedes his preface to the poem, "*a reply to Greek and Latin with the bare hands*" (Williams 1946, 2), then Marlatt's most recent long poems can be read as a reply to patriarchal discourse with the hands, and the ears, the tongue, the voice, the throat, the limbs, and the embrace. Just as Williams translates from the written tradition of British literature, with its sonorous and symbolic residues of Greek and Latin verse, into the grain of the American voice, so Marlatt translates from patriarchal source texts such as etymological dictionaries into a provisional, fluctuating, impermanent, as-yet-unknown feminist interlanguage or (m)other tongue. As Fred Wah tells us in his introduction to Marlatt's *Net Work,* "The most important books for her when she's writing are dictionaries" (Wah 1980a, 9). Dennis Cooley, in his article "Recursions Excursions and Incursions: Daphne Marlatt Wrestles with the Angel Language," muses that Marlatt's fascination with etymology has always been there in her work and is increasingly present. "The inclination brings together her interest in origins *and* in reflexive writing within a system. They announce further an engagement in a textual world, and not in any way direct or raw experience, the dictionary presiding over them" (Cooley 1989, 72), he writes. Cooley improvises upon Marlatt's etymological exploration of the word 'indigene' to suggest that

> Everywhere Marlatt seeks the essential self. . . . To be [indigenous], in place, first, primary, born to the language when word and world would be one, were one. When, presumably, the roots Marlatt rinses out under her stream of words and documentation, will restore words to authenticity and remove the detritus that time has deposited on them. (Cooley 1989, 78)

One of the strengths of Cooley's analysis of Marlatt's recourse to the dictionary is that, unlike Lola Tostevin, he allows two apparently contradictory possibilities to co-exist in her work, namely, the desire for a return to an "unconditioned language" (*Ana Historic,* 75, quoted in Cooley 1989, 78) and a recognition that there is no such thing as unconditioned language.

One must be cautious, however, about equating Marlatt's use of the dictionary or etymological associations as a compositional device with a recourse to origins and a privileging of an unmediated discourse where words and things operate in a reciprocal exchange. Such an assumption forgets that the dictionary too is a socially constructed tool for, among other purposes, maintaining separate spheres of high and low languages. The entry of a given word in the dictionary removes that word from its lived context and installs it in an apparently neutral but in fact socially and politically determined milieu. In his very provocative article " 'The Dismal Sacred

Word': Academic Language and the Social Reproduction of Seriousness" Allon White draws to our attention that the very first English
dictionary, Robert Cawdrey's *A Table Alphabeticall* (1604), was produced specifically with women and "any other unskilfull persons"
in mind. The preface to this dictionary advertised the volume as
follows:

> A Table Alphabeticall, conteyning and teaching the true
> writing, and understanding of hard usuall English wordes,
> borrowed from the Hebrew, Greeke, Latine, or French. &c.
> With the interpretation thereof by plain English words,
> gathered for the benefit & helpe of Ladies, Gentlewomen,
> or any other unskilfull persons.
>
> Whereby they may the more easilie and better under-
> stand many hard English wordes, which they shall heare
> or read in Scriptures, Sermons, or elsewhere, and also be
> made able to use the same aptly themselves. (quoted in
> White 1983, 8)

As White points out, the "hard wordes" defined in English dictionaries are largely Latin words used by the 'high' discourses of religion
and formal education (book-learning). White convincingly demonstrates that the codification of these hard words estranges women
from their own national language or mother tongue:

> Holding out the tantalising promise to the reader that she
> will gain skill and power through the purchase of the book,
> it nevertheless places her precisely as an outsider to her
> own national language, by and in the very act of producing
> the "table alphabeticall". These words are not *her* words,
> they belong to others, the learned men who *constitute*
> *themselves as learned* by producing the separation of lan-
> guage assumed and reproduced in dictionary-making. . . .
> The borrowing of hard words from Hebrew and the Clas-
> sics not only ensures the authority of religious and classical
> learning (the institutions of which excluded women com-
> pletely until very recently) it produces an exclusive lexicon
> for the "high" language generally which, codified and
> systematised in dictionaries, reproduces and objectivates
> its authority too (and even today the frequency of use of
> latinate terms is a clear indicator of sociolect). (White
> 1983, 8).

By means of their self-referential structure, dictionaries play a seminal role in the maintenance of the hierarchy between high and low (major and minor, serious and comic, masculine and feminine) languages: that which is to be taken seriously is defined in and by its own words (White 1983, 11). It is in this sense, then, that Marlatt's transgressive etymological translations between official derivations and slang, high culture and pop, masculine and feminine, and so on function as a reply to Greek and Latin, and English, and many other languages as well. In what follows I will track one of a multitude of possible readings through the translation poetics of *How Hug a Stone.*

How Hug a Stone, the narrative of Marlatt's trip to England with her son in 1981 to visit her mother's side of the family, opens with the dedication "for Edrys who was also Tino." This double naming triples with the reader's realization that Edrys/Tino was the woman whom Marlatt knew as 'mother.' A series of maps reproduces the itinerary of this return to her mother's mother country, which Marlatt had last visited in 1951 when she was nine, en route to Canada with her family as emigrants from Malaysia. Part 1, "Crossings-over," referring to the Atlantic ocean crossings during these different trips, recalls the etymological roots of the word 'translation': to transport, to carry across, transfer. These crossings-over or translations parallel the translation of the emigrants into and by another language and culture that began upon their arrival in British Columbia. Under the title of Part 1 are the titles of the first four poems of *How Hug a Stone,* which (as names of departures and destinations) anticipate and merge into the map reproduced on the page following. Thus the poems announce themselves too as crossings-over, as translations.

The "departure" poem is delayed, however, by the intercession of italicized notes which collect under the first map of the city of London and immediate environs. One of the sentences in italics informs the reader of the language estrangement the travellers begin to experience right away: *"melodic repeats of English, speech patterns volleying back & forth 2 seats away—we can't catch all of it"* (Marlatt 1983, 14). Marlatt and her son, "two living letters" (Introduction), travelling by plane and train over various geographies, are immediately immersed in the necessity of intralingual translation from

English to English. As they are translated bodily across the ocean, the movie on the plane is an "Agatha Christie version of what we fly to" (15). The movie's plot has an "enraged mother at the heart of it," and the windows onto the geography below are closed for the duration of this movie, obscuring the travellers' spatial translation from one continent to another.

Speeding through the English landscape by train "it is the rackety clacking of the wheels that is familiar, or this sideways motion" (16). It is also the son's getting a cinder in his eye, because this event recalls for Marlatt a similar experience of her own as a child and being asked by *her* mother "*didn't i tell you?*" (16). Bodily motion (swaying with the train) and bodily accidents reproduce the 'familiar' as 1) something repeated and 2) pertaining to the family. Their bodily closeness and intimacy makes mother and son 'familiar' to one another. Miming her mother, Marlatt goes through the repetition of removing a cinder from a child's eye.

He is also 'familiar' in that he reminds the writer of herself as a child. In the next poem-entry, "grounded in the family," Marlatt's step-brother recalls for her the time, thirty years previous, when "i am the child" (17). The step-brother, who "has named every flower in all four directions," catches moths in order to "fix them in their families" (17), to assign them to their scientific categories. This meaning of the word 'family' as the taxonomy of species both contrasts with and accretes to Marlatt's linguistic exploration of the 'moth' in 'mother'[1] and her improvisation upon 'family' in terms of 'hostess,' 'hostage,' 'host,' and 'guest.'

The poem "narrative continuity" continues the analysis of the word 'familiar.' Here "this house is familiar," although in terms of language "what was familiar now is relic." The language itself has aged during just thirty years of Marlatt's transplantation in another country:

> relics i recognize, even family phrases i've heard from his
> mother in Canada. crossings-over. as my childhood family
> had its language, covert because "so English" in North Van.
> & my mother driven wild: why can't they teach you how
> to speak? when i brought the colloquial home, flaunting
> *real fine* with *me 'n her*. (*How Hug a Stone*, 19)

Relics of Old English in contemporary British speech are a kind of "word henge to plot us in the current flow" (Marlatt 1983, 19). Immersed in "a constant stream of speech" Marlatt notes, and notates, *How Hug a Stone* with English expressions and expostulations. Along with shared speech, she also notices physical, genetic and emotional similarities such as "Mephistophelian brows" and "the full feminine mouth i see in my sister, the moods of my mother." But even as her son "imitates an English accent" he is "finding it hard to breathe, allergic to the nearest thing we have to a hereditary home" (24).

Just as the antiquity of English speech makes it redolent with the flowers of rhetoric and poetry, so Marlatt incorporates the rhetoric of flowers into her poem entitled "June near the river Clyst, Clust, clear. Clystmois this holding wet & clear" (25). Her English step-brother knows the Latin names for plants and insects, but Marlatt favors the ordinary names of "cow parsley, stinging nettles, campion, 'day's eyes' & snails all colours coiled in their leaf byways," although she does connect the Latin *phleum pratense,* otherwise 'timothy,' grass of the meadow, "a masculine given name, god honouring," with her son's phlegmatic allergic reaction. Working from the following two lines of an old poem or expression, " 'Sweet an' dry an' green as't should be, An full o' seed an' Jeune flowers,' " she translates inter- and intralingually: "jeune the young, green June delayed by rain. June why do you punish me?" (25).[2]

In the next poem 'the familiar' takes on additional meanings. Marlatt's cousin informs her that the red dirt of Devon is "sandstone parent material risen from the sea." The etymology of parent, to get, beget, give birth, from *parcae,* the Fates, connects the mother with the mythological spinners of one's destiny. But these connections are not made through the dictionary or mythology alone. Because of the family connection with Devon, and because her mother's ashes were scattered over the sea after her death, for Marlatt the phrase "sandstone parent material" connects "my mother's trace" with literal Devon bedrock. Furthermore, her aunt's spinning wheel sits "in the family room," and the aunt tells Marlatt that the fleece she is currently spinning is "the real thing." Genealogy becomes a function of that which is actually in the air (words and phrases commingling with the smell of fleece) and under foot (sandstone). Etymology allows Marlatt not to find the universal in the particular but instead to take the universal (or Latin) down to the sensory and bodily particularities of "dirt of Devon fields, sheep turd & grass smell" (26).

The definition *"Familia.* household servants" (27) introduces yet other dimensions of the familiar—class, social position and gender construction. The television is playing an episode of *A Town Called Alice,* the story of life in a small town in the Australian interior, and Marlatt begins to connect her childhood in Australia with the life there of her mother as a young woman and then young mother of three. Marlatt's grandmother speaks with the singsong intonation of what her son describes as the speech of *"all colonials deprived of an English education. it's what we call Anglo-Indian"* (28). In this musical, dark-veined speech the grandmother describes the beauty of her daughter Edrys as an eighteen-year-old girl dressed for her first public occasion. Her story of her daughter's dress ends with the words "and she looked a *dream"* (29). In her own intonations, Marlatt interprets this story of the dress as *"her* [the grandmother's] dream, the one my mother inherited, *her* dress, my mother lending her body to it. as i refused, on a new continent suffocated in changing rooms thick with resentment: you don't understand, *everybody* wears jeans here & i *want* a job. refusing the dream its continuity" (29). The grandmother relates how, just a few months prior to her wedding day, Edrys had told her she wanted to be not just a wearer of such dresses but a dress designer and maker. Through these narratives of the early life of Edrys runs the smell of coalsmoke, linking her in *her* daughter's mind, via the sensory allusion of this smoke smell, to the etymological root of coal, *geulo-,* ember from India. Using this olfactory memory as a guide, Marlatt tries to remember back to her own first years as the baby in the family in Australia: "did they burn coal in that house in Melbourne? smell of damp linen, of coal ash, of kerosene on the asphalt outside" (30). The smell of coal, familiar to the body, is translated intersemiotically with the word 'coal' to push back memory, family history and understanding.

Marlatt's son, Kit, on the other hand, occupies himself with tape-recording the sound of the English phone and the imaginary tale of himself stalking, not the family or the familiar, but "wildness."

Speaking into the recorder, he casts himself as "Adventurous Marlatt" "always on the Safari, always having to fight Wild Animals" (36). His mother, meanwhile, is trying to understand the "wildness" of her mother, her panic, "pan-ic (terror of the wild)" (55). She realizes that her dead mother—ember from India, become "bits of porous bone, fine ash" (55) scattered over the sea—completed her autobiography as the rebellious schoolgirl and young woman (wild mare), become mother (*mère*), and eventually returned to the sea (*mer*). It was the third translation (*mer*) which she refused. She refused to translate or be translated. She never really made that final crossing-over. It was this failed translation which eventually led to her madness, her wildness. Her last wish was for her ashes to be scattered over the Pacific ocean, "a different sea-coast off a different rock" (55) representing the ocean she would not ultimately cross.

With Kit ill with allergies and a virus, and dealing with her own cold and her sorrow at her mother's circumscribed life and premature death, Marlatt takes on some of her mother's pain and panic: "there is no limit. something in me is in shock, like a bird beating wildly against a branch—lost, panicked. why are we going through this?" (71). Terror, she discovers, springs not only from encountering "Wild Animals" and poisonous snakes but from entrapment within the family and other institutions (such as boarding schools far from home) and from having a child fall sick. "Stories can kill" (51), Marlatt writes, both those romantic stories which leave us with "a script that continues to write our parts in the passion we find ourselves enacting" (73) and those stories which are "unwritten, de-scripted, un-described" (35). The dictionary definition of 'evil' is 'exceeding the proper limit.' Marlatt asks "what is 'the limit'? for either the dead or the living?" (68). Our desire is to go beyond "the limit of the old story," "to redeem them [our ancestors], or them in ourselves, our 'selves' our inheritance of words. wanting to make us new again: to speak what isn't spoken, even with the old words" (73). Though she comes in many guises (Edrys, Mary Gypsy, Mary of Egypt, Miriam, Mary of the Blue Veil, Sea Lamb sifting sand & dust, Bride of the Brown Day, etc.) the mother is "not a person." Not a single, unitary, temporally and historically isolated individual. "She is what we come through to & what we come out of, ground & source. the space after the colon, the pause (between the words) of all possible relation" (73). Mother is the "forgotten parts" of the old story; she is the mother tongue; she is the possibility of language and relation. She is what makes us want to speak what is not spoken. *"Narrative is a strategy for survival"* (75).

However, contrary to what Lola Tostevin and Frank Davey have argued, Marlatt is not in such passages advocating a return to the Great Mother, the essential feminine or an undifferentiated identification with her own mother. *How Hug a Stone* is not, as Davey suggests, a metaphysical "counter-narrative of a primal feminine" "which locates the human outside of social action in an archetypal predetermination" (Davey 1989, 46). The figure of the mother near the end of the text is *not* "the lithic mother" (45).[3] Marlatt resolutely *refuses* to map her personal quest for her dead mother onto the mythological story and associations of the circle of stones at Avebury. She writes:

> *she lives* stands for nothing but this longstanding matter in the grass, settled hunks of mother crust, early Tertiary, bearing the rootholes of palms. they bring us up, in among stone-folds, to date: the enfolded present waits for us to have done with hiding-&-seeking terrors, territories, our obsession with the end of things.

> how hug a stone (mother) except nose in to lithic fold, the old slow pulse beyond word become, under flesh, mutter of stone, *stane, stei*-ing power. (*How Hug a Stone,* 75)

Marlatt's own mother does not live on in some archetypal form from four thousand years back. Marlatt made it clear as long ago as 1974 that "I'm not really interested in the eternal by itself. I think that that's a danger, too; that's a seduction. I'm interested in the interaction between the eternal & what's time-bound, & what's particularly local. And I think you can only articulate the eternal thru that" (Bowering 1979, 58). For her, etymologies, mythologies and dreams are all "other languages or events that are recognizable in our own lives" (56). Even history, let alone mythology, may be no more accessible or real than "simply the shell we exude for a place to live in" (Marlatt 1983, 51). As she says, "*she lives* stands for nothing but this longstanding matter in the grass." The question which engages her is how to articulate the contemporary and local material world.

Marlatt concludes that difference from the mother ("& i can do nothing but stand in my sandals & jeans [attire her mother opposed] unveiled, beat out the words, dance out names at the heart of where we are lost, hers first of all, wild mother dancing upon the waves") (78-79), locating oneself "where live things are soaring" (77) and where rapture can be found in such ordinary experiences as feeding the pigeons in Trafalgar Square, and embracing not archetypes but actual stone and rock brings us up to date, to the enfolded present, in order "to speak to, call to (here, pigeon, come on, it's all right) the free & unobliged" (77). The mother is "first love that teaches a possible world" (78). It is to that possible world of his own Kit wants to return, the world of Vancouver which his mother has given to him, and which Marlatt had earlier claimed from her mother. All she can do is to stand unveiled and open to this possible world and the language she finds there, answering to the "claims of the dead in our world (the fear that binds). i am learning how the small ones live" (79).

The title "How Hug a Stone" is not "How *To* Hug a Stone." This is not a how-to book. It is not a recipe for how to connect with one's parents and grandparents through voyaging to their motherland, visiting selected tourist spots and, drawing on certain local myths and stories, writing up the results. *How Hug a Stone* is a question. It is a question as to the possibility of embracing the family of ancestors and of replying to the wild heartbeat. It asks how to mother one's children and how to mother oneself. The pictogrammic gesture of literally hugging a literal stone asks how we can deploy our bodies in relation to the physical world of which bodies are a part. Embracing the present, physical world gives us "*stei*-ing power," the power to take a stand, to make a place for ourself in the world, and to continue to dwell here. The Great Mother is, as Phyllis Webb's promotional blurb on the back cover clarifies, the mother language, stone-writing, type-writing, and the poetry of things. The "monumental" stones of Avebury are a writing in stone. To embrace one of these stones is simultaneously to embrace the physical *and* writing. In this embrace, one's body becomes a writing on stone, a pictogram, a hieroglyph.

The dead live on through love and through our shared fears over, and participation in, the accidents of life. They do not live on through symbolic regression to Greek or Latin, Druid mythologies, or English etymologies. The dead live on through passages or crossings-over, through acts of interlingual, intralingual and intersemiotic translation.

Notes

1   Laurie Ricou spotted "the word moth which flies within mother, '*moththe, math-,* worm" (Ricou 1987, 214-15). He concludes his article with the statement that "Marlatt is convincing. Following her etymologies does uncover a women's experience lost or hidden in the language. But then reading the moth in mother, reading the moth's woman-ness is uncomfortably like any other ingenious over-reading" (215).

Frank Davey takes exception to what he reads as Marlatt's use of "the phonological similarity of *moth* and *mother*" to point to "a male attempt to collect the woman" (Davey 1989, 42).

See also Lianne Moyes's analysis of the familiar and the unfamiliar in her article "Writing, the Uncanniest of Guests: Daphne Marlatt's *How Hug a Stone.*"

2   See also Susan Knutson's reading of this particular poem in her article "Daphne Marlatt and Nicole Brossard: Writing Metanarrative in the Feminine." Drawing on Marlatt's notebooks in the Literary Manuscripts Collection of the National Library of Canada, she relays interesting parallels drawn by Marlatt herself between the sacrificial rites of ancient agricultural cultures and Kit's illness. Knutson observes that Marlatt does not reify or reconstruct the old myths of the son's sacrifice in her text but actively 'misreads' the old story and thereby "spirals into the new, the not-yet thought, the future" (Knutson 1990, 38).

Hilary Clark has also written about how what she calls the hologrammic or palimpsestic narrative of *How Hug a Stone* "enables us to reintegrate our past into our present in order to go forward into a new, ghostly future, paradoxically divided yet more whole" (Clark 1990, 11).

3   See Davey's article, "Words and Stones in *How Hug a Stone,*" especially pages 45-46.

The passage Davey finds particularly problematical, namely, "how hug a stone (mother) except nose in to lithic fold, the old slow pulse beyond word become, under flesh, mutter of stone, . . ." (Marlatt 1983, 75), finds an echo in *Touch to My Tongue* where Marlatt describes driving east through the mountains as "alone nosing my way into the unnamed female folds of hill" (Marlatt 1984b, 25).

Ever since I began writing professionally, I have assumed that my Mother Tongue is English, period. Certainly my main sources of inspiration as a non-fiction writer have been English-language writers—Orwell, Mailer, Didion—and my sense of pleasure with language has been experienced mainly in English. But somewhere in the back of my consciousness is that Ukrainian language I heard all around me as a child: by what devious routes might it be asserting itself in my English syllables and syntax? What nostalgia and longing for the Slavic syllable is making itself felt as I choose English words and phrases? Perhaps this is my Mother Tongue—the one in which my baby mind was coddled and aroused—and English is my **Sister**-Tongue.

Myrna Kostash
"Ethnicity and Feminism"

We must also find, find anew, invent the words, the sentences that speak the most archaic and most contemporary relationship with the body of the mother, with our bodies, the sentences that translate the bond between her body, ours, and that of our daughters. We have to discover a language [*langage*] which does not replace the bodily encounter, as paternal language [*langue*] attempts to do, but which can go along with it, words which do not bar the corporeal, but which speak corporeal.

Luce Irigaray
"The Bodily Encounter with the Mother"

The Phantom Limb Syndrome: Writing the Body in *Touch to My Tongue*

Because Daphne Marlatt's immigrant experience emerges from a colonial British background, it is easy for readers to overlook the fact that she considers her immigration to Canada to have exercised a profound influence upon her senses of language, writing, and the body. In her essay "Entering In: The Immigrant Imagination" Marlatt reflects: "Looking back, i think that most of my writing has been a vehicle for entry into what was for me the new place, the new world" (Marlatt 1984a, 219). She talks about the cultural and linguistic differences she and her family encountered upon emigration from Malaysia to Canada: "We came from a colonial multicultural situation in Penang where five languages were spoken in our house (English, Malay, Cantonese, Tamil, Thai) to a city [Vancouver] which was then (1951) much more than it is today, decidedly WASP, conservative, and suspicious of newcomers. We spoke the same language but not the same dialect . . ." (220).[1] Not only words and accents but every quotidian detail—food, clothing, sports, pop culture, music, flora and fauna, the subjects of nightmares, etiquette, school subjects, and reading material—became a marker of difference. Marlatt enthusiastically adopted the accent, slang, habits and practices associated with the new dialect in order to make herself into a Canadian teenager. It was not until years later[2] that she began to feel that "like a phantom limb, part of me, that Penang past, not quite cut off, still twitched alive and wanted acknowledging" (221).

While the young Marlatt wrote her way into the world she wanted to be part of, multiplying her signifying capabilities in the process, her mother, whose role, identity and status changed with immigration from colonial memsahib in Malaysia[3] to isolated Canadian housewife, became increasingly nostalgic for things English. In trying to enforce Englishness, Marlatt's mother confined and reduced her engagement with the present and with the world outside the domestic sphere. As Marlatt writes: "My mother wanted to keep up 'English' in our values as we struggled very hard to become Canadian. This led to a deepening neurosis i could neither understand nor address" (Marlatt 1984a, 222). The mother, as a mother, made desperate hysterical attempts on her own behalf and that of her children to salvage her colonial British culture and dialect. Her daughter, on the other hand, embraced postcolonial Canadian culture, swam into the flow of differences within a single language, and learned the subtleties of intralingual translation. The daughter's sense of linguistic estrangement lead not to neurosis but "to a sense of the relativity of both language and reality." She acquainted herself with the idiosyncracies of language, its duplicity, and its figurative or transformational powers. As she says:

> When you are told, for instance, that what you call earth is really dirt, or what you have always called the woods (with English streams) is in fact bush (with its creeks), you experience the first split between name and thing, signifier and signified, and you take that first step into a linguistic world that lies adjacent to but is not the same as the world of things, and indeed operates on its own linguistic laws. (Marlatt 1984a, 222)

According to Marlatt, this first-hand experience of the split between signifier and signified extends for the postcolonial immigrant writer to an awareness of the duplicitousness of the second-person pronoun and the twin illusion of the unitary self. The sense "that the you you were in that place is not the same you as the you you are in this place, though the two overlap, produces a desire to knit the two places, two (at least) selves, somehow" (223).

This relationship between bodily memories and writing in the poem sequence of Marlatt's *Touch to My Tongue* is the explicit focus of this chapter. What I explore is how this erotic, lesbian feminist text composes the body and, conversely, how the body inscribes itself into the text. How does the split between signifier and signified function in the inscription of bodies gendered as feminine? As lesbian? How does Marlatt's postcolonial writing of the body incorporate the phantom limb of the colonial past? Whose limbs assume the nature of phantoms?

In *Touch to My Tongue,* the desire to explore the relation between the multiple selves constructed through language and place, and between these selves and an Other, finds its most obvious expression in the multiplicity of forms included in this slim volume. Like the five languages spoken in Marlatt's Penang home, in *Touch to My Tongue* the treated photographs, the prose poems, the poetic essay "musing with mothertongue," a glossary to several of the poems, and a statement by photographer Cheryl Sourkes about her photographs (from a series called "Memory Room") explore different approaches to signification and representation and signal to the reader the need to translate (in this case, intersemiotically between different media). Remarking upon the paradoxical relation between the desirable Otherness of the hieroglyph's opacity to phonographic meaning and its apparently transparent, visual readability and referentiality, Janice Williamson suggests that in Sourkes's treated photographs "the female figure becomes a kind of hieroglyph, or pictorial language which blurs the distinction between woman and writing" and that Marlatt's series of poems likewise take up "the hieroglyph's contradictory identity as both enigmatic otherness and proximity" (Williamson 1991, 178).

But the correlation of the hieroglyph with the body gendered in the feminine is not only an alliance of exotic Otherness. The apparent collusion of the feminine body with hieroglyphs and other visual signifying systems is reminiscent of Freud's theory of "somatic compliance," whereby the hysterical body is thought to comply "with the psychical demands of the illness by providing a space and a material for the inscription of its signs" (Doane 1987, 40). Freud and Freudians read the hysterical symptom as a sign or inscription on the woman's body; they believe that the hysterical body obeys the psychic imperative to transform itself into textual material. Indeed, Freud's notion of somatic compliance is figured upon a phallogocentric model of writing in which material substance (paper or flesh) is imagined as compliant with or subordinate to psychic demands. Although hysterical symptomatology has been analyzed intensively, the body's signifying production in general has remained relatively untheorized, with the result that we lack a vocabulary with which to discuss the significations of materiality and corporeality. However, the body must be always already textual, or hysterical transformation/translation could not take place. As Robyn Ferrell asks in her article "The Passion of the Signifier and the Body in Theory": "What else is hysteria, but the exhibiting of the body as a place of signification?" (Ferrell 1991, 174).

For instance, Marlatt's reference to her bodily memories of her Penang childhood as a phantom limb speaks of a kind of bodily semiosis which is typically overlooked or ignored because subsumed to the type of memory believed to have its seat in the mind. In "Sounding a Difference," she describes this kind of memory as "a murmur in the flesh":

> . . . the experience of being back there in Penang so many years later and remembering, and yet not consciously remembering, having a memory that was in the body somehow, but wasn't consciously accessible until I got there. I couldn't have said how to get from A to B, but at a certain point, rounding a corner, I got an immediate flash of what I would see when I got around that corner, and I could not have foretold it until I was in that actual movement around that particular spot. And memory seems to operate like this, like a murmur in the flesh one suddenly hears years later. (Williamson 1989, 49)

Aside from memories accessible to consciousness, the body's own motility links different times and places and different "selves." The movements and gestures in which memories are stored are the same ones in which such memories are released. The body signifies and collects remembrances in muscles, heartbeats, physical motions, and sensual impressions. As signifying material, as flesh, the body connects different *topoi*—for Marlatt, Penang past and Penang present. Walking along a street is an immersion in signs, symptoms, and remembrances; phantom limbs, odours, and unheard melodies accompany present stimuli and re-member the body past.

Touch to My Tongue begins with the speaker reading the other woman's face: "i see your face because i don't see mine equally flush with being." This facial flush nominates the speaker not as "self" but as Other. The flush of welcome and excitement of both their faces signifies the two women as, so to speak, Othering each other, "equally flush with being." At this same initial meeting, the speaker reads in the Other's face the traces of ethnicity, that very specific, if often ambiguous, sense of Otherness. What she sees in the lover's glow are "fjords in there," a Scandinavian heritage. Their respective sets of ancestors having emigrated from Scandinavia and India, being together in present-day Vancouver is a literal "co-incidence." They meet both in the present tense and "in these far places we find in each other." Their co-incidence in the time and space of Vancouver partakes of their shared sense of being from other places and times as well, not mythic time of course but family histories, cultural memories (the British claiming Bombay) and texts read (Sappho on the radio). Their selection of meeting place, "no not the Danish Tearoom—the Indonesian or Indian," reflects both of their ancestral and ethnic backgrounds—Scandinavian and colonial British in India. Later, separated by distance from her lover, the speaker realizes painfully and fearfully that "i can only be, no vessel but a movement running, out in the open, out in the dark and rising tide, in risk, knowing who i am with you" (Marlatt 1984b, 20).

Marlatt uses language in *Touch to My Tongue* to access not only cognitive recollection but the body's memories as well. To quell the loneliness and pain of the physical distance from her partner, the speaker calls the lover up, either on the phone or in memory. The renewal of the connection—the tones and timbres of their speaking voices and their bodily memories of each other—sustain them over the geographical distance. Separated by distance, the lovers are "turned out," presumably of their paradise, but they realize that in their lovemaking they are "turned inside out, beside ourselves." While the speaker's conscious mind imagines the possible dissolution of their relationship, her body remembers them together as "creatures of ecstasy," which helps to bridge the distance and the absence. Drawing on this body knowledge, these memories of rising "drenched from our own wet grasses, reeds, sea," they re-affirm their commitment both to one another and to the necessary reclamation of language, geography, and the social world.

If writing provides access to the body, so too the body informs writing and social practices. Whether she draws upon the logic of symbols, mythologic or etymologic, Marlatt attempts in the act of writing to connect memory with both present and future possibility. That is, she uses writing to recover lost memories. These recovered memories can in turn create new writing and social practices. As she says, "In a sense, it's almost like a racial memory, verified in the recording of the relationships of words to various civilizations. There is also a connection between memory and possibility. The invention of possibility which is utopian allows for a new practice" (Marlatt 1984b, 27).

As a postcolonial writer, Marlatt refuses the traditional notion of mythology as transcendental, transhistorical, and transpersonal and interprets it instead as contemporary, personal, local, even geographical. In a 1976 interview, "There's this and this connexion," she explicitly connects mythology with the reclamation of geography, terrain, habitat, and a sense of place. Questioned as to the connection between her interest in recording local reality in an authentic and accurate way and her interest in mythic reality and in writing out of what the questionner describes as "an almost religious sense," Marlatt responds as follows:

> Well, brother, what can I say to that that might be useful? . . . I *am* interested in mythic thought. Because it seems to me that myths—well myths are a language in themselves but they do tell us how the early or first inhabitants of a terrain saw themselves in terms of their terrain, they tell us about inhabiting a place, and they tell us about the powers of the earth we inhabit which we've lost the sense of. (Cooley et al. 1977, 32)

Marlatt's postcolonial usage of mythology is as another language in which to access the real and the local, another language for translation. Insofar as it is local, mythology is not a narrative of the imaginary or utopian but a map of the earth and its previous inhabitants. It is not the deferral but the actualization of the real in language, time, and space. For her, mythology is someone else's mother tongue. A translation effect, mythology is not a religion but a language which connects the hungry ghosts of the ancestors with the desiring bodies of the living inhabitants of a given locale.

Marlatt's feminist and postcolonial poetics coalesces around her translative use of etymmology and mythology. In the poem "yes" (Marlatt 1984b, 21), for instance, she explores both contemporary and past associations of the word "jade." She begins from the word's dictionary meanings of " 'worthless woman, wilful girl.' " "JADE a sign on the road announces," but she translates it as an advertisement for "stone of the flank," recalling the possessive weight of her ex-husband's hand upon that part of her body during sleep. She associates the word with her own exhaustion and spiritlessness, her jadedness, during that period of her life. She also remembers that the jade stone has traditionally been thought to be a cure for kidney disease. She contrasts heterosexual marriage—ceremonially marked by the mythological figure of Hymen and by the breaking of the bride's hymen—with the experience of her lesbian love relation and the feeling of being "broken open by your touch," without loss, abandoning the "need for limits" and "the urge to stand apart." The image of the wedding ring and the "white band the skin of years hidden under its reminder to myself of the self i was marrying" is replaced by the ring of "our mouths' hot estuary, tidal yes we are, leaking love and saying it deep within." For Marlatt, the wedding band symbolizes both heterosexual marriage and "this small open space that was mine" prior to her marriage. "This small open space that was mine" refers both to psychic space, a sense of self, and to the body. Thus, for her, her former wedding ring symbolizes an attempted somatic compliance between psyche and body.

By contrast, with her lesbian lover, lovemaking is both love *and* its utterance. This other "yes," "redefined, it signals us beyond limits in a new tongue our connection runs along" (21), is pronounced "*yu*" (23). "*Yu,*" the notes in the glossary to *Touch to My Tongue* inform us, is "the Indo-European root of 'you,' second person pronoun; also an outcry as in Latin *jubilare,* 'to raise a shout of joy' (as the initiates at Eleusis might have done on seeing the luminous form of the risen Kore)" (36). It is not a promissory "yes," as in a wedding ceremony

185

where the words "I do" or "I will," supplemented by a wedding ring, promise to love, honour, etc. This other "yes" ("*yu*") does not promise to love from this day forth. It does not enact or exact a promise; it enacts love. "*Yu*" does not promise to love; it loves. It raises a shout of joy in the Other. In their lesbian relation, lovemaking and the jubilant cry of "*yu*" literalize the body of the Other and/as love. Love is at once symbolized and desymbolized. Love is desymbolized insofar as the lesbian lovers represent this desire without loss or finitude not as a single gold band but as a limitless procession of rings (of desire, of fulfillment). Nevertheless, love *is* symbolized because if to say "yes" is to promise, then the lovers promise with their bodies: "Tidal yes we are, leaking love and saying it deep within" (21).

Similarly, in the poem entitled "kore" (23), the lesbian love relation both accumulates elements of the mother-daughter relation and deconstructs them at the same time. Even as the mythological parallel is drawn, it is reduced, played down and problematized within the context of the poem. For example, within the poem it is undetermined which lover plays the role of Demeter and which Persephone. The title, "kore," might suggest that not the poet but her lover is Kore. Yet the lover's eyelashes, "amber over blue," recall "(*amba*, amorous Demeter, you with the fire in your hand, i am coming to you)," which implies that the lover is Demeter instead. In interview with Janice Williamson, Marlatt has discussed the mother-daughter elements of her relationship. She says: "Well, we each get to play the daughter and we each get to play the mother. . . . That's why there is so much mother/daughter imagery running through *Touch,* and the confusion between Persephone and Demeter is a deliberate confusion" (Williamson 1985, 26).

Furthermore, along with this naming/unnaming, there is the complication of the second person pronoun. The poem chants "no one wears yellow like you," "no one shines like you," "no one my tongue burrows in." The description of lovemaking leads to the statement, in parenthesis, "(here i am you)." As the poem works toward orgasm, as "lips work towards undoing," the mythological connotations of Demeter and Kore are stripped down to the etymological level, to the Indo-European root of the word "female," which originally meant "to suckle" but has diversified into "fetus" (that which sucks), "fellatio" (sucking) and "felix" (fruitful, happy) (Marlatt 1984b, 36). In other words, Marlatt uses the etymological evolution of the term "female" to radically complicate the pronoun "you" and the standard positionality of self and Other. The second-person pronoun, by virtue of Marlatt's translational accretion to it of its Latin root *jubilare,* "to raise a shout of joy," supplements Otherness with the cry, jubilation, and excess.

To say "you" in this translation is not only to designate or name that which is not the self. It is simultaneously to *enact* Otherness, and one's pleasure in the Other. Saying "you" is the exaltation experienced at the entering in to oneself of the Other. Thus it is not (or not only) that the self is discovered through intersubjective discourse or through intercourse. The Other is not simply a means to the solidification of the unitary self. Sex is not a detour through the Other toward a refreshment and consolidation of ego boundaries. "Extended with desire for you and you in me it isn't us" (24), as Marlatt writes in the poem following, refusing the reduction of two to one implicit in the traditional mathematics of love in the western world. "You" (*yu*) plus "me" does not equal "us."

Through such translations and deconstructions, Marlatt collapses dialectics and brings different dialects and different bodies into play. Bodies and lovemaking alter language. With the revision of established meanings, the body surges ahead of language, its materiality and its motility exceeding categorical thought. For Marlatt, language does not represent anything else: "it does not replace the bodies around us" (45). Like the phantom histories we carry with us encoded in our tissues, language "is both place (where we are situated) and body (that contains us), that body of language we speak, our mothertongue." If one brackets the ideas of representation and completion, then one can find both "alternate names" and "that tongue our bodies utter, woman tongue, speaking in and of and for each other" (27).

That tongue our bodies utter is the focal point of the poem "in the dark of the coast." In this poem, the lover converses with a small bird singing in the underbrush in a way analogous to how her body, her skin, answers to the touch of the Other. The lovers, reunited after the long period of separation, discover new things about each other. Marlatt writes: "i didn't know your hair, i didn't know your skin when you beckoned to me in that last place. but i knew your eyes, blue, as soon as you came around the small hill, knew your tongue" (30). The tongue she knew is both the literal organ of the tongue and perhaps a shared lovers' language not unlike "the hidden Norse we found." Paradoxically, distance, parting, absence, and mourning are very prominent in this poem about reunion and erotic fusion. The emphasis of the poem is not upon the merging of identities in one another, as in conventional love poetry, but upon how "your naked, dearly known skin—its smell, its answering touch to my tongue" creates a "separate skin we make for each other through." The hieroglyphs of embrace spell a new alphabet, a new skin, for their being together.

In the final poem of the sequence, "healing," it becomes evident in retrospect that the lover's body has translated itself into the text not only in the erotic content but in a number of other semes as well. As she tends to her lover's needs following gall bladder surgery, Marlatt is led to consult the dictionary for the etymology of the word "gall." Its etymological history includes words meaning to shine, words for colours (yellow), bright materials, bile or melancholy, glad, glass, glaze, and glee. These derivations of "gall" run through-out the entire series of poems, but perhaps the best example is the opening of the poem "kore": "no one wears yellow like you excessive and radiant storehouse of sun, skin smooth as fruit but thin, leaking light. . . . no one shines like you" (23). Similarly, in the poem "where we went," brightness, glass, and glaze appear: "we went to what houses stars at the sea's edge, brilliant day, where a metal crab jets water catching light, heaven and earth in a tropic embrace joined upright, outside glass doors people and cars and waterglaze" (28). Just as Cheryl Sourkes's photocollages intermingle with Marlatt's poems and poetic essay, so the lover's body inserts itself sympto-matically and erotically into the text. Just as the lover's skin produces an "answering touch to my tongue" (30), so her bodily symptoms translate themselves intersemiotically into her partner's poetic sequence.

The loved body transgresses the bounds of textual decorum and has its "say" within the text too. In hysteria, the erotogenic body bypasses the dichotomy between the real and the represented to translate itself directly into motor and speech "symptoms." Thus, if the body can translate itself into motility and speech, it would seem possible that it can translate itself into the tissue of written text. Or, just as the body carries memories in its tissues and limbs which can be translated into speech in the "talking cure" of psychoanalysis, so too corporeal information can be translated into writing. The material substance of the body translates itself intersemiotically into the material substance of language, signifier to signifier.

In the retrospective reading compelled by the ending of *Touch to My Tongue,* the lover's diseased gall bladder becomes a kind of phantom organ which permeates the entire text. Just as the body carries memories in *its* tissues, so too the tissue-text is imprinted not only with the lover's erotic body but her symptomatic body as well. The phrase "gall, all that is bitter, melancholy" (Marlatt 1984b, 32) refers to an historical organization of the body around four "humours" instead of according to the dualist mind-body split. Through techniques such as these, Marlatt translates intralingually, from English to English. She also translates interlingually from the dead languages of Latin, Greek, Old English, Old Norse, and others into contemporary Canadian English. The old roots and phantom residues of these languages serve as a source language from which to inscribe a new target language. Thirdly, she translates intersemiotically between the body and the text.

It is possible at this point to review and recontextualize the mother-daughter relationship described by Marlatt in her essay on immigration and recapitulated with differences in the relation between the lovers in *Touch to My Tongue.* As Marlatt depicts it now, during her teenage years the mother-daughter relationship revolved around a contest between colonial and postcolonial uses of language. In "Difference (em)bracing," an essay published in the 1990 collection *Language in Her Eye: Writing and Gender,* she refines her earlier remarks about the effects of her family's immigration to Canada (quoted near the beginning of this chapter) by nuancing more fully the class, gender, and family politics involved. She describes the tensions between her mother and her Canadianized daughters over the differences between the mother's mother tongue of "English English" and what the mother referred to as their "American" English and the battles over translation which ensued: "And so i engaged in long battles with my mother, each of us trying to correct the other, she correcting for purity of origin, while i corrected for common usage—each of us with different versions of 'the real thing' " (Marlatt 1990, 190).

It is crucial to remember that Marlatt's mother had been a memsahib in their Penang household and, moreover, as Brenda Carr reiterates, that the term "memsahib" is a derivative of "sahib," the white colonial male master of the household, and thus reflects the "mem's" subordinate status. While her mother functioned in many ways within her purview as an accomplice to the colonial project, she was also in equally many ways its victim. Though educated to the colonizing task with an English boarding school training, she was herself born in India into an Anglo-Indian family of two generations. As Marlatt confesses:

> Words were always taken seriously in my house because they were the weapons of that struggle [with her mother over reality]. But a woman's sense of herself in the language she speaks can only be denied so long before it transforms into a darker (side of the moon), a more insistent ir-reality, not *un*real because its effects are felt so devastatingly in its subject and those around her. Her words, her very style of speaking derided by her own children, her colonial manners and English boarding-school mores dismissed as inappropriate by Canadianized daughters who denied any vestige of them in their own behavior and speech, she withdrew into chronic depression and hypochondria. 'Unbalanced.' 'Loony.' But to deny: to completely say no to. A powerful mechanism. A form of colonialism at work within the family. (Marlatt 1990, 190-91)

Throughout this passage, Marlatt is ostensibly talking about her mother's enforcement of colonial and traditional heterosexual family relations, but the lack of nouns or pronouns in the final few phrases of the passage creates an ambiguousness which reminds us that repressive power relations cannot be attributed exclusively to the colonial side. Just as Marlatt's mother tried to enforce coloniality within the family, so too her daughters, denying their mother's speech and its accompanying reality, practiced a kind of postcolonial counter-enforcement upon her. Contrary to Sarah Harasym's argument that Marlatt erases the reality of the amah as a Third World woman in "In the Month of Hungry Ghosts" because she is preoccupied with questions of her own identity and with the workings of representation (Harasym 1991, 121-25), Marlatt's poetics are *not* based on representation but rather on translation, a practice which, I would suggest, derives largely from the language practices she learned battling her mother on Canadian ground(s) and from her more positive childhood interactions with her amahs in Penang.[4] Puzzling over the problem of speaking about differences and speaking to Others, Marlatt recalls:

> It wasn't sharing but difference in a multiplicity of ways i felt first as a child in Malaya where i was taught the King's (it was then) English, to mind my P's & Q's, to behave and speak 'properly,' when all the while i was surrounded by other languages that were not proper at all for a white colonial child, but which nevertheless i longed to understand, filled as they were with laughter, jokes, calls, exclamations, comfort, humming. Sometimes rocked to sleep, sometimes teased or scolded, sometimes ignored by the sounds of Cantonese, Malay, Thai, i stood on the fringe and longed to know what the stories were that produced such laughter, such shakings of the head. (Marlatt 1990, 189-90)

The five languages of her Penang home and the co-habitation within *Touch to My Tongue* of multiple signifying genres and forms are alike based on translation.

Touch to My Tongue celebrates both the lesbian love relation, which simultaneously supports and undetermines the mother-daughter relation, and a postcolonial delight in translation.[5] The multiple aspects of the mother figure touch upon Marlatt's mother, grandmother, and the elements of the mother/daughter relationship which are rehearsed in the relation between herself and her female lover. The dynamics between or among mothers and Others become radically complex. The phantom limb which beckons Marlatt to re-visit Penang one year after her mother's death also takes her to the land of her amahs, those women who spoke Cantonese, Malay, Thai, who were bi- or multilingual. Having "completely [said] no to" her mother, she completely says yes/yu to her lesbian lover. Like her amahs in Penang, the lovers translate. In other words, they practice what Bharati Mukherjee calls "the 'step-mother tongue' in which post-colonial writers write, 'implying as it does the responsibility, affection, accident, loss, and secretive roots-quest in adoptive family situations' " (quoted in Hutcheon 1991, 81). The "phantom limb" is not only the contained, if redolent, colonial past then; nor is it only a metaphor. The phantom limb of Marlatt's Penang past embraces each of her colonial and her postcolonial mothers' bodies.[6]

Therefore, while the lesbian Other is a different Other than the mother as Other, or the Third World woman as either mother or Other,[7] saying "yes" to her lover is also a way of saying a belated "yes" to these her several mothers. As Luce Irigaray states emphatically in her essay "The Bodily Encounter with the Mother": "It is also necessary, if we are not to be accomplices in the murder of the mother, for us to assert that there is a genealogy of women" (Irigaray 1991, 44). Arguing against the Oedipal basis of psychoanalysis, Irigaray's model in that article for a genealogy of women is primarily nuclear family based, but I am arguing here that a genealogy of women, a history of encounters with mothers' bodies, can and must include mothers and daughters from outside the narrowly defined patriarchal and colonial family unit, must include, for example, Marlatt's relations with the amahs who cared for her as a child. Moreover, a genealogy of women will inevitably require the invention and multiplication of kinship terms supplementary to those of the phallic mother and daughter.

Meanwhile, at the conclusion of the poem sequence of *Touch to My Tongue,* Marlatt seizes on the word "glisten," one of the derivatives of "gall," and puts the letter "g" in parentheses so that the word translated in this fashion doubles as a visual (glisten) and an aural (listen) term. The lovers, taking turns playing mother and daughter, return to their bed, entwine their warm limbs, and (g)listen to a new (m)other tongue.

Notes

1   It is important to note that four of the five languages spoken in Marlatt's childhood home were those spoken by the servants. I will return to this crucial point later.

2   The death of her mother precipitated Marlatt's journey back to Penang in July 1976 (Thesen 1979, 2).

3   Brenda Carr's essay "The Western Woman and 'the Colonial Empire of the Mind': (Re)Constructing the Memsahib as (M)other in Daphne Marlatt's 'In the Month of Hungry Ghosts' " can be read as a kind of companion essay to the present one. (I want to thank Brenda Carr for reading an earlier draft of my paper and making provocative suggestions for revision.)

4   In her reply to Harasym, Carr suggests that the "limits of feminist discourses cut both ways: in privileging the amah, we may lose sight of the conditions of the sexed body for the memsahib. I would suggest that a more productive model might be one in which neither memsahib nor amah are read out as fully empowered or victimized. . . . In this way, while accounting for the obvious unevenness of their subject positionings in imperialism, the amah may be read for contradictory instances of her agency, while the memsahib may be read for contradictory instances of her disempowerment. . . ." (Carr 1992).

5   In the second poem of *Touch to My Tongue,* Marlatt explores together the Otherness of the lover and of the mother figure. In the absence of her lover, the figure of the great mother in the first poem becomes for the speaker that of the terrible mother, she who "takes back what she gives, as you might, or i might," in the second (20). The allusion at this point to the double figure of the great mother/terrible mother does not reflect a nostalgia for a utopian or prelapsarian order. Rather the figure of the maternal conjures up Marlatt's own personal, familial background.

6   African American writer Toni Morrison's new novel *Jazz* contains a passage which configures an absent father as a kind of phantom limb. The passage extends over three paragraphs. I quote a mere portion:

> Only now, he thought, now that I know I have a father, do I feel his absence: the place where he should have been and was not. Before, I thought everybody was one-armed, like me. Now I feel the surgery. The crunch of bone when it is sundered, the sliced flesh and the tubes of blood cut through, shocking the bloodrun and disturbing the nerves. They dangle and writhe. Singing pain. . . .
>
> And no, I am not angry. I don't need the arm. But I do need to know what it could have been like to have had it. It's a phantom I have to behold and be held by, in whatever crevices it lies, under whatever branch. Or maybe it stalks

treeless and open places, lit with an oily sun. This part of me that does not know me, has never touched me or lingered at my side. This gone-away hand that never helped me over the stile, or guided me past the dragons, pulled me up from the ditch into which I stumbled. . . . When I find it, will it wave to me? Gesture, beckon to me to come along? Or will it even know who or what I am? It doesn't matter. I will locate it so the severed part can remember the snatch, the slice of its disfigurement. Perhaps then the arm will no longer be a phantom, but will take its own shape, grow its own muscle and bone, and its blood will pump from the loud singing that has found the purpose of its serenade. Amen. (Morrison 1992, 158-59)

7   Monique Wittig argues that the dialectical use of the term "Other" preserves the economy of the Same and deprives the said Other of subjecthood even before having gained it. Despite the multiplication of different categories of Otherness, she says, "[b]oth the figureheads of the dominators and of the dominated have adopted this point of view" and Otherness remains an essentialist position, defined solely in relation to the Same or the One.

In this regard, my retention of the term "Other" would seem to weaken somewhat my argument at this point. However, it would be premature in a discussion of the intersemiotic translation between bodies and texts, an area only just beginning to be theorized, to attempt to jettison all familiar language. Moreover, I have marked, where appropriate, the compromised nature of both the "Other" and the related concept of "the self," notions which continue to determine how we conceive of bodies.

We have seen previously that, caught between the sense we give to reality and the non-sense patriarchal reality constitutes for us, we are most often forced to adapt our lives to simultaneous translation of the foreign tongue.

Nicole Brossard
The Aerial Letter

My body writes a tongue with a warm breath. A silence, where I am. I recover my body. Marked noun in its place a woman's language emerging from not quite a country not quite a language not quite a voice that slips away zigzags bolts the stiffening.

France Théoret
The Tangible Word

The Reorganization of the Body:
"musing with mothertongue"

The body is not nature. The body is not a woman. The body is not a mute. No. The body is a persistent and perpetual translator. *Jouissance* ceaselessly circulates and recirculates pictogrammic, ideogrammic and phonetic signifiers so as to avoid congealing the body around a single organ, a single frozen drop of flesh. The body is not only a sum of its visceral organs but a series of contiguous libidinal surfaces and striations. The body is its own signifier. The body is a lifesize, mobile and audible pictogram.

"Musing with mothertongue," the poetic essay which follows the serial poem, glossary and photocollages in Daphne Marlatt's *Touch to My Tongue*,[1] elaborates upon the relation between language and body in her work. Marlatt has always evinced a strong drive to literalize the body. For her the issue is, given this body, how do we stay contained within it and not interpose our own ego between ourselves and that body?[2] How do we avoid constructing, or at least how do we from time to time puncture, or punctuate, the interior volume of a logocentric self which reduces the body to gross matter?

In the following passage from a 1988 interview, Marlatt talks about how her view of the relation between language and body led her, in her novel *Ana Historic,* to defer the seemingly inevitable lovemaking between the characters Annie and Zoe. She did not want the narrative's ending to be a conclusion, she says, but only another beginning:

> I suppose this has to do with where I place myself against Christianity, which has taught us to defer bliss to life after death. But language itself, especially writing, is another kind of deferral. In the humanist tradition it was thought to be a vehicle pointing to what was real beyond the writing. And we've now come to think of it very differently as a signifying process present to itself. To speak of what has been excluded from the world of literature, which is women's desire, and to make that present in a language of presence is a big challenge. (Williamson 1989, 52)

If writing is a signifying process present to itself alone (or, alternatively, deferred only from itself rather than from a transcendental signified), then the problem of how to speak of women's desire (largely absent from discourse, latent within the body) in such a writing is addressed by our desiring, deferring and deferred bodies. Just as writing refers to writing, so the desiring body, as, for example, in Marlatt's poetry, signifies itself. The desiring body, the body of *jouissance,* has its own compositions and positions. Desiring and loving bodies collect a history, a language and a skin of their own.

Because "my body does not have the same ideas I do" (Barthes 1975, 17), it must not be spoken of and represented in standard models of spoken and written composition only. Some of the methods feminist writers implement for addressing the absence of the body gendered as female within a language of presence are not to defer to phallogocentric authority, not to defer speaking or writing, and not to defer pleasure. To refuse to defer to the real and/or the transcendental signified is to position oneself *not* in logocentric presence but rather in the intervals between words, phonemes, gestures, arms, lips, pelvic bones, tongues, etc. It is to defer deferral. If, as Marlatt insists, we are simply not given the real out there, then there can be no absence pure and simple. This writing in the intervals between bodies and among body surfaces is what I call intersemiotic translation or 'writing under embrasure.'

The body cannot be divided from language, because language

is, as Marlatt writes, "a living body we enter at birth" (Marlatt 1984b, 45). Language shapes, configures and partially but not entirely determines our bodies. Our bodies are part language. Our physiological body parts are also grammatical organs, diagrammed, conjugated, and mobilized by cultural inscriptions. In bpNichol's phrase, syntax equals the body structure (Nichol 1985, 25-31).[3] Syntax is not identical with but equivalent to the body structure. Most assuredly though, for Marlatt language "does not stand in place of anything else, it does not replace the bodies around us" (Marlatt 1984b, 45). Language, in other words, is not *only* referential. The body of language is also our horizon, "placental, our flat land, our sea." Both *topos,* "place (where we are situated)", and trope, "body (that contains us),"[4] the flesh of language is the flesh of our world. Language as a living body envelops our lived world and lived body. As Marlatt said in 1974 with regard to Gertrude Stein's work, "Well, she sees language as a code. I dont want it to be a code. I want it to be the transmitting itself" (Bowering 1979, 68). Throughout her work Marlatt consistently demonstrates a concern for access to the physicality both of the body and of language. For her, articulation, especially by women writers, is "a visceral event" (68).

A crucial aspect of the physicality of language is what Marlatt calls its musicality. In "musing with mothertongue" she says that "language is first of all for us a body of sound" (Marlatt 1984b, 45). Language's physicality derives primarily from its oral/aural qualities. For babies, as we know, the world and their selves are not separate. The outside world is body as well. Children learn language nonreferentially because, as Marlatt insists, "language is literal. . . . Any word is a physical body. It's [sic] body is sound, so it has that absolute literal quality that sound has, which connects it up with sounds around it" (Bowering 1979, 69). For her, language is evocative rather than referential. "It can never be referential, because you simply arent given, in reality, that other out there" (79). It is only a gradual and lifelong process whereby we figure out "what the words are actually saying" (Marlatt 1984b, 45).

Language works by evocation, not invocation. Thought works by association. The physical bodies of words provoke each other into utterance by attraction along an associative, metonymic chain. Association is "a form of thought that is not rational but erotic

because it works by attraction" (45). Like attracts like. Even difference attracts liking. Words, like lovers, "call each other up, evoke
each other, provoke each other, nudge each other into utterance"
(45). The rhetoric of our thinking is erotic. Thus for Marlatt the
simile is more than a comparison between two objects using the
words 'like' or 'as.' In her view, words, phonemes and syllables like
one another.[5] She uses 'like' as a verb rather than as a preposition.

Marlatt also uses the fulcrum of the word 'like' not to subsume
one term by another but to highlight the metaphoricity of the body.
In common rhetorical usage, the tenor of a metaphor is the discourse or subject which the vehicle illustrates or illuminates.[6] A
comparative term is invoked to clarify, brighten, or render poetic a
primary term. The traditional definition and usage of the simile is
essentially Platonic in that two things, essentially unlike, are juxtaposed by virtue of a resemblance in a single aspect of their being.
In the simile it is forms which are analyzed and compared. The
traditional use of the simile thus reinforces metaphysics. In this
formal analysis there is no room for erotic attachments. However,
as Marlatt points out, the Germanic *lik-* refers to "body, form; like,
same" (45). Therefore the etymology of 'like' can be read as positing
a different (not an original) dynamic at work in similes.[7] The idea
of sameness is present in this new dynamic, but it is not necessarily
a sameness in the sense of an irreducible similarity of being, essence
or nature. It is sameness by virtue of the mutuality of attraction or
the pull of two or more bodies toward one another. Erotic attraction
is not always or even necessarily based on similarity: erotics is based
upon the play of both sameness *and* difference. Rather than producing analogy, this other kind of simile is based upon the physical
attractions of speech and the sounds of a given language or languages. Thus Marlatt might define the simile as the process of
attraction between two bodies (words as particles of language, or
human bodies) by virtue not of the fundamental similarity of a single
aspect of their being, and thus a reduction of the two to one, but
rather by virtue of their multiple and contingent physical, that is,
signifying, attributes.

Marlatt's erotics of rhetoric works to develop parallels between
the human body and the body of language without privileging either
term, tenor or vehicle, of that simile. In the following passage,

quoted in another context in "Unlimited Inc.orporation," Marlatt explores some of the attractions between our physical body and the material body of language[8] and in the process traces out familiar, forgotten and novel circuits of exchange between these two bodies:

> hidden in the etymology and usage of so much of our vocabulary for verbal communication (contact, sharing) is a link with the body's physicality: matter (the import of what you say) and matter and by extension mother; language and tongue; to utter and outer (give birth again); a part of speech and a part of the body; pregnant with meaning; to mouth (speak) and the mouth with which we also eat and make love; sense (meaning) and that with which we sense the world; to relate (a story) and to relate to somebody, related (carried back) with its connection with bearing (a child); intimate and to intimate; vulva and voluble; even sentence which comes from a verb meaning to feel. (*Touch to My Tongue*, 46)

As I have already argued, Marlatt does not invoke the serendipitous similarities between the language used to describe the body and that used to refer to language itself to transport us back to some ur-text, some utopian or matriarchal era, or to some original innocence of connection between body and language. Rather she uses this attraction between parts of the body and parts of speech to form new alliances. She translates, forging sense where there has been only non-sense, aspects of our lives which have been invisible to us because, as she says, "in a crucial sense we cannot see what we cannot verbalize" (Marlatt 1984b, 47).

When she draws an analogy between poetry as a form of verbal speech and lovemaking as a form of organ speech (Williamson 1985, 28), Marlatt is using the word 'speech' metaphorically in order to point to the signifying capacities of the body itself. In turn, this new awareness of the body's sign production rereads or unsettles that which we presently understand as verbal speech, poetry and texts. As readers, we must become oriented to traces of the body in the text. We must not assimilate these traces as metaphoric. As if we were reading a translation, which we are, an intersemiotic translation, we must not privilege only the target *text*. Instead we must read the marks, gestures and postures of the body too. Within this translation model, we must allow ourselves to be "lured beyond equivalence" to "a new skin."[9] The reader reading, like the writer writing, must climb into a pictogrammic body.

Marlatt's emphasis on sound and speech, though, does not place her solely within an oral poetics. She draws upon the lineage of poetry "which has evolved out of chant and song, in riming and tone-leading" (Marlatt 1984b, 45). However, her poetics also derives out of the prelinguistic and nonreferential significations of the child and the current gaps in our language vis-à-vis the inscription of women's bodies. Etymologies, which she uses liberally to generate her texts, depend upon dictionaries and literacy. Moreover, *Touch to My Tongue* includes photocollages not just as illustrations but as instructions in how to read the interlingual, intralingual and intersemiotic translations of the poem series. That is, Marlatt does not preconfigure the body as external to words nor as entirely coded by them either. She strives *not* to locate the body in either of these epistemes but instead to continue to translate between epistemes.[10] For her, just as the text metaphorizes or translates the body, so the body metaphorizes the text.[11] When body and text as two material substances or tissues are invited to attract, metaphorize and translate one another, different textual practices are initiated, and different bodies constructed.[12] The body is both translatable and untranslatable: translatable in this intersemiotic exchange between two material substances; untranslatable in that like a proper name or any other untranslatable word it transfers nothing except itself as pure signifier. The smooth and slippery body, like the proper name, announces paradoxically 'translate me' and 'don't translate me.'

In addition to sound, etymology is another force of attraction among words that allows various forms of translation to take place. Etymologies form the "history of verbal relations (a family tree, if you will) that has preceded us and given us the world we live in" (46). Indeed, Marlatt's translation poetics contains a genealogical component.[13] Language and its history of verbal relations, etymology, like our own mother's body, is "the given, the immediately presented, as at birth" (46-47). Hence language and the etymon are part of the phenomenological horizon of our lives, which is never really given (in the same way that etymologies do not allow us to time-travel back to a prelapsarian, maternal or matriarchal condition). As a feminist writer, Marlatt "take[s] issue with the given, hearing the discrepancy between what our patriarchally-loaded language bears (can bear) of our experience and the difference from it our experience bears out" (47). Because both history and language are constructions, says Marlatt, we can change the reality we live in: "We're not stuck in some authoritative version of the real" (Williamson 1985, 52).

Of course, one very important aspect of the authoritative version of the real which is also a function of translation is gender difference. Marlatt lists some of women's experiences which have been invisible to patriarchal language—gestation, menstruation, body cycles, breast-feeding, intimacy, and lovemaking. If the real is a construction, and if the body is the medium of the real, then through translation between the body and language the body can be reconstructed, re-realized, reorganized. Marlatt describes the act of writing as a translation between the prelinguistic given (this given can be equally the body or the external world) and language. She states that "Everything is prelinguistic, & as soon as you get into linguism, language, humming it, uttering it, you get back into the problem of translating. . . . Plus the fact that it's even more complicated than translating, because language has its own presence & its own insistences & its own connections, which you have to take into account all the time" (Bowering 1979, 58-59).

Here it is necessary to make a distinction between prelinguistic and presignification. The body conceived of in phallogocentric terms exists *prior* to language. However, it is accurate to say that the body is prelinguistic only if language in turn is conceived to be totally absorbed by or identical with its referential functions. The problem is that theories of signification based upon representation override the development of alternate theories of both the body's and language's signifying potential. We lack a vocabulary for thinking about different signifying practices of the body. Some, such as dance, have been culturally assimilated as art forms extraneous to language (although certain contemporary dance choreographers incorporate language into dance).[14] Others less assimilated, such as hysteria and lesbianism, can provide clues to alternative signifying practices. These not yet completely theorized practices are sources of information about the body.[15] Without retaining the phallogocentric body then, but without wholly discarding it either for the moment, since it is the only one most Western cultures recognize, we must add other signifying practices of the body to those such as speech and writing.

Just as certain experiences of women's bodies have been rendered invisible within patriarchal discourses, so aspects of the body of language have been equally overlooked or misread. In order to address these absences, Marlatt turns to a poetics of translation. In "Translating *MAUVE*: Reading Writing" Marlatt sums up what are for her the similarities between writing and translating. In either activity what she is doing is "sensing [her] way through the sentence, through (by means of) a medium (language) that has its own currents of meaning, its own drift. So that what one ends up saying is never simply one with, but slipping, in a fine displacement of, intention" (Marlatt 1989b, 27-28). To some measure, both body and language elude signification. When Marlatt writes about the call of feminist writers in Québec for a writing which returns us to the body and the "largely unverbalized, presyntactic, postlexical field it knows" (Marlatt 1984b, 48), she clarifies that what she means by this postlexical field is the site of the erotic attraction and proliferation of words. Within a translation poetics the term 'postlexical' can be read not only as pre-existing and exceeding the limits of the dictionary. Instead of a regression toward a dubious site of origins, it can also be read as a translation, using the etymological roots of words contained in the dictionary, toward a language which no one at present speaks or writes or performs but which perhaps subsequently we *will* be able to inhabit. In the meantime, experimental feminist writers such as Marlatt translate toward a target text and target language. Marlatt and writers like her write in a (m)other tongue or 'interlanguage,' a separate, yet intermediate, linguistic system situated between a source and a target language (Toury 1980, 71).

At this point in her poetic essay, the penultimate paragraph, where the figure of a new woman writer emerges, Marlatt accretes to the problem of "the given," which she had previously used solely in a phenomenological sense, the same associations Hélène Cixous borrows from Marcel Mauss on the logic of the gift (Cixous 1981, 252, 263-64). The given is not just that which pre-exists. It also partakes of the nature of a gift. Like Cixous's figure of the woman writer, Marlatt's "Alma," "inhabitant of language, not master, not even mistress, . . . in having is had, is held by it [language], what she is given to say. in giving it away is given herself . . ." (Marlatt 1984b, 48). Alma is the writer as translator. Her writing/translating works off of "that double edge where she has always lived, between the already spoken and the unspeakable, sense and non-sense" (48). Her source language is ordinary speech and writing, but her target language is not. This is translation between the articulate (the already spoken) and the inarticulate (the unspeakable), language (sense) and the body (non-sense), the vernacular and an unknown language, the mother tongue and a (m)other tongue. Marlatt touches on a similar point when she says in an interview "okay, interface is a better word for the meeting of what is knowable & what is unknowable. So all writing is a kind of translation. . . . From that which is inarticulate but sensed, deeply sensed. . . . In translation you're always making choices because you cant get the whole, the original, in fresh" (Bowering 1979, 57). There is always excess, spillage and loss of signifiers and signifieds in translation. At the present stage in her work, the seepage inherent to translation has become an intrinsic part of Marlatt's theory of language, writing and the body.[16] The gift is, paradoxically, this seepage, this loss, this drift.

In the final paragraph of "musing with mothertongue" *topos,* "place (where we are situated)," and trope, "body (that contains us)," have coalesced again:

> language thus speaking (i.e., inhabited) relates us, "takes us back" to where we are, as it relates us to the world in a living body of verbal relations. articulation: seeing the connections (and the thighbone, and the hipbone, etc.). putting the living body of language together means putting the world together, the world we live in: an act of composition, an act of birthing, us, uttered and outered there in it. (*Touch to My Tongue,* 49)

Language speaking is language inhabited by a body. This body in turn is situated in a network of verbal relations. Marlatt's use of the terms 'speaking,' 'articulation' and 'composition' are inconclusive with regard to the differentiation between writing and speech. When she refers to language speaking, she immediately modifies that term with 'inhabited' so as to insist on the bodily incarnation and articulatory or joining function that signifying in general enacts. The root of 'inhabit,' 'ghabh,' means, among other things, to give or receive, which in the context of Marlatt's modification creates a kind of equation such that to speak is to inhabit is to give or receive. Language speaking is language inhabiting our bodies, but there is always a surplus of the given, of both body and language. Language exceeds us. There are many languages and discourses which are unheard by us. In turn, the materiality of our bodies supercedes the referentiality of language.

Thus Marlatt's conception of the relation between the body and language is close to the idea of hysterical translation.[17] Unlike Cixous, who theorizes an alternate relation between body and language on the basis of the hysterical body, Marlatt's focus is the lesbian body. However, what is important to note in terms of the present discussion is that hysterical bodies and lesbian bodies alike disclose both the feminine erotogenic body and processes of signification in general.

Hysteria, as the name suggests, was traditionally thought of as a reorganization of the body caused by the wandering or displacement upwards of the womb. Freud's theory of somatic compliance, conversion or the transposition of psychic pain into physiological symptoms superceded this view. But hysterical *translation* is not the translation of psychic blockage or pain into bodily symptoms. It is not the expression or imitation of madness, or of femininity. Hysterical translation is the intersemiotic translation from one signifying system to another. Hysterical translation does not represent[18] the body as ill, pathological or diseased; it presents the body as pictogram. The movements of the hysterical body are "the perceptible appearance of a signifying system or a language that plays upon the visible" (David-Ménard 1989, 20). Insofar as it marks the physiological body off from the signifying but nonverbal body (21), hysteria is an anti-metaphysic, a new epistemology, a new ontology. Ironically then, hysteria thus rethought not as the picaresque wandering of the womb nor as a dutiful somatic compliance but as a translative process along the lines of the translation between writing and speech, for example, does in fact lead to a reorganization of the body.

Therefore when Cixous, for one, posits women writers as hysteric she is not suggesting that they are afflicted with that malady. Contemporary experimental women writers do not recapitulate the gestures of hysteria as illness, nor do they valorize this sense of hysterical illness. The woman writer is not the double of the classic hysteric, because the writer writes. Inasmuch as she writes, she may draw on the philosophies posed by the hysterics. The same is true of Marlatt's tracing the significations of the lesbian body. Just as Jean Martin Charcot found hysterics to be photogenic because of their play with the language of visibility, so Marlatt explores and translates the erotogenic 'organ speech' of the bodies of lesbian lovers. The erotogenic body is the literal body, but it is not the essentialist body we have inherited from Cartesian metaphysics. The erotogenic body is located in the spaces between signifiers. Between one kiss or embrace and the next. Literally, between two mouths.

For Marlatt, then, orality is not entirely tied to speech, conversation, the vernacular, or even whole words. She differentiates within and supplements the traditional model of signification.[19] Asked in an interview about the relation of writing to speaking in her work, she responds, "I think my writing is fairly oral":

> When I'm writing, I'm writing it as I'm hearing it. . . . But, I'm not too concerned with it on the page. When I was writing verse, when I was using the space of the page, then it would get in the way of the words coming out . . . . I'm concerned with how it sounds, with how you speak it, and how it can be heard. . . . What most intrigues me is what I think of as the sound body of the work. What kinds of sounds bounce off, echo off, call up other sounds. How the rhythms elongate or slow down, or suddenly pick up and run (Williamson 1985, 29).

Marlatt focuses on the sound body of language less for the sounds of speech than for the sheerly physical sounds of language—semiotic, prelinguistic or postlexic. Although she is concerned with speaking and hearing the vernacular in her work, she is more responsive to and absorbed by the purely material element of sound.

Marlatt's concern with the sonority of words and the materiality of the body is not incompatible though with composing on the typewriter. When George Bowering remarks in " 'Syntax Equals the

Body Structure' " that "you can almost bypass the body when you're composing on the typewriter, that it's the brain just using part of the body to get out onto the page" (Nichol 1985, 27), she objects, declaring that she does not feel that the body is not present in such compositional circumstances: "I always compose on a typewriter, and I don't feel that the body isn't there. In fact, I find that there's a kind of rush possible on the typewriter—because you can type that fast—that equates very definitely with certain body states" (27). The difference in opinion between Bowering and Marlatt on this point stems from the fact that he is working from a conventional distinction between oral and written forms, whereas she differentiates within the oral model.

Marlatt's project is to diffuse the mother tongue beyond and in excess of logocentric or patriarchal speech. Sensing her way through the sentence, she performs a bidirectional translation between the physical organs, senses and perceptions of the body and a language yet to be spoken by anyone. Moreover, by factoring in the signifying practices of bodies themselves, she diversifies orality and disperses signification beyond the privileged organs of the phallogocentric body to other corporeal surfaces. "Poetics," she writes, "is not a system of thought but a tactic for facing the silence" (Marlatt 1985a, 36). Instead of a strategy for hearing-oneself-speak, "poetics is a strategy for hearing" (38). Her poetics does not give a hearing to the evidence of the phallogocentric self but rather to "every comma, every linebreak, each curve thought takes touching nerve-taboo, the empty space where speech, constrained by the 'right form,' the 'proper word,' is gripped (passive voice) by silence" (38). Marlatt's poetics translates between the audible and the inaudible, the visible and the invisible, speech and writing, the body and language. Her poetics is not a method of composition as much as it is a way of translating the body, of composing and reorganizing it.

Marlatt's writing proposes that the mother tongue both is and is not our first language (which in fact is usually a father tongue spoken and transmitted to us by our mothers). She writes toward a (m)other tongue that will de-territorialize the phallogocentric body. She wants both to map other areas of the body with language and to translate the body literally into her texts. For Ezra Pound a 'periplum' was the geography "not as you would find it if you had a geography book and a map, but . . . as a coasting sailor would find it" (Pound 1934, 43-44). For Daphne Marlatt, the periplum is the body as mapped by the tongue in translation. Writing this (m)other tongue is a literal and a littoral translation.

> it moves mouth to ear (nipple to mouth), the fine stream
> that plays in time across a page, under pressure from all
> there is to say, so much we start again, starting from the
> left, starting from the silenced, body the words thrum.
> waiting to hear with all our ears. listening in, on . . .
> ("Listening In," 38)

Body Inc.

Notes

1   I am using the version of "musing with mothertongue" published in *Touch to My Tongue*. Page references are to that book. As the essay is quite short, and as my analysis proceeds through it in the order in which it is written, readers may not find it difficult to consult one of the two other published versions. The essay appeared independently in the first issue of the journal *Tessera* [in *Room of One's Own*, 8.4 (1984): 53-56] and in Dybikowski and others, eds., *In the Feminine: Women and Words/Les Femmes et les Mots, Conference Proceedings 1983*, pp. 171-74.

2   Here I am deliberately echoing American poet Charles Olson's statement that "Objectism is the getting rid of the lyrical interference of the individual as ego, of the 'subject' and his soul, that peculiar presumption by which western man has interposed himself between what he is as a creature of nature (with certain instructions to carry out) and those other creations of nature which we may, with no derogation, call objects" (Olson 1973, 156). In her work Marlatt considers this problem from the position of a western woman.

3   I discuss Marlatt's contribution to this discussion with bpNichol and George Bowering near the end of the present chapter.
     See also Marcel Mauss on what he calls 'body techniques.'

4   I am using the term 'trope' here in a very general way—as figure of speech. As Gérard Genette demonstrates, a figure is simply one signifier offered as the signified of another signifier. In actuality, both signifiers are merely signifiers. Neither can be legitimately claimed as the literal of the other. Both are literal signifiers (Genette 1982, 47). Hence I am using this sense of the word 'trope' to underscore the literalness of the body in Marlatt's writing.
     This sense of 'trope' as two signifiers in a relationship of otherness parallels the relation between two languages, bodies or words.

5   See Marlatt's comments on metaphor in Bowering, "Given This Body," 43.

6   C. Hugh Holman, *A Handbook to Literature,* based on the original by William Flint Thrall and Addison Hibbard, 3rd ed. (Indianapolis: Odyssey Press, 1972) 525.

7   This is not to suggest that there is a prior or original meaning to the word hidden in etymology that authorizes such interpretation. What I am suggesting is that Marlatt uses such a root to think otherwise, to translate beyond metaphysics.

8   We must remember that the word 'body' is just that. 'Body' is no more referential to the human body than it is, for example, to the body of language.

9   Marlatt quotes part of Colin Browne's letter to her in "Translating MAUVE." Browne had written to her asking whether she would like to

participate in a translation project involving the work of Québecoise writer Nicole Brossard. He gave the series the name 'transformances,' ostensibly to distinguish what he wanted from more traditional and faithful interlingual translations. Marlatt quotes one of his definitions of 'transformance' as " 'reading reading, writing writing, writing reading—that flicker pan-linear, lured beyond equivalence: a new skin' " (Marlatt 1989b, 28).

10   This may also partially account for the current disagreements about her work and the censuring responses to it of critics who are searching for consistency and a purity of poststructuralist, reader-response or Marxist conscience. I am thinking of articles by, respectively, Tostevin, Davey and Harasym.

Marlatt read Maurice Merleau-Ponty in the late sixties, very early in her career, yet she does not use his term 'flesh,' as it is usually translated. She retains the word 'body.' Thus she avoids placing her work within a strictly phenomenological poetics either, acknowledging that, like Merleau-Ponty, we are still struggling with Descartes and the mind-body problem.

11   In Marlatt's *Rings* (1971), for example, a long poem about her pregnancy and the birth of her son, the title and overall shape, form or design of that long poem metaphorizes psychic confusion as well as various literal rings (wedding ring, the ring of the cervix, the cyclical rhythms of women's bodies).

12   Here I am using 'metaphorize' and 'translate' in a similar way. Both terms contain the sense of 'to transport' or 'carry across.' I am letting them float together for the moment in order to invoke Barbara Freeman's work on Cixous's metaphorization of the body and Gérard Genette's work on the metaphor as one signifier masquerading as the signified of the other.

13   Just as the movement between languages for poet Fred Wah involves primarily intralingual translation as a substitute for interlingual translation between English and Chinese (a language which he does not know), the translation in Marlatt's poetry is also intralingual from English to English. Wah's translation poetics emerges from a desire to connect with his *father;* Marlatt's translations using etymologies take on a new importance in *How Hug a Stone,* the first book in which she begins to deal with her *mother's* life as an immigrant and with what she has inherited from her.

14   See Elizabeth Dempster's article "Women Writing the Body: Let's Watch a Little How She Dances" for a discussion of the dancing body as a locus of signifying practices. Tracing a history of modern dance, Dempster argues that for postmodern choreography "The body was no longer to be trained to the task of interpreting or illustrating something other than its own material reality. Postmodern dance does not present perfected, ideal or unified forms, nor bodies driven by inner imperatives, but bodies of bone, muscle and flesh speaking of and for themselves" (Dempster 1988, 46).

15   For a critique of representation, especially as it relates to translation and the body, see my article "The Body as Pictogram: Rethinking Hélène Cixous's *écriture féminine*," *Textual Practice*. 6(2): 225-46.

16   See Marlatt's use of the metaphor of seepage in her account of "Translating MAUVE."

17   As Jacques Derrida observes in "Roundtable on Translation": "When one speaks of hysteria, of oneiric or hysterical translation, one is speaking of translation in [Roman] Jakobson's third sense, the passage from one semiotic system to another: words-gestures, words-images, acoustic-visual, and so forth (Derrida 1985b, 108).

18   Hysterical translation does not re-present the body in the sense of presenting it over again, a second time. As David-Ménard argues, the hysterical body itself thinks (David-Ménard 1989, 12). Her book is very helpful on the ways in which a pervasive dualism conditions Freud's theorization of hysteria.

19   As Marlatt suggests in "Writing our Way Through the Labyrinth," writing, unlike reading, seems to her to be phallic, singular, proprietory, and self- rather than other-directed. As she says, "writing can scarcely be for women the act of the phallic signifier" (Marlatt 1985b, 49). Women, she suggests, are "lost" inside of the labyrinth of language. We must "(w)rite [the word itself is an intralingual translation] our way . . . in intercommunicating passages" (49).

THE PROMISE OF TRANSLATION

The person who becomes a writer is a person who starts to notice the language itself instead of what it signifies. Language is a problem very early for the potential writer. In my own case, I can remember different stages of the problem. My parents were bilingual in English and German, but they stopped speaking German the day I was born, because they wanted me to be assimilated and totally English-speaking; they were marvellously successful—I learned no German, maybe two curse words. And there's a sense of guilt in me about that silence that my birth occasioned. Some of the kids in my own generation grew up bilingual and it mystified me completely that they had this other alien tongue. That no doubt contributed to my sense of language as a visible rather than an invisible thing.

Robert Kroetsch
Labyrinths of Voice

The Promise of Translation

The fragments and musings of Robert Kroetsch's essay "For Play and Entrance: The Contemporary Canadian Long Poem" weave in and around a series of unspoken questions as to the nature and status of the promise. If a given language is ours but not 'originally' or uniquely, and if it is a language imposed by, and therefore largely indistinguishable from, the language of the colonial powers which suppressed our or our neighbour's familial, ethnic, tribal, provincial, or group tongue, then how do we negotiate and sign a social contract in this language? Can we make a promise in a foreign language? In what language(s) can we compose and sign our own Constitution? How do we live up to the promises of the postcolonial contract, those promises made not to the Fatherland but to ourselves and on our own behalf? To whom are we promising in this language which is neither native nor foreign? And how do we draft a poetic license in such a language?

The promise, as we have seen in "Translation, Infidelity and the Sadness of the Sad Phoenician," is performative. It does what it says it does, even if the acts trailing in its wake are not carried out (translated) to the letter. The promise enacts the real. In addition, whether spoken or written, the promise also brings with it a performative signature effect. The signature is a synonym for 'yes.' 'Yes' has no meaning other than that it is an answer to the demand or desire of an Other. 'Yes' is the end to a monologue; even 'no' implies 'yes' in this respect, since it says 'yes' to the Other even as it withholds its affirmation to a deed. 'Yes,' then, means 'yes, yes,' a double 'yes.'[1]

By working in the delay and deferral between the failure or impossibility of the Roman translation of Greek and the parallel dilemma in postcolonial Canada with regard to the languages of the so-called founding nations France and England, translation poetics foregrounds the differences between and among languages. Unhiding the hidden, then, is translation. The radical process of rooting the borrowed word in authentic experience is translation. But does translation poetics pronounce 'yes' or 'no' to language?

Because a writer's commitment is to language, the problem of promising in a foreign language is very complex. In an essay called "The Art of Translation," Timothy Brennan compares the narrative strategies of postcolonial writers Gabriel García Marquez and Salman Rushdie. In the following passage, he describes the position of the postcolonial writer with regard to the language of the colonizers:

> As he attributes his choice of form to the inheritance of European colonisation, García Marquez wilfully inverts the common neo-colonial dilemma of having to write in the language of the former colonisers. For it is not a question of a language involuntarily accepted but of an entire artistic outlook voluntarily assumed. The logic behind this new emphasis is plain. It places responsibility for the present on the only ones today capable of mastering the situation, instead of reliving the sins of the past. By proclaiming that his discourse derives from imperialism's early myth-makers, he envisions an influence so deep that it infuses all thought. But at the same time, the influence is *their own* possession, and therefore capable of being transformed for constructive purposes. The power of the former rulers is in fact diminished, for the conqueror himself has apparently been conquered by a reality which he is powerless to describe in any way other than the language of fantasy. . . .

> Both García Marquez and Rushdie in this way temper
> and subvert the routine appeals by writers of anti-colonial
> commitment to 'native' discourse by showing not only the
> inevitability but the benefits of what has been left behind.
> Their discourse, instead of telling a story reviling Europe-
> ans for their dishonourable past, stylistically alludes to that
> past and appropriates it for their own use. (Brennan 1989,
> 68-69)

Writing in the language of the colonizers García Marquez and
Rushdie say 'yes' to that language. In saying 'yes,' however, they do
not affirm or accept their colonization; instead they appropriate it,
art and artifact, as their own. They translate intralingually, and this
act of translation says, in effect, both 'yes' and 'no' to the language
and terms of the contract of colonization.

Translation, then, is a way of promising in two languages at
once. A contra-diction that speaks 'yes' and 'no' in the same breath,
translation redistributes the promise and the contract. Derrida,
reading through the screen of Walter Benjamin's transcendental
language in the essay "The Task of the Translator," does not use the
kind of political language Brennan uses, but his conclusions are
nonetheless similar. In the following passage, he interprets what
Benjamin means by the 'language of the truth' and 'the pure
language':

> Translation promises a kingdom to the reconciliation
> of languages. This promise, a properly symbolic event
> adjoining, coupling, marrying two languages like two
> parts of a greater whole, appeals to a language of the truth
> ("Sprache der Wahrheit"). Not to a language that is true,
> adequate to some exterior content, but to a true tongue,
> to a language whose truth would be referred only to itself.
> It would be a matter of truth as authenticity, truth of act
> or event which would belong to the original rather than to
> the translation, even if the original is already in a position
> of demand or debt. (Derrida 1985a, 200)

The covenant, contract or promise of a people among themselves
breached, the national language or languages swallowed, the voice
and the breath taken away in the act of colonization, there is in the
failure to translate an attendant loss of authenticity of act or event.

The consolation for the absences introduced by colonization[2] is, to use a word particularly resonant in the Canadian postcolonial context, the accord of tongues. In translation "one language gives to another what it lacks, and gives it harmoniously, this crossing of languages assures the growth of languages. . . . This perpetual reviviscence, this constant regeneration (*Fort-* and *Auf-leben*) by translation is less a revelation, revelation itself, than an annunciation, an alliance and a promise" (Derrida 1985a, 202). The promise is to language: that it will continue to be reborn, that it will survive. What the affinity, kinship or coupling of two or more languages aims at is "the being-language of the language, tongue or language *as such,* that unity without any self-identity, which makes for the fact that there are languages and that they are languages" (201). The postcolonial writer writing in the language of the colonizer is, in fact, translating. As Kroetsch predicts, "One nice thing that has happened to English is its own unravelling. I'm sure India is going to have a new version of English that will almost have to be translated" (Neuman and Wilson 1982, 119). He postulates that the oral tradition plays an important role in intralingual translation. Speech, he believes, overrides much of the rigid codification and inauthenticity which writing can impose upon language. Through such intralingual translation, authenticity—the truth of act or event—is restored to language or languages. Translation, in other words, revivifies the promise.

Translation, for Kroetsch, is a compositional method, a poetics. Perhaps more than any other signifying practice, translation practices the *différence,* deferral and delay between signifiers. This play of differance is foregrounded both in Kroetsch's musings about the vernacular and in his notes on the contemporary long poem in Canada. He metaphorizes delay and deferral as foreplay to the act of making love. Poets are compared to lovers—lovers of the Other, lovers of language. Following upon the excerpt from bpNichol's *The Martyrology,* which opens Kroetsch's essay on the long poem by translating, intralingually, the words 'purpose' and 'porpoise' and thematizing the act of writing, Kroetsch sets up the fundamental problematic of the long poem, namely, the search for a method of delay which would replace narrative, no longer a tenable method for contemporary poets:

> In love-making, in writing the long poem—delay is both—delay is both technique and content. Narrative has an elaborate grammar of delay. The poets of the twentieth century, in moving away from narrative, abandoned (some willingly, some reluctantly) their inherited grammar. Poets, like lovers, were driven back to the moment of creation; the question, then: not how to end, but how to begin. Not the quest for ending, but the dwelling at and in the beginning itself. (Kroetsch 1989b, 117-18)

The poem of the failure of system, grid, monism, cosmologies, and inherited story is the long poem. The long poem is the poem of the failure of the promises inherent in system and grid. The length of the long poem allows for the exploration of our "disbelief in belief." The long poem, therefore, promises failure, and delivers on its promise, as much as a promise can ever be fulfilled. That is to say, the long poem does succeed. "The failure of language becomes its own grammar of delay" (Kroetsch 1989b, 120).

Given his metaphor of the writing of the long poem as love-making, it is significant that the first example Kroetsch cites of a love poem is Phyllis Webb's *Naked Poems*. In this short long poem, the lovers are lesbian, not heterosexual.[3] Of course, and Frank Davey has noted this as well, in lovemaking it is the heterosexual male who sometimes must delay orgasm, not necessarily his partner nor, we might add, the lesbian lover. Davey writes:

> Kroetsch argues in ["For Play and Entrance"] that this impulse to prolong is a wish to delay; in this argument he reads the energy of the long poem as sexual energy, and delay as postponement of a terminating orgasm. This theory, in my subjective view, has unhappy implications for the life-long poem (not to mention the life itself should it bear any close relationship to the poem), and contains at least a hint of exclusively male perspective; not surprisingly, it is linked by Kroetsch to a view of the Canadian long poem as a narrative of disappointment and failure. I simply don't see the long poem this way; for me, in Kroetsch's metaphor, it requires recurring orgasm, movement from surprise to surprise, is prolonged not only to delay but to continue, it anticipates more rather than postpones the most. Individual sections of the poem can culminate, come briefly to rest, as well as lead into new

> moments in the larger work. This is how I read *Allophanes,*
> Kroetsch's own *Seed Catalogue,* Dudek's *Atlantis*—as mov-
> ing in the joy of continuing and varied culmination rather
> than in a fear of ending. (Davey 1983, 185)

Davey's reservations about Kroetsch's model of delay are worth taking into account. If delay and deferral are not always the procedure or protocol in lovemaking, then Kroetsch's analogy between lovemaking and writing the long poem does not always hold.

The referential validity of the analogy to actual sexual technique, however, is less important than its function within the text of Kroetsch's essay. That is to provide an example of "A method, then, and then, and then, of composition; against the 'and then' of story" (Kroetsch 1989b, 120). There is no single method for composing the contemporary Canadian long poem. Kroetsch's multiple metaphors for writing the long poem—lovemaking, fishing, archaeology, birthing, phenomenological erasure, travelling, doubling, etc.—are testimony to this fact.[4] As Kroetsch says, "The story as fragment *becomes* the long poem: the story becomes its own narrative; i.e., our interest is in, not story, but the act of telling the story" (120). The story has always already been told; what grips us now is the act of its telling. Kroetsch says of Fred Wah's *Pictograms from the Interior of B.C.:* "The pictograms are a language and a story; at once, a language and a story. But we have lost the connection" (122). We have lost the code that will allow us to translate the language of the pictograms into story. Thankfully, therefore, the language cannot be overwhelmed by narrative. Instead translation can take place over and over and over without limit. We are no longer so entranced by the story; rather we are entranced, admitted, into the composition of the poem and the process of translation. Story is delayed while translation is performed jointly by writer and reader.

In the same way that ordinary interlingual translation is a method, of which a translation is the product or result, so the long poem is "A method, then, and then, and then, of composition" (Kroetsch 1989b, 120), as well as the composition itself. This is not just semantic serendipity. Unlike representational aesthetics, in which the thing represented is *not* the thing as such but a linguistic substitute and the reader reads to decode the meaning of the substitution, the process of converting one system of signs into another in translation *is* the translation. Source text and target text are both texts. Process is not subordinate to product. A translation is never final, definitive or exhaustive. This accounts, in part, for the frequent presence of palimpsests in long poems. The text being translated is often visible on the same or the facing page. Writer and reader collaborate in the ongoing translation. The time of writing and the time of reading are allowed to overlap.

Delay and deferral, let us not forget, are not just sexual, but temporal, procedures. As the story goes, translation came into being as a deferral of cosmology, grid, system, and tower: architects constructing the Tower of Babel arose from their beds one morning to discover their grand scheme deferred and to learn the necessity to translate. The long poem does not attempt to come full circle by returning to any 'originary' translation, since the journey of the return to origins is also part of a cosmology. Both Kroetsch and Davey see the temporal duration of the long poem as a deflection of the old cosmologies of apocalypse and ending. The opening paragraph of Davey's essay dwells on the time of the long poem:

> The first sign we see in the long poem is its length, promising to the reader that its matter is large in depth or breadth. Its length also speaks about time—that the writer will take his time, engage time, encompass its passage. Unlike the collection of 'occasional' poems, it says that time is not a series of discrete and unique occasions, but is large, can be viewed as large, can be apprehended, measured and entered, that there is time—time at least to read a long poem. There is even in the length of the long poem an announcement of futurity—in the commitment of the poet to enter a continuing structure . . , in the exemplary motion of line following line, page following page, section opening into section. (Davey 1983, 183)

One of the large matters engaged by the long poem is "that there is time." More so than self-reflexivity, the 'frame' of the long poem is its length. The promise of the long poem is the promise of time. In Canada, says Kroetsch, we embrace "the nightmare and the welcome dream of Babel" (Kroetsch 1989b, 71). Lovers, we embrace the promise and the time of translation. Translators, we say 'yes,' we sign, we authenticate our own 'true' tongue; and we say 'no,' we perpetuate the non-accord of tongues and the survival of language itself.

RENÉ DESCARTES'S VALORIZATION of reason and method as a universal language mimes the Babelian scene. He wrote his *Discours de la méthode* in French, the vernacular, rather than in Latin, the 'universal' language, in order to argue that natural reason and method constitute the true universal language. As Derrida shows, this choice was not the subversive gesture it might appear.[5] Within the French juridico-political context of the time during which he was writing his treatise, Descartes's act "follows the monarchist state tendency" and "the direction of power and reinforces the installation of French law" (Derrida 1984a, 104). It was in the interests of the French state to extend the usage and influence of the French language. Under the guise of making a concession toward French as the maternal tongue, the nation's subjects were moved "into the trap of their *own language,* as if the king were saying to them: in order to be subjects of the law—and of the king—you will finally be able to speak your French mother tongue . . ; it is as if one gave them back to the mother in order to better subjugate them to the father" (99). However, at the same time as French was being extended, the provincial dialects were being abolished. Thus, the French language moved into the space vacated by Latin. Derrida illustrates:

> . . . to plead in favour of a dialect, as to plead any cause in justice, *translation was necessary;* you had to learn French. Once you had learned French, the claim of dialects, the 'maternal' reference, was destroyed. Try to explain to somebody who holds both power and the power of law that you want to preserve your language. You would have to learn his to convince him. Once you have appropriated the language of power, for reasons of rhetorical and political persuasion, once you master it well enough to try to convince or to vanquish, you are in turn vanquished in advance and convinced of being wrong. The other, the king, has demonstrated through the fact of *translation,* that he was right to speak his language and to impose it on you. By speaking to him in his language, you acknowledge his law and authority, you prove him right, you countersign the act that proves him right over you. A king is someone

who is able to make you wait or take the time to learn his
language to claim your rights, that is, to corroborate his.
(Derrida 1984a, 99-100)

Descartes's strategy of writing in French, in addition to securing a
certain readership in the foreign courts where French was fashion-
able, served the interests of a pedagogy aimed, as his letters reveal,
at feeble minds and women (Derrida 1984a, 104).

Universal reason is designed to bypass both the paternal,
written language of Latin and the maternal or 'natural' spoken
languages. Descartes attempts both to sever the dead hand of Latin
and to excise the speaking tongue and with it corporeality in
general. His manoeuvres efface writing, speech, the body, and sexual
difference. As Derrida writes:

> Order, the straight and essential path, that which goes
> from what is less easy to what is easier, would be an
> *intelligible* order, hence 'desexed', without a body. The
> necessary passages in the order of demonstration (the
> doubt of sensible things, the *I think, I am, God exists,* etc.)
> are sexually neuter or indifferent. The *cogito* is related, in
> its thinking as in its utterance, in the grammar of its
> sentence, to a subject which bears no sexual mark, because
> it is a *res cogitans* and not a body. As always, this neutrali-
> zation produces ambiguous effects. It opens up for women
> access to a universal community and to philosophy (which
> one might consider as progress); but the cost is a neutrali-
> zation of sexual difference, which is now relegated to the
> side of the body, inessential to the act of the *cogito,* to
> intuition, to reason, to the natural light, etc. The subjec-
> tivity of the subject which is thus founded in the Cartesian
> movement would remain--whether it is a question of the
> body or of language--sexually undifferentiated. . . .
>
> . . . In this battle for the French language and against
> Latin and the School, the place of women is essential, at
> least in certain social spheres, and first of all at Court.
> Because they have never been taught Latin and the disci-
> pline of the School, women are supposed to have a better
> rapport with the mother tongue, a better feel for language.
> They are in short the true guardians of the vernacular.
> (Derrida 1984a, 111-12)

Derrida suggests that the extension of natural reason to women paradoxically neutralizes sexual difference. It is to enlist women, like the common people whose dialects were being outlawed at this time, in an enterprise which erases at once their difference and their diversity among themselves. Furthermore, insofar as 'woman' represents corporeality, the desexed, nondifferentiated inclusion of women acts as a supplement to the privilege accorded the *cogito* at the body's expense.

As opposed to universal reason, translation, in the sense I have developed throughout this book, can *only* be practiced by the body. Translation, tongue tied to the signifier, can only pass through the body of the translator. A body, but not some imaginary universal body, not a body extrapolated on the basis of the idea of universal reason. Not any body and every body. Translation will not pass through the 'pure,' 'universal' language of reason and its body, but only through the physical, temporal, particular body and its ability to write and speak in more than one language. This body does not succumb to 'pure language,' any more than it does to 'pure reason.' The body translates between *given* languages, mothers' tongues and vernaculars.

> So i bought rock 'n roll records, put away my mother's copies of Keats and Tennyson, wore white bucks and jeans and pencil-line skirts. I loved the principles of democracy as we argued them out in school, loved Canadian history with its romance of the coureurs de bois, the Métis uprising, Simon Fraser tracing rivers, Pauline Johnson and Emily Carr recording a culture as exotic as any Malay kampong's—yet here it had something to say about the plants and rocks and animals we lived and would go on living among. (Marlatt 1984a, 221)

WHEREAS IN THEIR ESSAYS on the long poem Kroetsch and Davey metaphorize the writing of the long poem as the time and timing of lovemaking, Daphne Marlatt's notes on her long poem *Steveston,* "Long as in Time? Steveston," configure time itself as inspiration. For Marlatt as well, "the long poem takes on time, proposes an open future as it embraces a closed past, successive, linear" (Marlatt 1979a, 316). She did not set out to write a long poem, she says, so much as to "explore the place Steveston through a lengthening line. Hearing it push time—that came first." She relates the double sense of the word 'inspire' (breathing in and breathing upon or into, outward) to taking the time for a deep breath, time to be. To inspire is to take time and to take time on. Time is the body breathing and living in the world.

Steveston engages time in the particulars of a place, not a representative place but a particular Japanese-Canadian fishing village on the west coast of British Columbia prior to 1974. "The world I was writing was & is a world I in the company of everyone could continue to live in: creation, goes on being created as writing enacts it." Immersed in the particulars of the place and taking her time, poet and world permeate one another. Her literal breathing, her aliveness in her body and in the world, is her inspiration.[6] She positions herself, in her body, as a translator between inner and outer. Her body as translator is the pivotal point in her world and in her work.

In a recent essay on translation, Marlatt writes that "Translation has always stood in an intimate relationship to writing for me, not the same but similar to, and it is this shade of difference . . . that is exactly the area . . . that the process of translation works. . . . For me translation is about slippage and difference, not the mimesis of something solid and objectified out there" (Marlatt 1989b, 27). Translation works (in) the area of *différance*. In both writing and translation, "what one ends up saying is never simply one with, but slipping, in a fine displacement of, intention" (28). Marlatt's terms— difference, displacement, slippage—are comparable to Kroetsch's 'delay' and 'deferral' and Davey's 'prolongation.' Each points to the play of *différance* at the root of the composition of the contemporary Canadian long poem.

As we have seen, *différance* deconstructs the conventions of mimesis and representation, which typically use the bodies of others, often though not always those of women, as a supplement. As Sherry Simon says, "Both women and translators are the 'weak' terms in their respective hierarchies, sexual and literary" (Homel and Simon 1988, 52). Thus the drift and slippage inherent in translation are important to Marlatt as a feminist writer. The doubling involved in translation—"there are two minds (each with its conscious and unconscious), two world-views, two ways of moving through two different languages" (Marlatt 1989b, 28)—is compounded when, as in the case of Marlatt translating Nicole Brossard's *MAUVE,* the two writers involved are "aware of the displacement that occurs between their own experience as women and the drift that is patriarchally loaded in their language." Then, Marlatt says, you have both drift and resistance, immersion and subversion, working together. Moreover, her translation of *MAUVE* involves the interlingual translation of a text which is composed, in part, as an intralingual translation: "Meaning operates strangely in [*MAUVE*], seeping from one phrase to others around it, leaking back and forth between fragments, definitely not progressing in linear fashion." This is the translation of one interlanguage into another.

The words Marlatt uses—the excess, slippage, drift, leakage, stain, bruise, and curve of translation—reflect the 'interference' of the bodies of the two women in translation. For Marlatt, translation takes place not only between two languages and two texts but between two tongues, two mouths. Moreover, the mouths of women speak of "another real and another (dorsal) mouth" (Marlatt 1989b, 29).[7] The relationship of one mouth to another (those of the self and the Other, the translator and the other writer) doubles that between "the living body and its mental impress," that divergence of the body from its virtual image, especially the body of woman because it has been "much imaged." This "resistance" of the body has been analyzed by Elizabeth Grosz. As she suggests:

> The body can thus be seen not as a blank, passive page, a
> neutral ground of meaning, but as an active, productive,
> 'whiteness' [sic] that constitutes the writing surface as
> resistant to the imposition of any or all patterned arrange-
> ments. It has a texture, a tonus, a materiality that is an
> active ingredient in the messages produced. It is less like
> a blank, smooth, frictionless surface, a page, and more like
> a copper-plate to be etched.

The Cartesian valorization of reason as a universal language reduces the body to a symptom of the self and aligns that body-symptom with the symbolic, social order. As Andrea Nye explains in her feminist reading of the history of the ideal form of rationality, logic:

> Logic proclaims itself the unreadable language, the lan-
> guage which has detached itself from confusion and pas-
> sion, the language which has transcended natural
> language embedded in sensual lives, mutably imprinted
> with social, economic, or personal concerns. The logician
> does not speak; he does not tell the truth; he exhibits it.
> All vestiges of his speaking voice are transcended, all
> reference to his situation, to his sex, his place in time or
> space. Logic is the perfect transparency of a language
> which does not need to be read. (Nye 1990, 4)

Nye's description of logic and the logician sounds uncannily like descriptions of the "logic" and bodies of hysterics.

Against this abstraction and symptomatization of the body, Grosz and Marlatt view the body as 'intextuated' (Grosz) and resistant to, rather than totally compliant with, social inscriptions.[8] This is not to suggest, however, that they set the body up as a counter-universal against 'universal reason.' Feminist writers are not simply reversing the Cartesian mind-body binary, as anti-essentialists claim. It makes no more sense to say that the body is a universal than to say that reason is. However, by factoring translation, writing, and other signifying practices through the body, instead of only through the signifying systems always already comprehended by (because constitutive of) consciousness—representation and mimesis—the body can be reinscribed and new accents heard.

The promise of translation for Marlatt is multifaceted. For feminist writers, the notion of fidelity—the fidelity of language to event in the promise, in marriage, and in translation—is problematic. Against fidelity, Marlatt posits excess, slippage, difference, leakage, and so on. Unfaithful translation, translation unfaithful to the traditional translation contract, provides a method for deconstructing the Cartesian 'universal reason' which has operated to erase her body's differences, to alienate its drives and significations, and to subject her to the Law of the Father. The liquid hydraulics of translation (leakage, seepage) supplant the mechanics of representation and mimesis.[9] Translation involves her in an intimate, dialogic relation with an Other. In the words of Susanne de Lotbinière-Harwood and Nicole Brossard, " 'I am already a translation by being *bilingue,* I am already a translation by being lesbian feminist, I am already a translation by being a woman' " (quoted by Mezei 1988, 49).

I have been suggesting that translation is a method opposed to method, a kind of anti-method method. It is now possible to modify that phrase. Translation is not a method in the Cartesian or common sense of the term, not even an anti-method. Rather translation is a poetics. Although the parallel is instructive in terms of understanding the nature and extent of their project, feminist writers are *not* repeating Descartes's gesture of writing in the vernacular. They do not write in some universal feminine or maternal language, nor do they seek to invent one. Furthermore, they do not write *in* the (m)other tongue either, since that language does not exist as a language independent unto itself and is instead an interlanguage. They write toward an Other language, the language, that is, both of another body than the one Western cultures have inherited from Descartes and the language of an Other's body. Their inspiration is in the interpenetration and permeability between the particulars of the intextuated body and the lived world (which is not necessarily the so-called 'real' world, or the world of 'real' men). Neither text nor body is the site of origins. The site of origins is endlessly displaced, though translation continues to take place. Since transcendental signifiers will not translate, the phallus translates itself out in feminist translation poetics. It no longer stands as the signifier which governs all other signifiers, organizing bodies, both masculine and feminine bodies, according to its drives.

> . . . or when you arrived in China in 1916 only four years old unable to speak Chinese and later in the roaring twenties when each time Grampa gambled away your boat passage so you didn't get back to Canada until 1930 languageless again with anger locked up in the immigration cells on Juan de Fuca Strait . . . (Wah 1985b, 69)

FRED WAH'S TRANSLATION POETICS is connected very closely with genealogy, ethnicity, the death and absence of his father, and memory. By virtue of the premature death of his father, Wah finds himself in the position of heir and survivor in a genealogy. In reply to Lola Lemire Tostevin's questions about tracing his ancestry back almost exclusively through his male parent, he explains that he has written far more about his father than his mother because his father died but his mother is still alive and because his father's story is more exotic. Tostevin probes to discover why he would consider the Chinese element of his background more exotic than the Swedish on his mother's side. Wah replies:

> More exotic because it's more mysterious. The story around my grandfather and father is more mysterious than the story around my mother and her parents from Sweden. That's a fairly clear story—European move to Canada, etc. . . . But my Chinese grandfather untypically married an English woman. Also when I was a kid in elementary school, we had to fill out these forms on registration day and one of the things we had to put down was our racial origin and the teacher told me to put down "Chinese." We weren't allowed then to put down "Canadian." That wasn't considered a racial origin. It's illegal now to ask for anyone's racial origin in Canada, but at that time you wrote down where your father came from. It had nothing to do with the mother. (Tostevin 1988a, 43; ellipsis is Tostevin's)

Wah goes on to remind Tostevin that the last section of *Waiting for Saskatchewan* is called "Father/Mother Haibun," in which he "intentionally tried to engage some of the mother stuff partly as a way of exorcising this father obsession and also as a way of moving towards dealing with the mother thing because I am half Swedish." Where this has taken him, he says, is to his grandmothers, particularly the English woman who married his Chinese grandfather. He has, in his answer, in the course of talking about his female ancestors, returned to the father.

In the Canadian context, however, Wah's surname is not only the privileged signifier of the name and authority of the father. The surname 'Wah' is also a prime signifier of 'ethnic' identity and marginalization. Born and raised in Canada by a Chinese father and Swedish mother, and carrying a Chinese name, Wah confesses to having little idea what race or ethnicity feel like. He says he does not know what it feels like to feel 'Chinese.' It is important to realize, though, that Wah's father tongue is not a single or unitary language. His father, born in Canada and English speaking, was sent to China at age four to be educated. Having been separated from his family and plunged into the Chinese language just after acquiring English, he remained in China until as a young man he was finally returned to Canada, no longer speaking or understanding any English. His father's radical linguistic estrangement complicates the alliance of Fred Wah's father tongue with the Lacanian 'name of the Father.' Part of the mystery of the father's story for Wah lies in the fact that his father tongue is inaccessible, foreign, other, displaced. In effect, Wah's father tongue is a kind of mother tongue. His memories of his father—cooking Chinese food for his children, the rhythms and body movements of work in his café, the click of dominoes in games played with other Chinese men, his signature brush cut, Wah's recent investigations of his own unspecific and unnamed anger he feels has to do with his father's exile from language —are similar, if not identical, to the kind of bodily experiences Julia Kristeva associates with the semiotic. Wah's translations of his proper name help to heal the wound inflicted two generations ago by immigration and the translation of his name from Chinese into English. 'Wah' functions in Wah's texts as a cartouche allowing the son to translate in the direction of his Chinese genealogy and thereby to release some of the repressed or otherwise previously inaccessible bodily experiences and emotions associated with his inheritance of that genealogy and the 'ethnic' identity imposed by immigration into a foreign culture.

CAN WE MAKE A PROMISE in a foreign language? No, but we can always try to translate. Contemporary Canadian long poems promise to take time, to defer endings, to delay apocalypse until that ending is rewritten and changed. But the long poem is not simply a postponement of the end of history. It is a technology for survival, for living and for living on. It is through translation that this promise of living on is carried out. If it is true that the Homeric epic poem comprised the encyclopaedia and pedagogy of the Greeks (a manual for shipbuilding, navigation, etc.), then the contemporary long poem is also an encyclopaedia for daily living. An encyclopaedia of signifying forms, the long poem translates different signifying practices (picto-ideo-phonographic writing, speech, performance, hysterical practice, photographs, pictographs, documentary materials) into one another in a process which claims authentic language for this culture and renews language itself. "We write poems, in Canada, not of the world, but to gain entrance to the world. That is our weakness and our strength," says Kroetsch. "Dare to enter. Dare to be carried away, transported" (Kroetsch 1989b, 132).

Translation cannot be abstracted, systematized, methodized, or subjected to universal reason. It can only take place via the body. The body compounds the difficulties of translation because the body itself is a site of delay, deferral, *différance,* and resistance. As Wah's pictogram " nv s ble/ tr ck" and its accompanying pictograph demonstrate, part of the invisible trick translation performs is, by playing with visibility and invisibility, inscription and erasure, writing and speech, to reinscribe the body in a way different from its inscription through representation, mimesis and universal reason. The long poem then is an 'owner's manual'[10] for the body. Translating, the long poem composes the body Canadian.

Notes

1   I am paraphrasing my notes from a seminar given by Jacques Derrida at the International Summer School for Semiotic and Structural Studies, University of Toronto, June 25, 1984.

2   See Kroetsch's catalogue of such absences in section 4 of *Seed Catalogue.*

3   Kroetsch quotes the section ("Flies") in which one lover records noticing a pair of flies on the ceiling making love, thus further decentering his own metaphor of lovemaking.

4   Frank Davey discusses several methods by which writers of the contemporary Canadian long poem have replaced narrative: place; language itself; the recurrent image; linguistic and narrative adventure, game and play; collage; symphonic form; and geography. Davey is concerned to preserve the element of narrative in the long poem. He sees these other methods as supplanting *sequential* narrative, not narrative as such. He suggests that "In recent years narrative makes a comeback as the narrative of composition" (Davey 1983, 184-85).

5   Derrida comments on the word 'natural' in Descartes's phrase 'natural reason':

> But the meaning of the word 'natural' in the expression 'natural language' is clearly opposed to its meaning in 'natural reason'. It is quite clear, but this first paradox must be emphasized: a natural language is native or national, but also particular and historical; it is the least commonly shared thing in the world. The natural reason that Descartes talks about is presumably universal, ahistorical, pre- or metalinguistic. We are dealing here with two determinations of naturality. (Derrida 1984a 92)

6   In a book on *The Concept of Method* Justus Buchler compares the Coleridgean and Cartesian concepts of method. His comparison can be related to Marlatt's phenomenological method and/or inspiration. Buchler writes:

> The "leading idea" of Coleridge supplies impetus and stimulus, and is most fully exemplified where "inspiration" is present. But the Cartesian rule is designed precisely to obviate dependency on inspiration, or more generally, dependency on contingent stimuli and indeterminate devices. The way ahead is to be prescribed by formulae, reason being in a sense the capacity to provide such formulae. The rule . . . ensures economy; for diffuseness, regardless of the success it may permit, generates distraction and confusion, and courts irrelevancy, which is the basis of imperfection. (Buchler 1961, 71)

Marlatt's poetics, based on inspiration as literal breathing and on entering into the flux of time and chance, is clearly and deliberately antithetical to the sense of method we have inherited from writers such as Descartes.

7   One can hear an echo from Marlatt's two mouths to Irigaray's two lips. Or is it an echo, since echoes bounce from ear to ear. Maybe a kiss. Perhaps when two lips speak together, it is not only what is heard, as many critics worry, but the fact of their speaking, their movement, their banishment of silence (or not) and what is created between them that is important.

8   Many theorists influenced by Michel Foucault have discussed the inscription of the body by discourses. However, much remains to be done with regard to the problem of the reciprocal inscription of discourses and texts by the body. Grosz and her Australian colleagues Moira Gatens and Vicki Kirby have made significant beginnings in this area. See also Jane Gallop.

9   Françoise Meltzer describes the economy of psychoanalysis as hydraulic:

> Psychoanalysis, in other words, has not only an economy which is hydraulic (mirroring the nineteenth-century physics from which it springs), but has as well an economy of seepage: each apparent object, whether in dream, literature, or psychic narrative, splashes over onto at least one "something else." Not only is there always a remainder, but the remainder generally proliferates, multiplies, from more than one quotient, such that the original "thing" in question becomes merely the agent for production. Its status as thing-in-the-world is easily lost. (Meltzer 1987, 215-16)

Meltzer notes that psychoanalysis has also seeped into many other disciplines. For example, she quotes Shoshana Felman, who posits a dialogue between literature and psychoanalysis as between two different bodies of language and between two different modes of knowledge (217). As Patrick Mahony has argued, Freud's work has contributed substantially to translation theory as well.

Barbara Godard picks up on the physics metaphor in her remarks about feminist writing/translation: "This theory of translation as production, not reproduction, focusing on the feminist discourse as it works through the problematic notions of identity and reference, is at odds with the long-dominant theory of translation as equivalence and transparency which describes the translator as an invisible hand mechanically turning the words of one language into another" (Homel and Simon 1988, 50). I share Godard's view that in feminist writing the whole body of the translator is becoming visible and substantially changing our concept of translation.

Carol Maier has published a very interesting article about how she dealt with the feminist issues which came to the fore during her translations of texts by Cuban-born, male poet Octavio Armand. Maier, realizing that translation "seemed to offer a way of learning to let go in a language, of knowing intimately the body of a particular text and creating a new body through the pleasure of shared experience" (6), decided, for example, to summon the absent mother in his work and give voice to her. She concludes that the resulting translation "is his tongue, but I know that it is also mine" (7).

10   *Owners Manual* is the title of one of Wah's books. In an interview with me in 1986 he said:

> And *Owners Manual* is a book that deals with the body. The owner is yourself. . . . I'm kind of humorously interested in the fact that we've got these wonderful owner's manuals for our cars but not for our bodies. . . . There are poetry owner's manuals. Certainly *The Odyssey* is a great owner's manual. *The Epic of Gilgamesh* and *The Divine Comedy* are great owner's manuals. But to be just intentional about it . . .(Banting 1986, 17)

Wah's *Owners Manual,* published after *Pictograms from the Interior of B.C.,* is a book of poems in which the associated pictographs are not included. Wah removed them because he "didn't want the trans aspect to be there" (17). When we read this owner's manual then, this book about the body, we cannot help but translate, and our own bodies take the place of the missing pictograms.

WORKS CITED

Allen, Donald, and Warren Tallman, eds. 1973. *The Poetics of the New American Poetry*. New York: Grove Press.

Allen, Jeffner, and Iris Marion Young, eds. 1973. *The Thinking Muse: Feminism and Modern French Philosophy*. Bloomington and Indianapolis: Indiana University Press.

Amos, Flora Ross. 1920. *Early Theories of Translation*. New York: Columbia University Press.

Banting, Pamela. 1986. "An Interview with Fred Wah." *Brick* 27:13-17.

———. 1992. "The Body as Pictogram: Rethinking Hélène Cixous's *écriture féminine*." *Textual Practice* 6(2): 225-46.

———. 1993. "The Reorganization of the Body: Daphne Marlatt's 'musing with mothertongue.'" In *ReImag(in)ing Women: Representations of Women in Culture,* eds. Shirley Neuman and Glennis Stephenson, 217-32. Toronto: University of Toronto Press.

Barber, E.J.W. 1974. *Archaeological Decipherment: A Handbook*. Princeton: Princeton University Press.

Barbour, Douglas. 1982. Review of *Owners Manual,* by Fred Wah. *Books in Canada* 11(8): 32-33.

Barthes, Roland. 1970. "To Write: An Intransitive Verb?" In *The Languages of Criticism and the Sciences of Man: The Structuralist Controversy,* eds. Richard Macksey and Eugenio Donato, 134–156. Baltimore and London: Johns Hopkins Press.

———. 1975. *The Pleasure of the Text*. Trans. Richard Miller; note by Richard Howard. New York: Hill and Wang.

———. 1977a. "The Death of the Author." In *Image-Music-Text,* Fontana Communications Series, selected and trans. by Stephen Heath, 142-48. Glasgow: Fontana/Collins.

———. 1977b. *Roland Barthes by Roland Barthes*. Trans. Richard Howard. New York: Hill and Wang.

———. 1982. *Empire of Signs*. Trans. Richard Howard. New York: Hill and Wang.

Baxter, Meaghan, Jeff Derksen, and Angela Hryniuk. 1984. "An Interview with Fred Wah." *Writing* 9:45-49.

Benjamin, Walter. 1968. "The Task of the Translator." In *Illuminations,* ed. and intro. Hannah Arendt, trans. Harry Zohn, 69-82. New York: Schocken Books.

Bensmaïa, Réda. 1987. *The Barthes Effect: The Essay as Reflective Text.* Theory and History of Literature 54. Trans. Pat Fedkiew. Foreword Michèle Richman. Minneapolis: University of Minnesota Press.

Bloom, Alfred H. 1981. *The Linguistic Shaping of Thought: A Study in the Impact of Language on Thinking in China and the West.* Hillsdale, NJ: Lawrence Erlbaum Associates.

Bowering, George. 1979. "Given This Body: An Interview with Daphne Marlatt." *Open Letter* 4th ser. 3:32-88.

————. 1980. "The Poems of Fred Wah." Introduction to *Loki is Buried at Smoky Creek: Selected Poems,* by Fred Wah. Vancouver: Talonbooks.

————. 1985. "Stone Hammer Narrative." *Open Letter* 6th ser. 2/3:131-44.

————. 1989. "On *Ana Historic:* An Interview with Daphne Marlatt." *Line* 13:96-105.

Brandt, Di. 1987. *Questions i asked my mother.* Winnipeg: Turnstone Press.

————. 1988. "Questions I Asked Dennis Cooley about the Vernacular Muse." *Prairie Fire* 9(3): 94-96.

Brennan, Timothy. 1989. "The Art of Translation." *Salman Rushdie and the Third World: Myths of the Nation.* London: Macmillan.

Brossard, Nicole. 1988. "From Radical to Integral." In *The Aerial Letter,* trans. Marlene Wildeman, 103-17. Toronto: The Women's Press.

Brown, Russell. 1984. "Seeds and Stones: Unhiding in Kroetsch's Poetry." *Open Letter* 5th ser. 8/9:154-75.

Buchler, Justus. 1961. *The Concept of Method.* New York and London: Columbia University Press.

Carr, Brenda. 1992. "The Western Woman and 'the Colonial Empire of the mind': (Re)constructing the Memsahib as (M)other in Daphne Marlatt's 'In the Month of Hungry Ghosts.' " Unpublished paper.

Catford, J.C. 1965. *A Linguistic Theory of Translation: An Essay in Applied Linguistics.* Language and Language Learning 8.

London: Oxford University Press.

Chan, Anthony B. 1983. *Gold Mountain: The Chinese in the New World.* Vancouver: New Star Books.

Chao, Yuen Ren. 1947. *Cantonese Primer.* New York: Greenwood Press.

Cixous, Hélène. 1981. "The Laugh of the Medusa." In *New French Feminisms: An Anthology,* eds. Elaine Marks and Isabelle de Courtivron, 245-64. New York: Schocken Books.

———. 1991. *"Coming to Writing" and Other Essays.* Intro. Susan Rubin Suleiman. Ed. Deborah Jenson. Trans. Sarah Cornell, Deborah Jenson, Ann Liddle, Susan Sellers. Cambridge, Mass. and London: Harvard University Press.

Clark, Hilary. 1990. "Living with the Dead: Narrative and Memory in Woolf's 'A Sketch of the Past' and Marlatt's *How Hug a Stone." Signature* 4:1-12.

Cohen, Keith. 1977. "The *Délire* of Translation." *Sub-stance* 16:85-88.

Con, Harry, Ronald J. Con, Graham Johnson, Edgar Wickberg, William E. Willmott. 1982. *From China to Canada: A History of the Chinese Communities in Canada.* Ed. Edgar Wickberg. Toronto: McClelland and Stewart, in association with the Multiculturalism Directorate, Dept. of the Secretary of State and the Canadian Government Publishing Centre, Supply and Services Canada.

Conley, Verena Andermatt. 1984. *Hélène Cixous: Writing the Feminine.* Lincoln and London: University of Nebraska Press.

Cooley, Dennis. 1987. *The Vernacular Muse: The Eye and Ear in Contemporary Literature.* Winnipeg: Turnstone Press.

———. 1989. "Recursions Excursions and Incursions: Daphne Marlatt Wrestles with the Angel Language." *Line* 13:66-79.

Cooley, Dennis, David Arnason and Robert Enright. 1977. "There's This and This Connexion: An Interview with Daphne Marlatt." *CVII* 3(1): 28-33.

Corner, John. 1968. *Pictographs (Indian Rock Paintings) in the Interior of British Columbia.* Vernon, B.C.: privately published.

Culler, Jonathan. 1982. *On Deconstruction: Theory and Criticism after Structuralism.* Ithaca, NY: Cornell University Press.

Davey, Frank. 1983. "The Language of the Contemporary Canadian Long Poem." *Surviving the Paraphrase: Eleven Essays on Canadian Literature..* Preface Eli Mandel. Winnipeg: Turnstone Press.

————. 1988. *Reading Canadian Reading.* Winnipeg: Turnstone Press.

————. 1989. "Words and Stones in *How Hug a Stone." Line* 13:40-46.

David-Ménard, Monique. 1989. *Hysteria from Freud to Lacan: Body and Language in Psychoanalysis.* Trans. Catherine Porter. Foreword Ned Lukacher. Ithaca and London: Cornell University Press.

De Man, Paul. 1986. "Conclusions: Walter Benjamin's 'The Task of the Translator.' " In *The Resistance to Theory,* foreword by Wlad Godzich, 73-105. Theory and History of Literature 33. Minneapolis: University of Minnesota Press.

Dempster, Elizabeth. 1988. "Women Writing the Body: Let's Watch a Little How She Dances." In *Grafts: Feminist Cultural Criticism,* ed. Susan Sheridan, 35-54. London and New York: Verso.

Derrida, Jacques. 1976. *Of Grammatology.* Trans. Gayatri Chakravorty Spivak. Baltimore and London: Johns Hopkins University Press.

————. 1979. "Living On / Border Lines." In *Deconstruction and Criticism,* ed. Harold Bloom et al., trans. James Hulbert, 75-176. New York: Seabury Press.

————. 1981a. *Dissemination.* Trans. and introduction by Barbara Johnson. Chicago: University of Chicago Press.

————. 1981b. *Positions.* Trans. and annotated by Alan Bass. Chicago: University of Chicago Press.

————. 1984a. "Languages and Institutions of Philosophy." *Recherches Sémiotiques / Semiotic Inquiry* 4(2): 91-154.

————. 1984b. *Signéponge / Signsponge.* Trans. Richard Rand. New York: Columbia University Press.

————. 1985a. "Des Tours de Babel." In *Difference in Translation,* ed. Joseph F. Graham, 165-207. Ithaca and London: Cornell University Press.

————. 1985b. *The Ear of the Other: Otobiography, Transference, Translation.* English editor Christie McDonald. Trans. Peggy Kamuf of the French edition edited by Claude Levesque and Christie McDonald. Lincoln and London: University of Nebraska Press.

————. 1986. *Glas.* Trans. John P. Leavey, Jr. and Richard Rand. Lincoln and London: University of Nebraska Press.

————. 1987. "Passe-Partout." *The Truth in Painting.* Trans. Geoff

Bennington and Ian McLeod, 1-13. Chicago and London: University of Chicago Press.

————. 1988. "Letter to a Japanese Friend." In *Derrida and "Différance,"* eds. David Wood and Robert Bernasconi, trans. David Wood and Andrew Benjamin, 1-5. Evanston: Northwestern University Press.

————. 1989. *Mémoires for Paul de Man*. Revised edition. Trans. Cecile Lindsay, Jonathan Culler, Eduardo Cadava, Peggy Kamuf. The Wellek Library Lectures. New York: Columbia University Press.

Diringer, David. 1962. *Writing*. New York: Praeger.

Doane, Mary Ann. 1982. "Film and the Masquerade: Theorising the Female Spectator." *Screen* 23(3/4): 74-87.

————. 1987. "Clinical Eyes: The Medical Discourse." *The Desire to Desire: The Woman's Film of the 1940s*. Theories of Representation and Difference. Bloomington and Indianapolis: Indiana University Press.

Drutz, N.M. 1981. Review of *Breathin' My Name with a Sigh,* by Fred Wah. In *Canadian Book Review Annual, 1981,* eds. Dean Tudor and Ann Tudor, 176-77. Toronto: Simon and Pierre.

Dybikowski, Ann, et al., eds. 1985. *In the Feminine: Women and Words / Les femmes et les mots, Conference Proceedings 1983*. Edmonton: Longspoon Press.

Dyck, E.F. 1987-88. "Trope as Topos in the Poetry of Robert Kroetsch." Review of *Advice to My Friends,* by Robert Kroetsch. *Prairie Fire* 8(4): 86-93.

Easthope, Antony. 1983. *Poetry as Discourse*. New Accents. London and New York: Methuen.

————. 1986. "The Male Body." *What a Man's Gotta Do: The Masculine Myth in Popular Culture*. London: Paladin Grafton Books.

Emerson, Caryl. 1986. "The Outer Word and Inner Speech: Bakhtin, Vygotsky, and the Internalization of Language." In *Bakhtin: Essays and Dialogues on His Work,* ed. Gary Saul Morson, 21-40. Chicago and London: University of Chicago Press.

Enright, Robert. 1987. "Literary Landscaping: A Symposium on Prairie Landscape, Memory and Literary Tradition." *Border Crossings* 6(4): 32-38.

Felman, Shoshana. 1983. *The Literary Speech Act: Don Juan with*

J.L. Austin, or Seduction in Two Languages. Trans. Catherine
Porter. Ithaca, NY: Cornell University Press.

———. 1985. "Writing and Madness, or Why This Book?" In
Writing and Madness (Literature/ Philosophy/ Psychoanalysis),
trans. Martha Noel Evans and Shoshana Felman, with Brian
Massumi, 11-32. Ithaca, NY: Cornell University Press.

Fenollosa, Ernest. 1936. *The Chinese Written Character as a Medium
for Poetry.* Ed. Ezra Pound. San Francisco: City Lights Books.

Ferrell, Robyn. 1991. "The Passion of the Signifier and the Body
in Theory." *Hypatia* 6(3): 172-84.

Foucault, Michel. "What Is an Author?" In *Language,
Counter-Memory, Practice: Selected Essays and Interviews,* ed.
and introduction by Donald F. Bouchard, trans. Donald F.
Bouchard and Sherry Simon, 113-38. Ithaca, NY: Cornell
University Press.

Freeman, Barbara. 1988. "Plus corps donc plus écriture: Hélène
Cixous and the mind-body problem." *Paragraph* 11(1):
58-70.

Fuss, Diana. 1989. *Essentially Speaking: Feminism, Nature &
Difference.* New York and London: Routledge.

Gallop, Jane. 1987. "Reading the Mother Tongue: Psychoanalytic
Feminist Criticism." *Critical Inquiry* 13(2): 314-29.

———. 1988. *Thinking Through the Body.* New York: Columbia
University Press.

Gagnon, Madeleine. 1981. "Body I." In *New French Feminisms: An
Anthology,* eds. Elaine Marks and Isabelle de Courtivron,
179-80. New York: Schocken Books.

Garbini, Giovanni. 1988. "The Question of the Alphabet." In *The
Phoenicians / Fenici,* under the scientific direction of Sabatino
Moscati, 86-103. Milan: Bompiani.

Gatens, Moira, 1991. *Femism and Philosophy: Perspectives on
Difference and Equality.* Bloomington and Indiana: Indiana
University Press.

Géfin, Laszlo. 1982. *Ideogram: History of a Poetic Method.* Austin:
University of Texas Press.

Genette, Gérard. 1982. *Figures of Literary Discourse.* Trans. Alan
Sheridan. Intro. Marie-Rose Logan. New York: Columbia
University Press.

Godard, Barbara. 1985. " 'Body I': Daphne Marlatt's Feminist
Poetics." *The American Review of Canadian Studies* 15(4):
481-96.

————. 1988. "Theorizing Feminist Discourse / Translation." In
Mapping Literature: The Art and Politics of Translation, eds.
David Homel and Sherry Simon, 49-51. Montréal: Véhicule
Press.

Goddard, John. 1986. Interview with Fred Wah. *Books in Canada*
15(7): 40-41.

Graham, Joseph F., ed. 1985. *Difference in Translation.* Ithaca and
London: Cornell University Press.

Grosz, Elizabeth. 1989. "Inscriptions and Body-Maps:
Representation and the Corporeal." Paper read to the
Women's Studies Program, University of Alberta.

Gunnars, Kristjana. 1984. "Words on Multilingualism." *Prairie
Fire* 5(2/3): 7-8.

————. 1987-88." 'Meditation on a Snowy Morning': A
Conversation with Robert Kroetsch." *Prairie Fire* 8(4): 54-67.

Haas, W. 1970. *Phono-Graphic Translation.* Mont Follick Series 2.
Manchester: Manchester University Press.

Harasym, Sarah. 1988. "Opening the Question: A 'Political'
Reading of Texts by Jacques Derrida, Gayatri Spivak, Roland
Barthes, and Daphne Marlatt." Ph.D diss., University of
Alberta, Edmonton.

————. 1991. "EACH MOVE MADE HERE (me) MOVES THERE
(you)." *boundary 2* 18(1): 104-26.

Havelock, Eric A. 1963. *Preface to Plato.* Oxford: Basil Blackwell,
1963. Reprint. New York: Grosset and Dunlap, 1967;
Harvard University Press, 1971.

————. 1986. "The Special Theory of Greek Orality." *The Muse
Learns to Write: Reflections on Orality and Literacy from
Antiquity to the Present.* New Haven and London: Yale
University Press.

Holman, Hugh. 1972. *A Handbook to Literature.* 3rd ed.
Indianapolis: Odyssey Press. Based on the original by
William Flint Thrall and Addison Hibbard.

Homel, David, and Sherry Simon, eds. 1988. *Mapping Literature:
The Art and Politics of Translation.* Montréal: Véhicule Press.

Hutcheon, Linda. 1985. *A Theory of Parody: The Teachings of
Twentieth-Century Art Forms.* New York and London: Methuen.

————. 1988. "Seeing Double: Concluding with Kroetsch." *The
Canadian Postmodern: A Study of Contemporary English-
Canadian Fiction.* Toronto, New York and Oxford: Oxford
University Press.

————. 1991. " 'Circling the Downspout of Empire':
Post-Colonial and Post-modern Ironies." In *Splitting Images:
Contemporary Canadian Ironies,* 69-95. Toronto: Oxford
University Press.

Irigaray, Luce. 1985. "When Our Lips Speak Together." *This Sex
Which Is Not One.* Trans. Catherine Porter with Carolyn
Burke, 205-18. Ithaca, NY: Cornell University Press.

————. 1991. "The Bodily Encounter with the Mother." In *The
Irigaray Reader,* ed. Margaret Whitford, 34-46. Oxford: Basil
Blackwell.

Jakobson, Roman. 1971. "On Linguistic Aspects of Translation."
In Vol. 2 of *Selected Writings,* 260-66. Word and Language.
The Hague and Paris: Mouton.

Johnson, Barbara. 1985. "Taking Fidelity Philosophically." In
Difference in Translation, ed. Joseph Graham, 142-48. Ithaca
and London: Cornell University Press.

Kamboureli, Smaro. 1984a. "Fred Wah: A Poetry of Dialogue,"
Line 4:44-62.

————. 1984b. "A Poem *out of* Love: An Interview with Robert
Kroetsch on *The Sad Phoenician." Open Letter* 5th ser.
8/9:47-52.

Kintz, Linda. 1973. "In-different Criticism: The Deconstructive
'Parole.' " In *The Thinking Muse: Feminism and Modern French
Philosophy,* eds. Jeffner Allen and Iris Marion Young,
113-35. Bloomington and Indianapolis: Indiana University
Press.

Kirby, Vicki. 1991. "Corporeal Habits: Addressing Essentialism
Differently." *Hypatia* 6(3): 4-24.

Kiyooka, Roy. 1990. "We Asian North Americanos: An
unhistorical 'take' on growing up yellow in a white world."
West Coast Line 3:116-118.

Knutson, Susan. 1990. "Daphne Marlatt and Nicole Brossard:
Writing Metanarrative in the Feminine." *Signature* 3:28-43.

Kolybaba, Kathie. 1985. "The Kolybaba Connection / The
Krafchenko Theft: Conversation (Avoided, Imagined, Faked,
Failed) with Cooley." Review of *Bloody Jack,* by Dennis
Cooley. *Border Crossings* 4(4): 43.

Kostash, Myrna. 1985. "Ethnicity and Feminism." In *In the
Feminine: Women and Words / Les femmes et les mots,
Conference Proceedings 1983,* eds. Ann Dybikowski et al.,
60-62. Edmonton: Longspoon Press.

Kristeva, Julia. 1980. *Desire in Language: A Semiotic Approach to Literature and Art.* Ed. Leon S. Roudiez. Trans. Thomas Gora, Alice Jardine and Leon S. Roudiez. New York: Columbia University Press.

——. 1981. "Women's Time." Trans. Alice Jardine and Harry Blake. *Signs* 7(1): 13-35.

——. 1984. *Revolution in Poetic Language.* Trans. Margaret Waller. Intro. Leon S. Roudiez. New York: Columbia University Press.

Kroetsch, Robert. 1975a. *The Ledger.* Ilderton, ON: Brick/Nairn.

——. 1975b. *The Stone Hammer Poems: 1960-1975.* Lantzville, BC: Oolichan Books.

——. 1977. *Seed Catalogue.* Winnipeg: Turnstone Press; rep. 1979.

——. 1979. *The Sad Phoenician.* Toronto: Coach House Press.

——. 1980. *The "Crow" Journals.* Edmonton: NeWest Press.

——. 1981. *Field Notes 1-8, a Continuing Poem: The Collected Poetry of Robert Kroetsch.* Don Mills, ON: General Publishing.

——. 1985. *Advice to My Friends: A Continuing Poem.* Don Mills, ON: Stoddart.

——. 1989a. *Completed Field Notes: The Long Poems of Robert Kroetsch.* Toronto: McClelland and Stewart.

——. 1989b. *The Lovely Treachery of Words: Essays Selected and New.* Toronto, New York, Oxford: Oxford University Press.

Leavey, John P., Jr. 1990. "Lations, Cor, Trans, Re, &c.*." In *The Textual Sublime: Deconstruction and Its Differences,* ed. Hugh J. Silverman and Gary E. Aylesworth, 191-202. Contemporary Studies in Philosophy and Literature 1. Albany, NY: State University of New York Press.

Lecker, Robert. 1986. "Bordering On." *Robert Kroetsch.* Boston: Twayne. (First published in 1982 under the title "Bordering On: Robert Kroetsch's Aesthetic." *Journal of Canadian Studies* 17(3): 124-33.)

Lenoski, Daniel. 1986. "Voicing Prairie Space: Interview with Dennis Cooley." *Line* 7/8:166-83.

Lentricchia, Frank. 1980. *After the New Criticism.* Chicago: University of Chicago Press.

Lingis, Alphonso. 1983. *Excesses: Eros and Culture.* Albany, NY: State University of New York Press.

Liu, James J.Y. 1962. "Some Grammatical Aspects of the Language of Poetry." In *The Art of Chinese Poetry,* 39-47.

Chicago and London: University of Chicago Press.

Lyotard, Jean-François. 1984. *The Postmodern Condition: A Report on Knowledge.* Trans. Geoff Bennington and Brian Massumi. Foreword Fredric Jameson. Theory and History of Literature 10. Minneapolis: University of Minnesota Press.

McCaffery, Steve. 1976. "Anti-Phonies," *Open Letter* 3rd ser. 5:87-92. Reprinted in 1986 as "Anti-Phonies: Fred Wah's *Pictograms from the Interior of B.C,*" *North of Intention: Critical Writings 1973-1986,* 30-38. New York: Roof Books and Toronto: Nightwood Editions.

Mahony, Patrick. 1980. "Toward the Understanding of Translation in Psychoanalysis." *Journal of the American Psychoanalytic Association* 28(2): 461-75. Reprinted in 1987 in *Psychoanalysis and Discourse,* New Library of Psychoanalysis 2. London and New York: Tavistock Publications.

Maier, Carol. 1985. "A Woman in Translation, Reflecting." *Translation Review* 17:4-8.

Man, Paul de. 1986. "Conclusions: Walter Benjamin's 'The Task of the Translator.' " *The Resistance to Theory.* Minneapolis: University of Minnesota Press.

Mandel, Eli. 1978. "The Ethnic Voice in Canadian Writing." In *Figures in a Ground: Canadian Essays on Modern Literature in Honor of Sheila Watson,* eds. Diane Bessai and David Jackel, 264-77. Saskatoon: Western Producer Prairie Books.

Marlatt, Daphne. 1971. *Rings.* Vancouver: Georgia Straight Writing Supplement. Reprinted in 1980 in *What Matters: Writing 1968-70.* Toronto: Coach House Press.

———. 1979a. "Long as in Time? *Steveston.*" In *The Long Poem Anthology,* ed. Michael Ondaatje, 316-18. Toronto: Coach House Press.

———. 1979b. "Steveston." In *The Long Poem Anthology,* ed. Michael Ondaatje, 81-123. Toronto: Coach House Press.

———. 1982. "The Measure of the Sentence." *Open Letter* 5th ser. 3:90-92.

———. 1983. *How Hug a Stone.* Winnipeg: Turnstone Press.

———. 1984a. "Entering In: The Immigrant Imagination." *Canadian Literature* 100:219-24.

———. 1984b. *Touch to My Tongue.* Edmonton: Longspoon Press.

———. 1985a. "Listening In." *Contemporary Verse 2* 9(2): 36-39.

————. 1985b. "Writing our Way through the Labyrinth."
Tessera 2 / La Nouvelle Barre du Jour 157:45-49.

————. 1988. *Ana Historic.* Toronto: Coach House Press.

————. 1989a. "Correspondences: Selected Letters." *Line* 13:5-31.

————. 1989b. "Translating MAUVE: Reading Writing." *Tessera*
6:27-30.

————. 1990. "Difference (em)bracing." In *Language in Her Eye:
Writing and Gender: Views by Canadian Women Writing in
English,* eds. Libby Scheier, Sarah Sheard, and Eleanor
Wachtel, 188-93. Toronto: Coach House.

Mauss, Marcel. 1979. "Body Techniques." *Sociology and
Psychology: Essays,* 95-122. Trans. Ben Brewster. London and
Boston: Routledge & Kegan Paul.

Meltzer, Francoise. 1987. "Editor's Introduction: Partitive Plays,
Pipe Dreams." *Critical Inquiry* 13(2): 215-21.

Merleau-Ponty, Maurice. 1970. "The Concept of Nature, II:
Animality, the Human Body, Transition to Culture." *Themes
from the Lectures at the Collège de France 1952-1960,* 88-98.
Trans. John O'Neill. Evanston: Northwestern University
Press.

Mezei, Kathy. 1988. "Tessera, Feminist Literary Theory in
English-Canadian and Québec Literature, and the Practice of
Translation as Betrayal, Exchange, Interpretation, Invention,
Transformation, and Creation." In *Mapping Literature: The
Art and Politics of Translation,* eds. David Homel and Sherry
Simon, 47-49. Montréal: Véhicle Press.

Miki, Roy. 1989. "Self on Self: Robert Kroetsch Interviewed."
Line 14:108-42.

Moi, Toril. 1985. *Sexual/Textual Politics: Feminist Literary Theory.*
New Accents. London and New York: Methuen.

Morrison, Toni. 1992. *Jazz.* Toronto: Knopf.

Moyes, Lianne. 1991. "Writing, the Uncanniest of Guests:
Daphne Marlatt's *How Hug a Stone.*" In *Beyond Tish,* ed.
Douglas Barbour, 203-21. Edmonton and Vancouver:
Newest Press and *West Coast Line.*

Munton, Ann. 1985. "The Long Poem as Poetic Diary." *Open
Letter* 6th ser. 2/3:93-106.

Neuman, Shirley. 1983. "Allow Self, Portraying Self:
Autobiography in *Field Notes.*" *Line* 2:104-21.

————. 1984. "Figuring the Reader, Figuring the Self in *Field
Notes:* 'Double or noting.' " *Open Letter* 5th ser. 8/9:176-94.

Neuman, Shirley and Robert Wilson. 1982. *Labyrinths of Voice: Conversations with Robert Kroetsch.* Western Canadian Literary Documents Series 3. Edmonton: NeWest Press.

Newnham, Richard. 1971. *About Chinese.* Helped by Tan Lin-tung. Markham, ON: Penguin.

Nichol, bp. 1978. "Transcreation: A Conversation with Fred Wah: TRG Report One: Translation (Part 3)." *Open Letter* 3rd ser. 9:34-52.

———. 1985. "The 'Pata of Letter Feet, or, The English Written Character as a Medium for Poetry." *Open Letter* 6th ser. 1:79-95.

Nichol, bp, Daphne Marlatt, George Bowering. 1985. " 'Syntax Equals the Body Structure': bpNichol, in Conversation with Daphne Marlatt and George Bowering." Ed. Roy Miki. *Line* 6:22-44.

Nye, Andrea. 1990. *Words of Power: A Feminist Reading of the History of Logic.* Thinking Gender. New York and London: Routledge.

Olson, Charles. 1966. "Mayan Letters." In *Selected Writings of Charles Olson,* ed. and intro. Robert Creeley. New York: New Directions.

———. 1973. "Projective Verse" and "Human Universe." In *The Poetics of the New American Poetry,* eds. Donald Allen and Warren Tallman, 147-58 and 161-74. New York: Grove Press.

———. 1974. *Additional Prose.* Bolinas: Four Seasons.

Ong, Walter J. 1967. *The Presence of the Word.* New Haven: Yale University Press.

———. 1982. *Orality and Literacy: The Technologizing of the Word.* New Accents. London and New York: Methuen.

Perloff, Marjorie. 1985. "The Word as Such: L=A=N=G=U=A=G=E Poetry in the Eighties." In *The Dance of the Intellect: Studies in the Poetry of the Pound Tradition,* 215-38. Cambridge Studies in American Literature and Culture. Cambridge: Cambridge University Press.

Pivato, Joseph. 1987. "Constantly Translating: The Challenge for Italian-Canadian Writers." *Canadian Review of Comparative Literature* 14(1): 60-76.

Pound, Ezra. 1934. *A B C of Reading.* New York: New Directions; reprinted 1960.

Quasha, George. 1977. "DiaLogos: Between the Written and the

Oral in Contemporary Poetry." *New Literary History* 8:485-506.

Ricou, Laurie. 1986. "Phyllis Webb, Daphne Marlatt and simultitude: Journal entries from a capitalist bourgeois patriarchal anglo-saxon mainstream critic." In *A Mazing Space: Writing Canadian Women Writing,* eds. Shirley Neuman and Smaro Kamboureli, 205-15. Edmonton: Longspoon Press/NeWest Press.

Ricou, Laurie. 1987. "Fred Wah." In Vol. 60 of *Dictionary of Literary Biography: Canadian Writers Since 1960,* 2nd ser., ed. W.H. New, 369-73. Toronto: Bruccoli Clark Layman.

Scobie, Stephen. 1986. "Surviving the Paraph-raise." *Open Letter* 6th ser. 5/6:49-68. Revised and reprinted in 1989, *Signature Event Cantext: Essays by Stephen Scobie.* The Writer as Critic Series 2. Edmonton: NeWest Press.

Serafin, Bruce. 1982. "It's a Struggle Without the Shine." Review of *Breathin' My Name with a Sigh,* by Fred Wah. *The Vancouver Sun,* 4 June 1982: L33.

Silverman, Kaja. 1988. *The Acoustic Mirror: The Female Voice in Psychoanalysis and Cinema,* Theories of Representation and Difference, ed. Teresa de Lauretis. Bloomington and Indianapolis: Indiana University Press.

Sokolov, A.N. 1972. *Inner Speech and Thought.* Trans. George T. Onischenko. Trans. ed. Donald B. Lindsley. New York: Plenum.

Spivak, Gayatri Chakravorty. 1984. "Love Me, Love My Ombre, Elle." *Diacritics* 14(4): 19-36.

Stanton, Domna C. 1989. "Difference on Trial: A Critique of the Maternal Metaphor in Cixous, Irigaray, and Kristeva." In *The Thinking Muse: Feminism and Modern French Philosophy,* eds. Jeffner Allen and Iris Marion Young, 156-79. Bloomington and Indianapolis: Indiana University Press.

Sutherland, Fraser. 1986. Review of *Waiting for Saskatchewan,* by Fred Wah, and *The Night the Dog Smiled,* by John Newlove. *The Globe and Mail,* 21 June 1986: C7.

Tedlock, Dennis. 1983. *The Spoken Word and the Work of Interpretation.* Philadelphia: University of Pennsylvania Press.

Théoret, France. 1991. *The Tangible Word (1977-1983).* Trans. Barbara Godard. Montréal: Guernica.

Thesen, Sharon. 1979. Introduction to excerpts from *Running In the Family,* by Michael Ondaatje and "In the Month of

Hungry Ghosts," by Daphne Marlatt. *The Capilano Review* 16/17:2-3.

Tostevin, Lola Lemire. 1988a. " 'Music. Heart. Thinking.': An Interview with Fred Wah." *Line* 12:42-56.

———. 1988b. *'sophie.* Toronto: Coach House Press.

———. 1989. "Daphne Marlatt: Writing in the Space That Is Her Mother's Face." *Line* 13:32-39.

Toury, Gideon. 1980. *In Search of a Theory of Translation.* Tel Aviv: The Porter Institute for Poetics and Semiotics.

Twigg, Alan. 1981. "Robert Kroetsch: Male." *For Openers: Conversations with Twenty-Four Canadian Writers,* 107-16. Madiera Park, BC: Harbour Publishing.

Ulmer, Gregory L. 1985. *Applied Grammatology: Post(e)-Pedagogy from Jacques Derrida to Joseph Beuys.* Baltimore and London: Johns Hopkins University Press.

Vološinov, V.N. 1973. *Marxism and the Philosophy of Language.* Trans. Ladislav Matejka and I.R. Titunik. Studies in Language 1. New York: Seminar.

Vygotsky, L.S. 1962. *Thought and Language.* Ed. and trans. Eugenia Hanfmann and Gertrude Vakar. Cambridge, MA: MIT Press.

Wachtel, Eleanor. 1986. "An Interview with Daphne Marlatt." *Capilano Review* 41:4-13.

Wah, Fred. 1965. *Lardeau.* Toronto: Island Press.

———. 1967. *Mountain.* Buffalo: Audit East/West.

———. 1972a. *Among.* Toronto: Coach House Press.

———. 1972b. *Tree.* Vancouver: Vancouver Community Press.

———. 1974. *Earth.* Canton, N.Y.: The Institute of Further Studies.

———. 1975. *Pictograms from the Interior of B.C.* Vancouver: Talonbooks.

———. 1977. "To Locate." Review of *Songs and Speeches,* by Barry McKinnon. *Open Letter* 3d ser. 7:110-11.

———. 1978. "Mrs. Richard's Grey Cat." *Open Letter* 6th ser. 9:53-63.

———. 1980a. Introduction. *Net Work: Selected Writing. By Daphne Marlatt.* Vancouver: Talonbooks.

———. 1980b. *Loki is Buried at Smoky Creek: Selected Poems.* Ed. and intro. George Bowering. Vancouver: Talonbooks.

———. 1981a. *Breathin' My Name with a Sigh.* Vancouver: Talonbooks.

————. 1981b. *Owners Manual.* Lantzville, BC: Island Press.

————. 1982a. *Grasp the Sparrow's Tail: A Poetic Diary.* Kyoto, Japan: privately printed.

————. 1982b. "Standing and Watching the Writing Writing." *La Nouvelle Barre du Jour* 118-119:156-58.

————. 1983. Review of *Considering How Exaggerated Music Is,* by Leslie Scalapino. *Brick* 18:9.

————. 1985a. "Making Strange Poetics." *Open Letter* 6th ser. 2/3:213-21.

————. 1985b. *Waiting for Saskatchewan.* Winnipeg: Turnstone Press.

————. 1986a. "Subjective as Objective: The Lyric Poetry of Sharon Thesen." *Essays on Canadian Writing* 32:114-21.

————. 1986b. "Which at First Seems to be a Going Back for Origins: Notes on a Reading of Some American Women Writers." In *A Mazing Space: Writing Canadian Women Writing,* eds. Shirley Neuman and Smaro Kamboureli, 374-79. Edmonton: Longspoon Press/NeWest Press.

————. 1987. *Music at the Heart of Thinking.* Writing West Series. Red Deer, AB: Red Deer College Press.

Webb, Phyllis. 1982. "Non Linear." In *The Vision Tree: Selected Poems,* ed. and intro. Sharon Thesen, 80-93. Vancouver: Talonbooks.

————. 1985. "The Muse Figure." In *In the Feminine: Women and Words/Les femmes et les mots, Conference Proceedings, 1983.* eds. Ann Dybikowski et al., 114-16. Edmonton: Longspoon Press.

White, Allon. 1983. " 'The Dismal Sacred Word': Academic Language and the Social Reproduction of Seriousness." *Journal of Literature, Teaching, Politics* 2:4-15.

White, David A. 1978. "Poetizing and Man." *Heidegger and the Language of Poetry.* Lincoln and London: University of Nebraska Press.

Williams, William Carlos. 1946. *Paterson.* New York: New Directions; rep. 1963.

Williamson, Janice. 1985. "Speaking In And Of Each Other: An Interview with Daphne Marlatt and Betsy Warland." *Fuse* 8(5): 25-29.

————. 1989. "Sounding a Difference: An Interview with Daphne Marlatt." *Line* 13:47-56.

————. 1991. "It gives me a great deal of pleasure to say yes:

Writing/Reading Lesbian in Daphne Marlatt's *Touch to My Tongue.*" In *Beyond Tish,* ed. Douglas Barbour, 171-93. Edmonton and Vancouver: NeWest Press and *West Coast Line.*

Wittig, Monique. 1992. *The Straight Mind and Other Essays.* Boston: Beacon Press.

Wood, David and Robert Bernasconi, eds. 1988. *Derrida and "Différance."* Evanston, IL: Northwestern University Press.

Yee, Chiang. 1973. *Chinese Calligraphy: An Introduction to Its Aesthetic and Technique.* Foreword Sir Herbert Read. 3d ed. Cambridge, Mass.: Harvard University Press. (First published in 1938, London and New York: Methuen.)